CHILDREN OF THE WHALES

Volume

12

On the Mud Whale

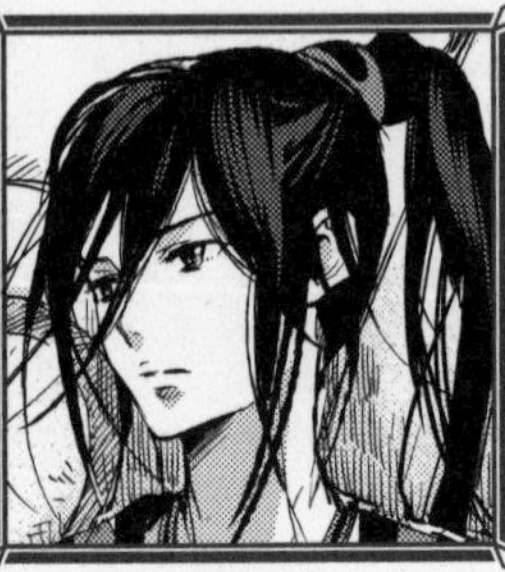

Ouni
(Marked, 16 years old)

A very powerful thymia user. His daímonas power is awakening, and he has now come face-to-face with Orca.

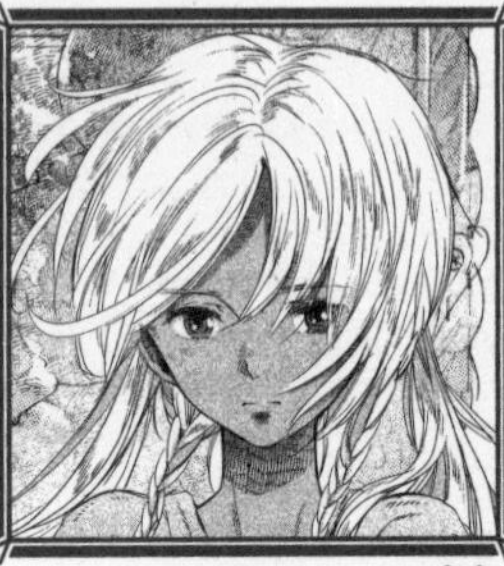

Lykos
(Marked, 14 years old)

A girl from the Allied Empire who comes aboard the Mud Whale. She sneaks into Amonlogia by herself and runs into Liontari.

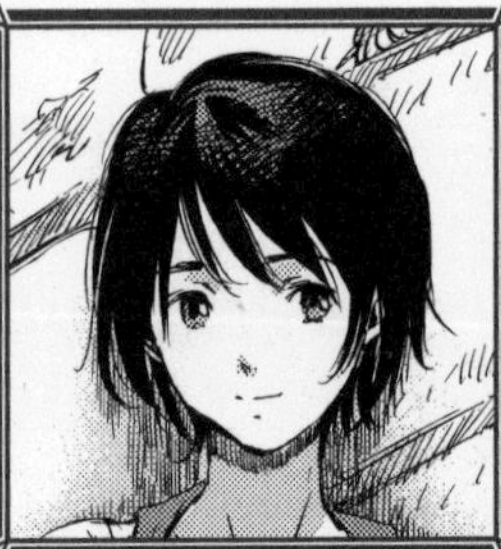

Chakuro
(Marked, 14 years old)

The young archivist of the Mud Whale. In order to save the hostage Unmarked, he and a group of Marked infiltrate Amonlogia.

Allied Empire

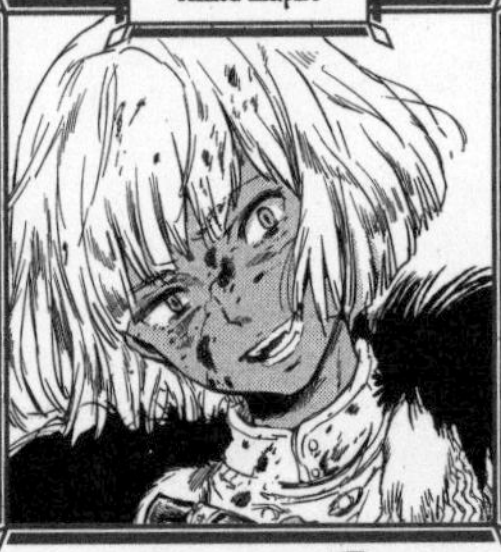

Liontari
(Marked)

Accompanied Orca on the Amonlogia invasion as a jester. He doesn't get along with the Insect Cage troops.

Allied Empire

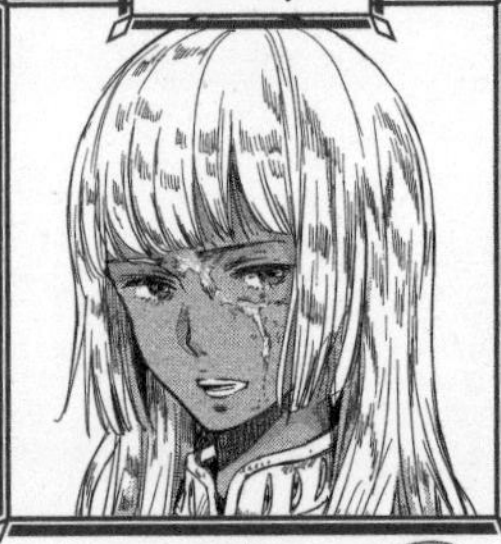

Orca
(Marked)

A high-ranking official from the Allied Empire and Lykos's brother. He invades Amonlogia and seizes the island's guardian, Kýma.

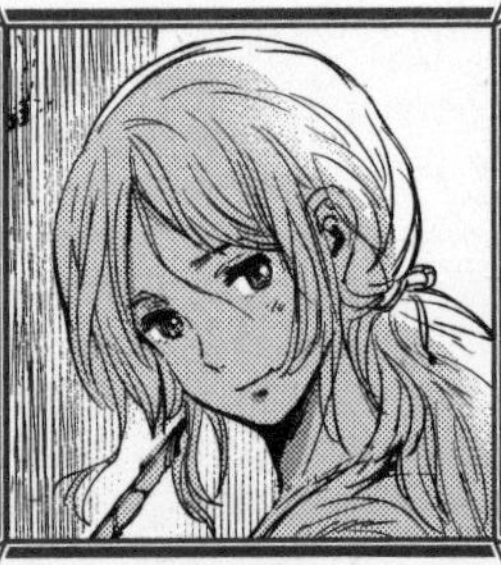

Suou
(Unmarked, 17 years old)

Mayor of the Mud Whale. Was being held prisoner with the rest of the Unmarked, but they have now been rescued.

Amonlogia

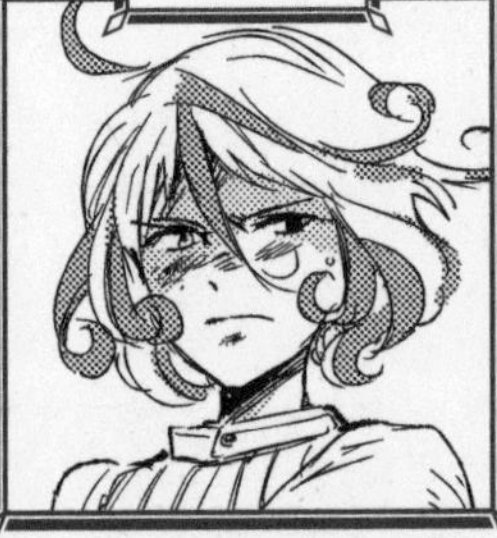

Rochalízo
(?, 17 years old)

The youngest son of the duke of Amonlogia. He is considered useless by his family, but he has decided to save the Mud Whale.

Amonlogia

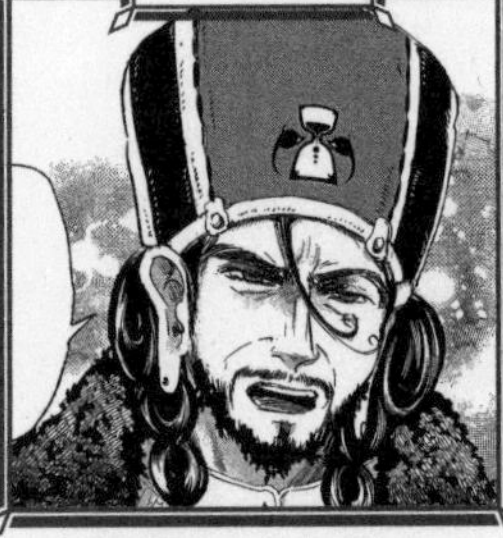

Dáchtyla

Duke of Amonlogia and Rochalízo's father. His greatest fear, the capture of Kýma, has come to pass.

Allied Empire

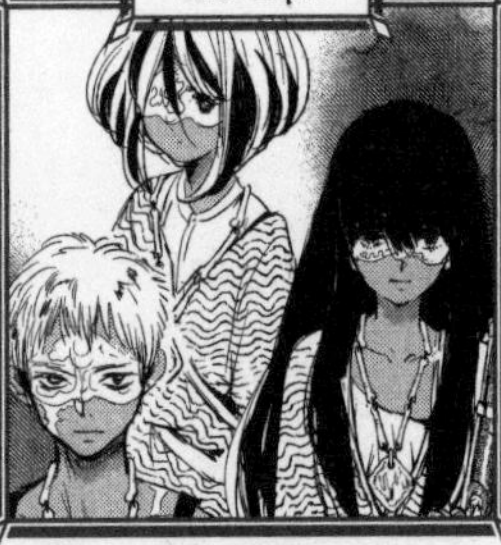

The Insect Cage
(Marked)

Children from an imperial mining settlement. They are Orca's personal army, and their loyalties lie with him.

Glossary of the Sea of Sand

The Mud Whale	A huge, drifting island-ship. Those in the empire who resisted giving up their emotions were exiled here, along with all their descendants.
Thymia	Telekinetic power derived from emotions.
The Marked	The 90 percent of the Mud Whale population who are thymia users. They are all short-lived.
The Unmarked	The members of the Mud Whale population who cannot use thymia. Unlike the Marked, they are long-lived.
Nous	A unique organism that obtains energy from peoples' emotions and gives people the power of thymia in return.
Nous Fálaina	A Nous that dwells deep within the Belly of the Mud Whale. Unlike other Nouses, it consumes the life force of humans rather than their emotions.
The Allied Empire	A large nation on the Sea of Sand that controls its citizenry through the Nouses and their absorption of emotions.
Daímonas	A legend from the empire. A being said to be able to destroy a Nous.

A Record of the Mud Whale and the Sea of Sand

Year 93 of the Sand Exile.

The Mud Whale drifts endlessly through the Sea of Sand, home to about 500 people who know nothing of the outside world.

Upon arrival in Amonlogia, the Unmarked of the Mud Whale are captured by Duke Dáchtyla. Chakuro and a team of Marked children sneak into the castle and successfully rescue Suou and the other Unmarked.

Meanwhile, the battleship Karcharías, led by Orca, has attacked Amonlogia. With an overwhelming show of thymia, Orca advances toward the ducal castle and makes short work of Dáchtyla's resistance. Orca breaches the chamber of the guardian of Amonlogia, the sotíras Kýma, and proposes a deal to turn humans into Nouses. Kýma, a creature of the Nous herself, agrees to his scheme. Then Chakuro and the others run into Orca after releasing the Unmarked from Dáchtyla's dungeon.

"The Mud Whale was our entire world."

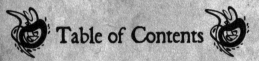 Table of Contents

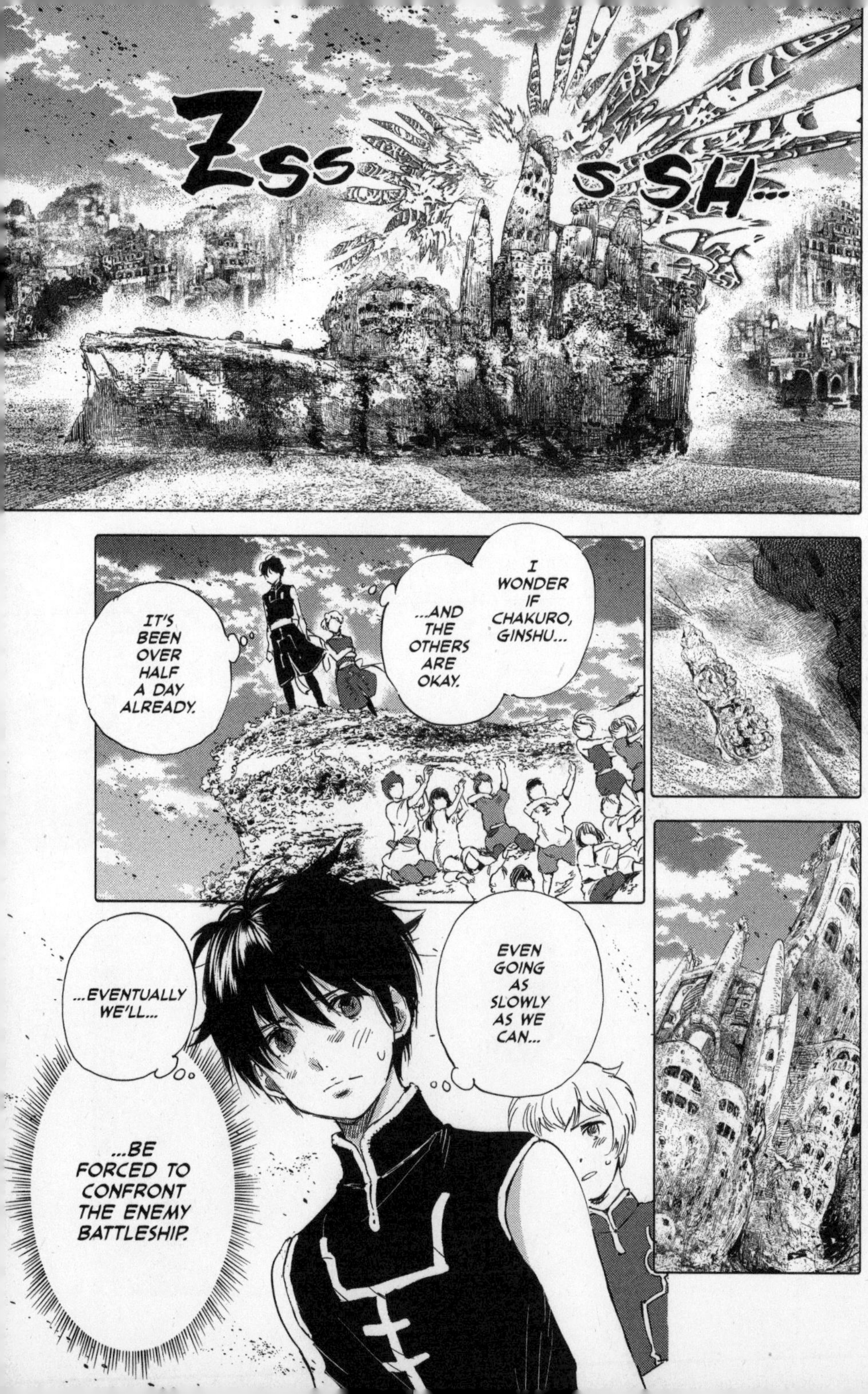
ZSS SSH...
I WONDER IF CHAKURO, GINSHU...
...AND THE OTHERS ARE OKAY.
IT'S BEEN OVER HALF A DAY ALREADY.
EVEN GOING AS SLOWLY AS WE CAN...
...EVENTUALLY WE'LL...
...BE FORCED TO CONFRONT THE ENEMY BATTLESHIP.

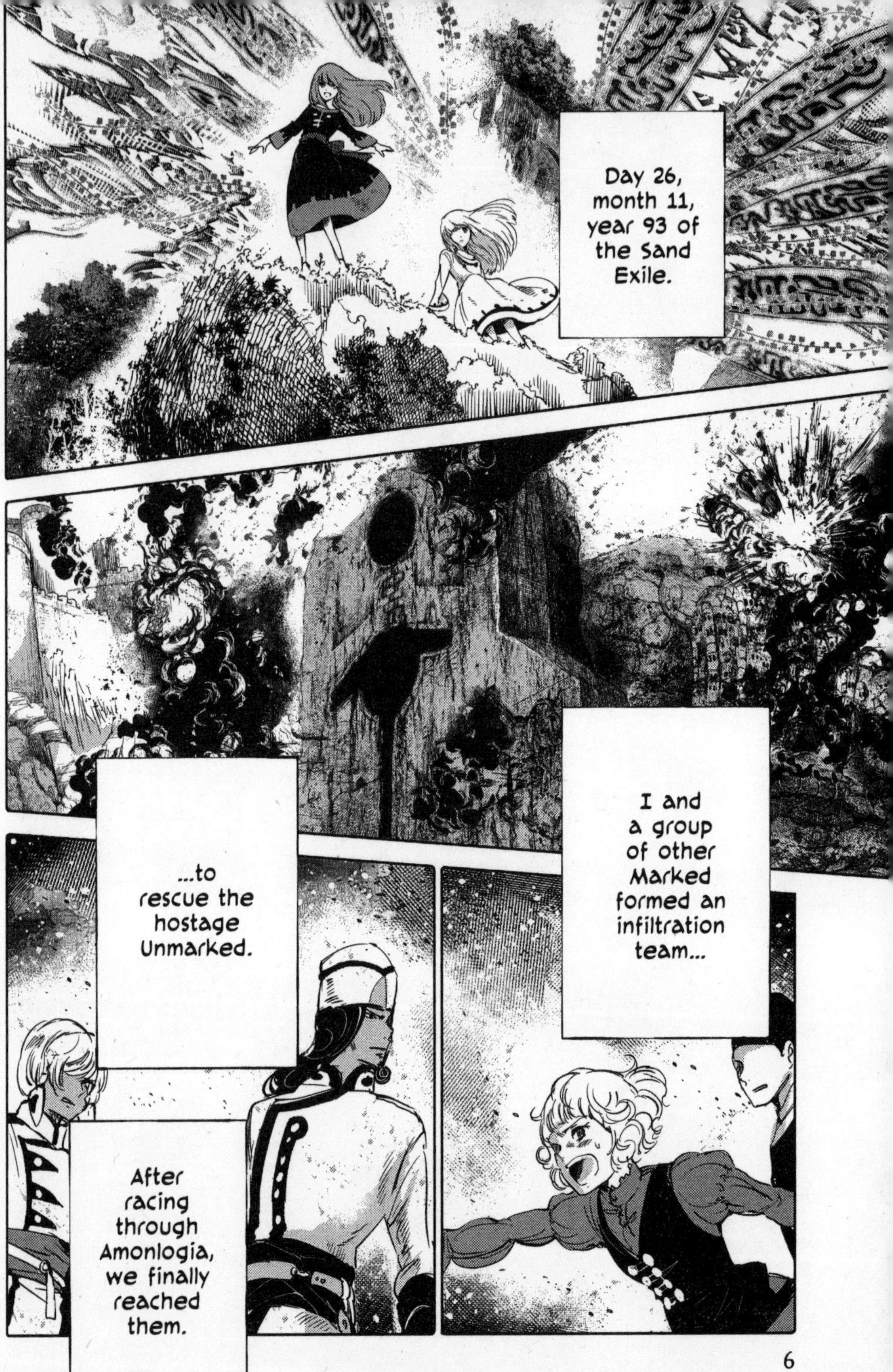
Day 26, month 11, year 93 of the Sand Exile.
I and a group of other Marked formed an infiltration team...
...to rescue the hostage Unmarked.
After racing through Amonlogia, we finally reached them.

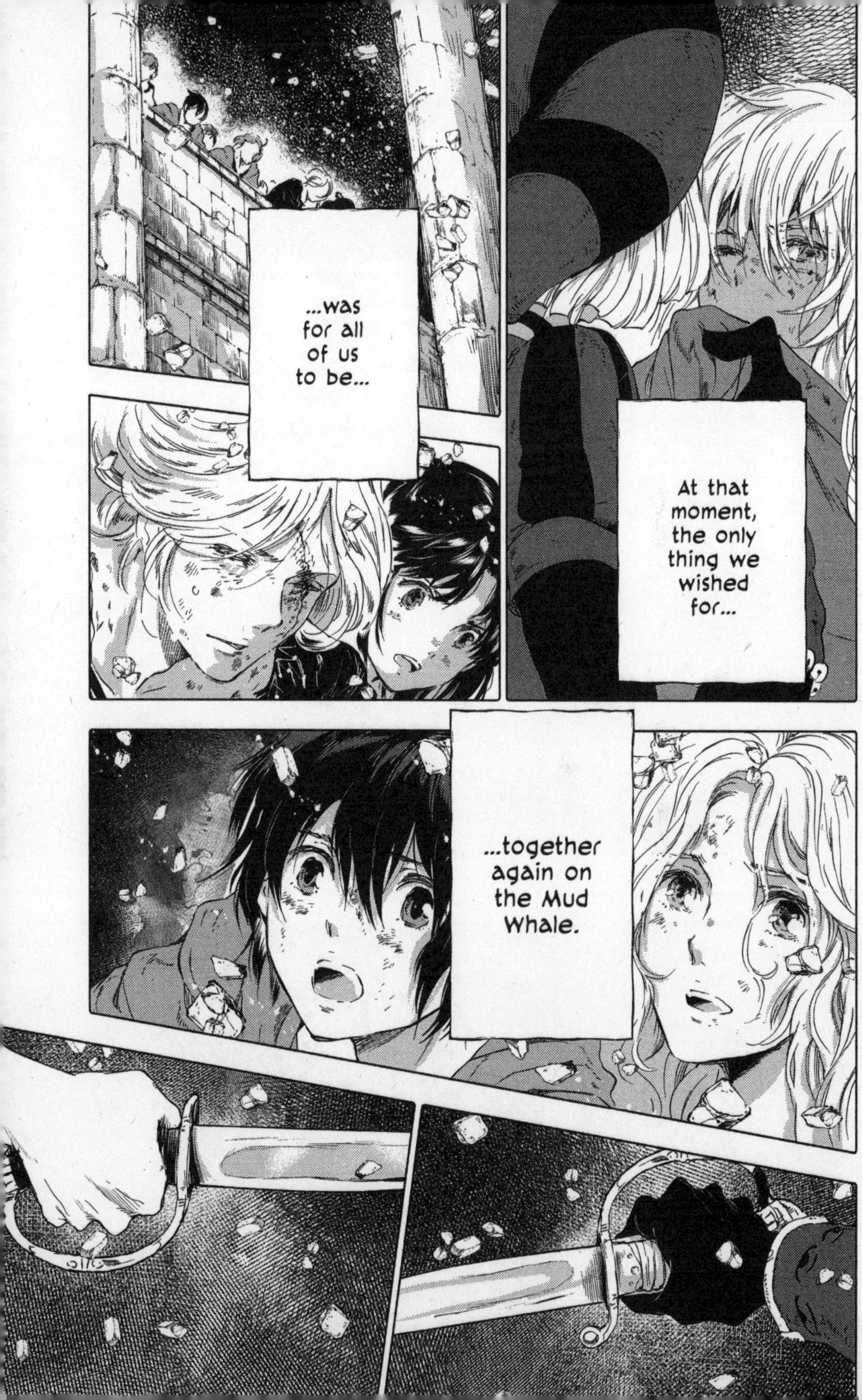
At that moment, the only thing we wished for...
...was for all of us to be...
...together again on the Mud Whale.

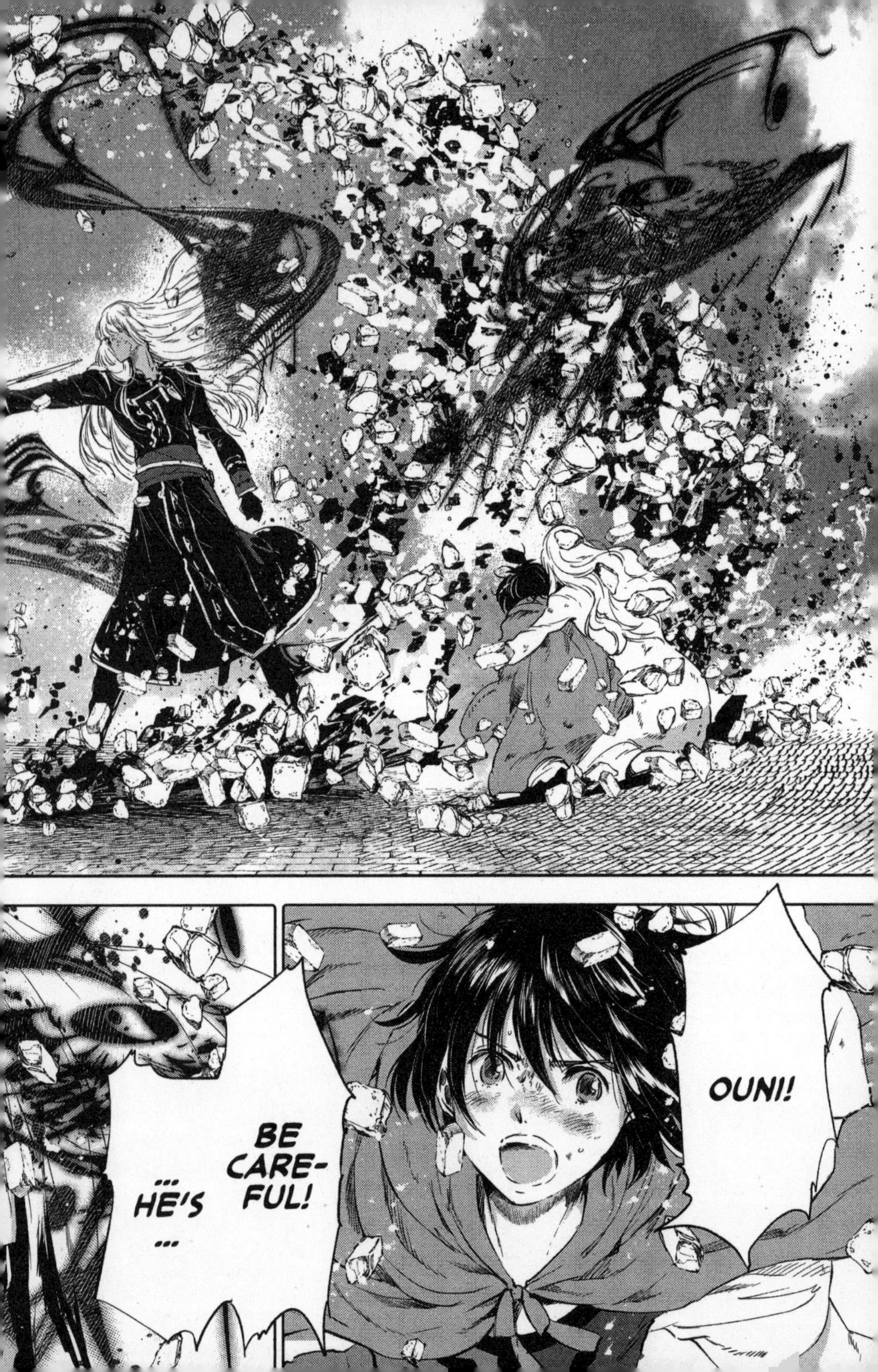
OUNI!
BE CAREFUL!
...HE'S ...

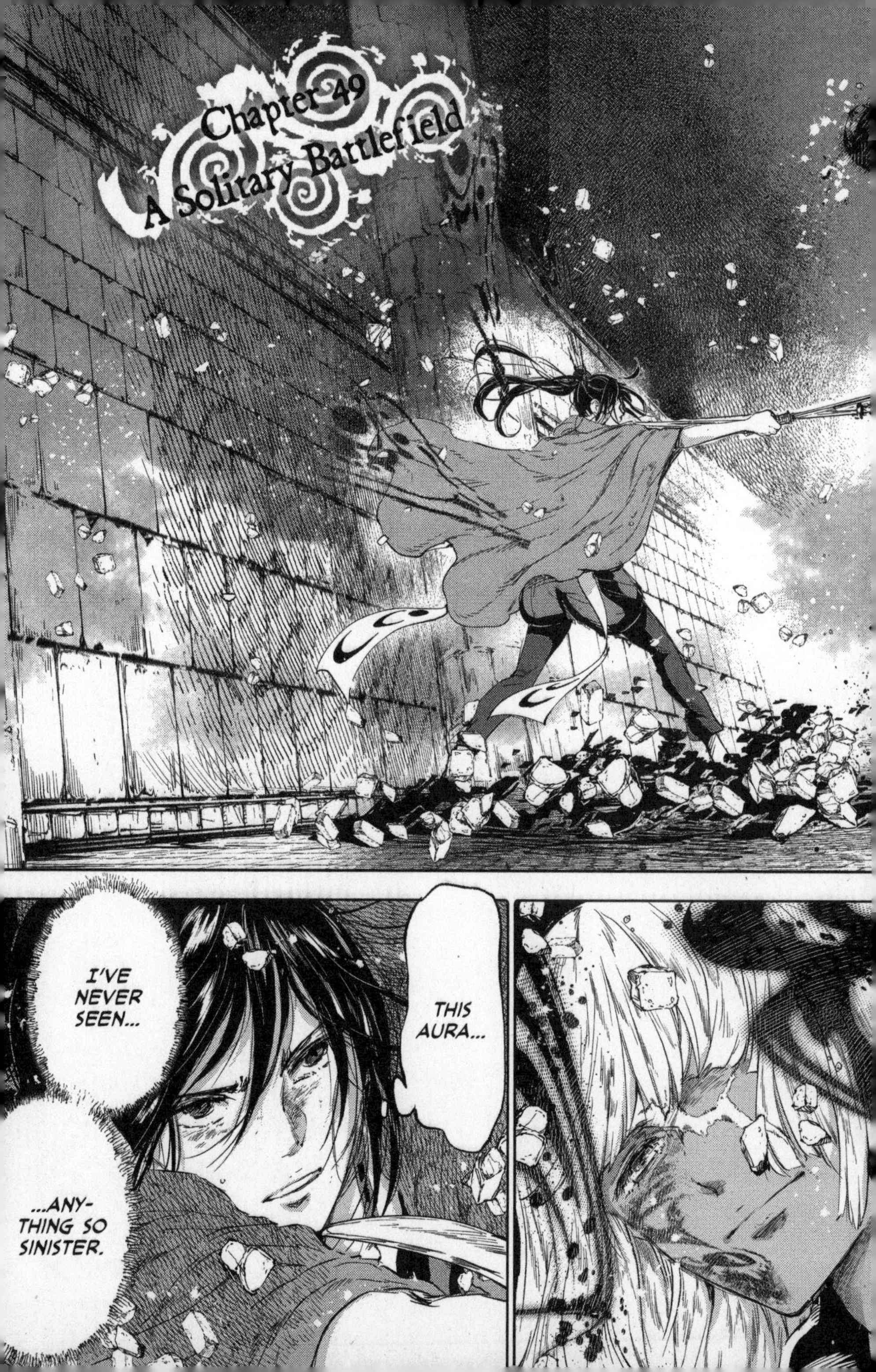
Chapter 49
A Solitary Battlefield
THIS AURA...
I'VE NEVER SEEN...
...ANY-THING SO SINISTER.

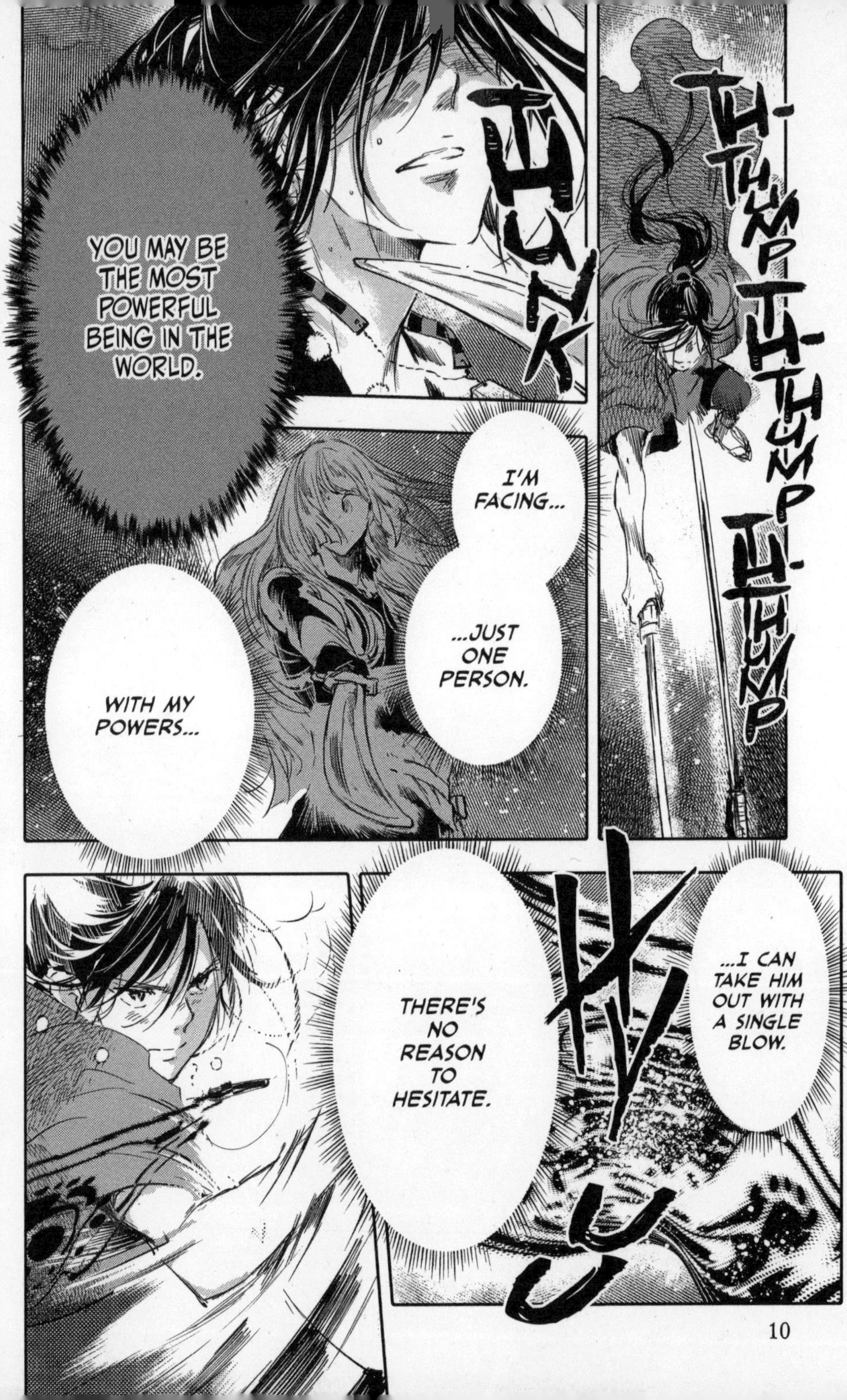
TH-THUMP TH-THUMP TH-THUMP
THUNK
YOU MAY BE THE MOST POWERFUL BEING IN THE WORLD.
I'M FACING...
...JUST ONE PERSON.
WITH MY POWERS...
...I CAN TAKE HIM OUT WITH A SINGLE BLOW.
THERE'S NO REASON TO HESITATE.

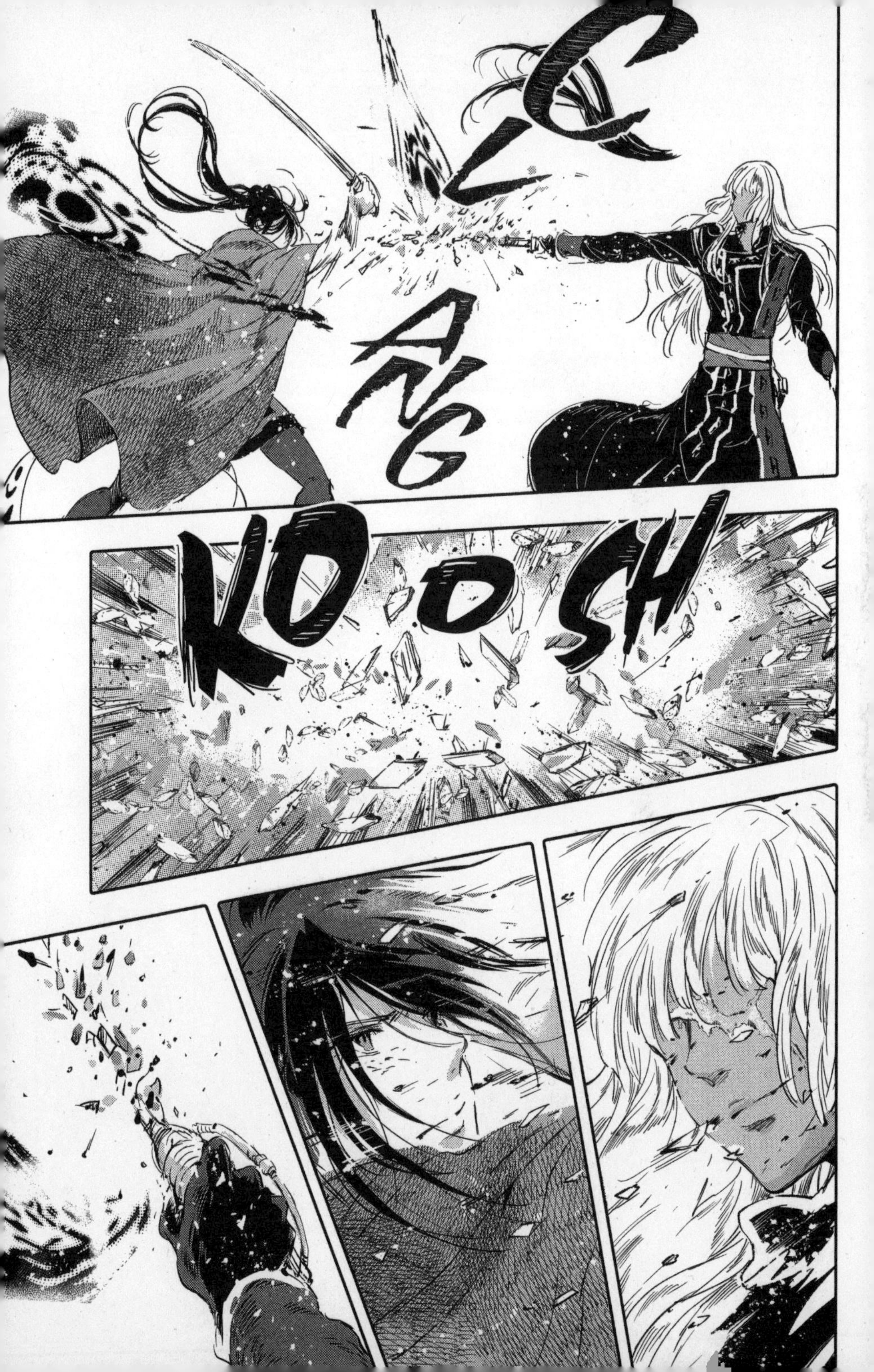
CLANG
KOOSH

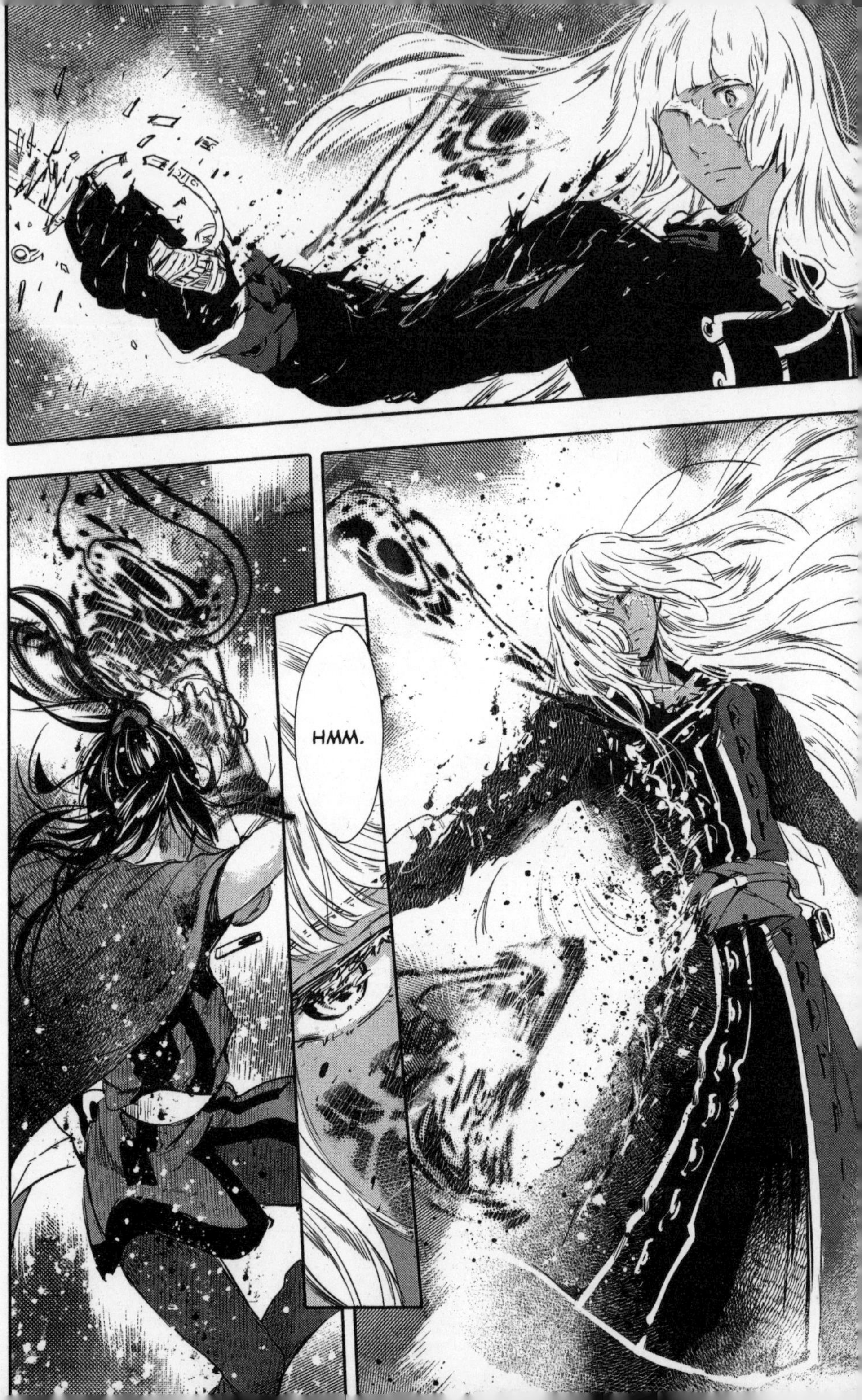
HMM.

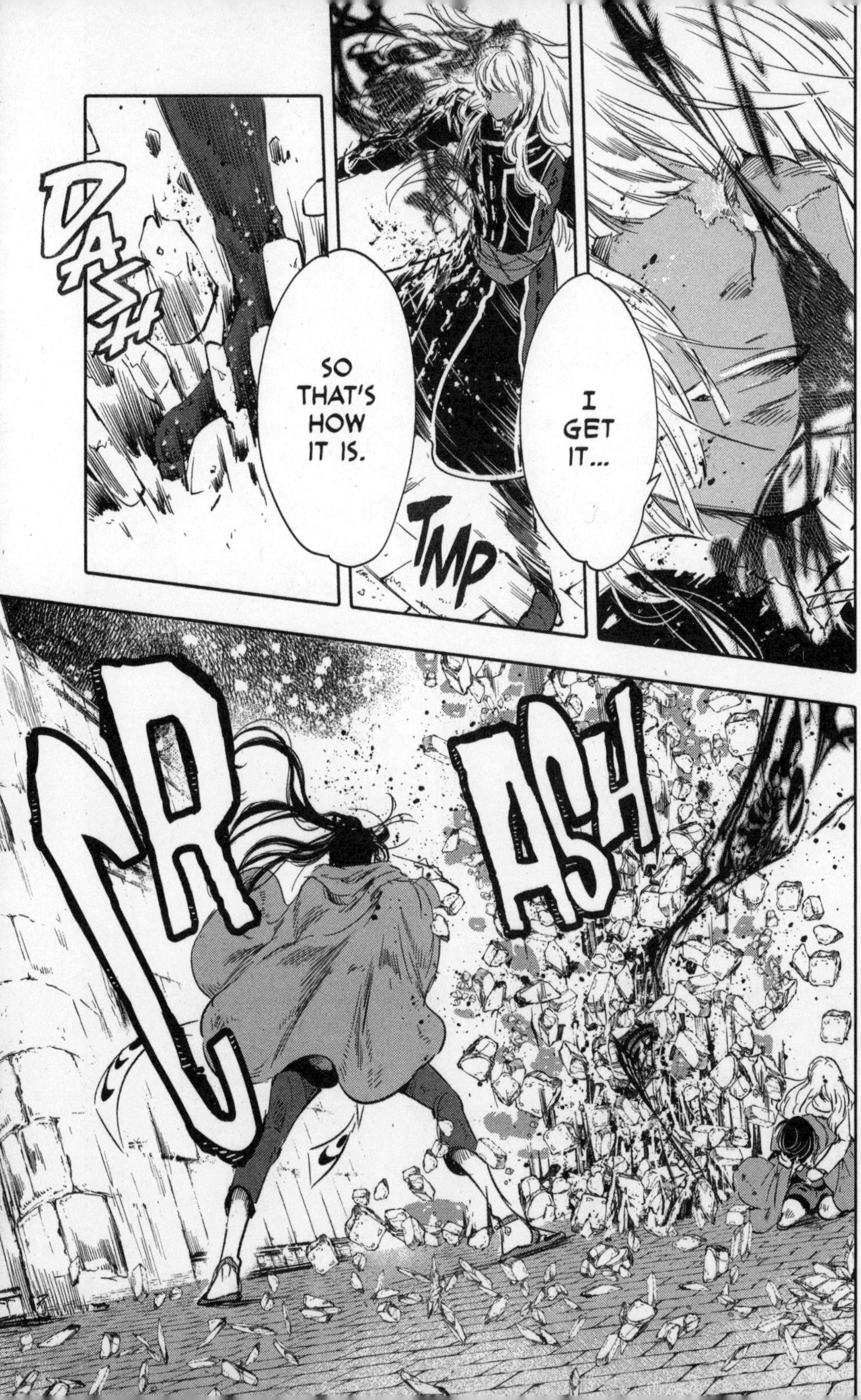
I GET IT...
SO THAT'S HOW IT IS.
TMP
DASH
CRASH

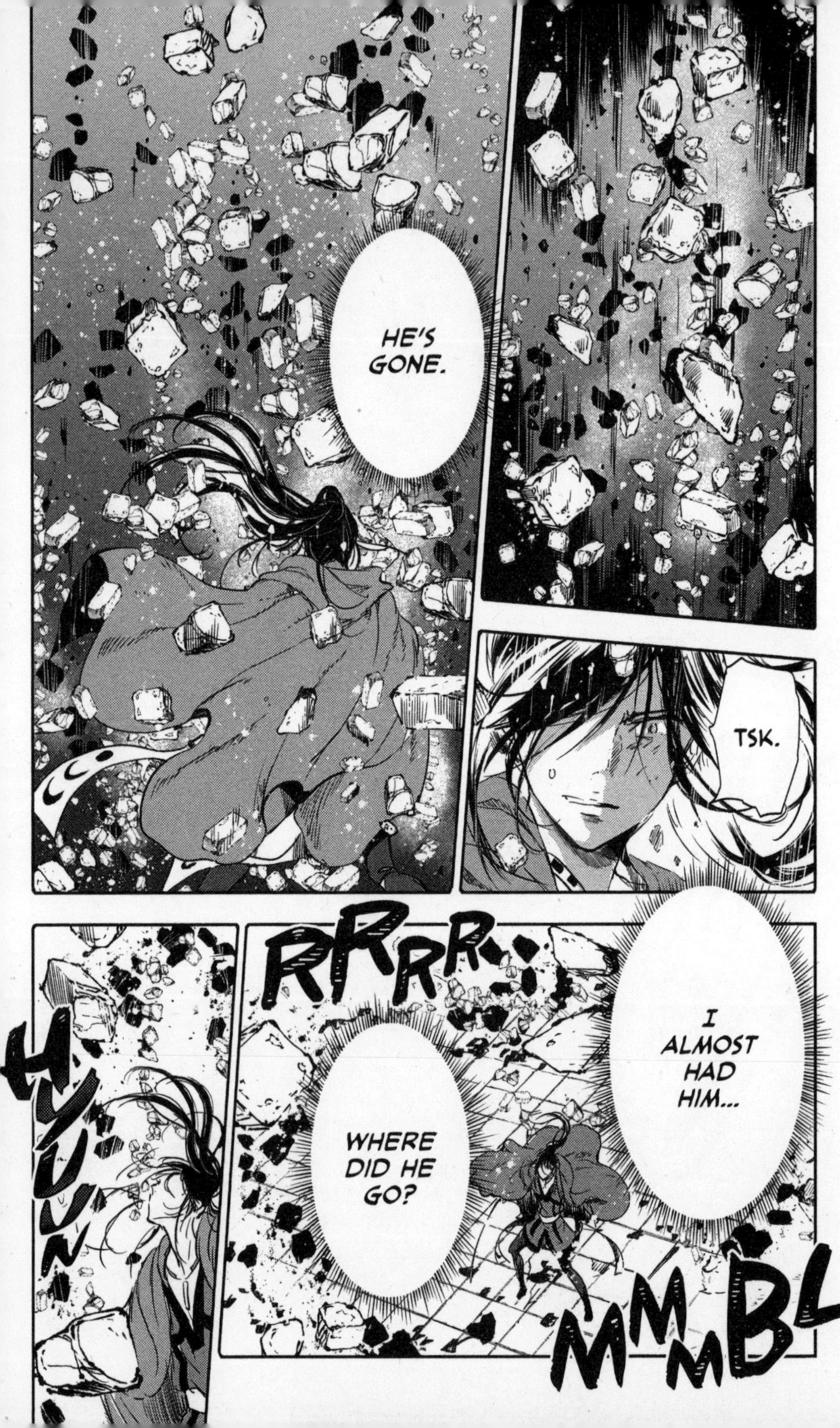
TSK.
HE'S GONE.
RRRR
I ALMOST HAD HIM...
WHERE DID HE GO?
MMMBL
HYUUUN

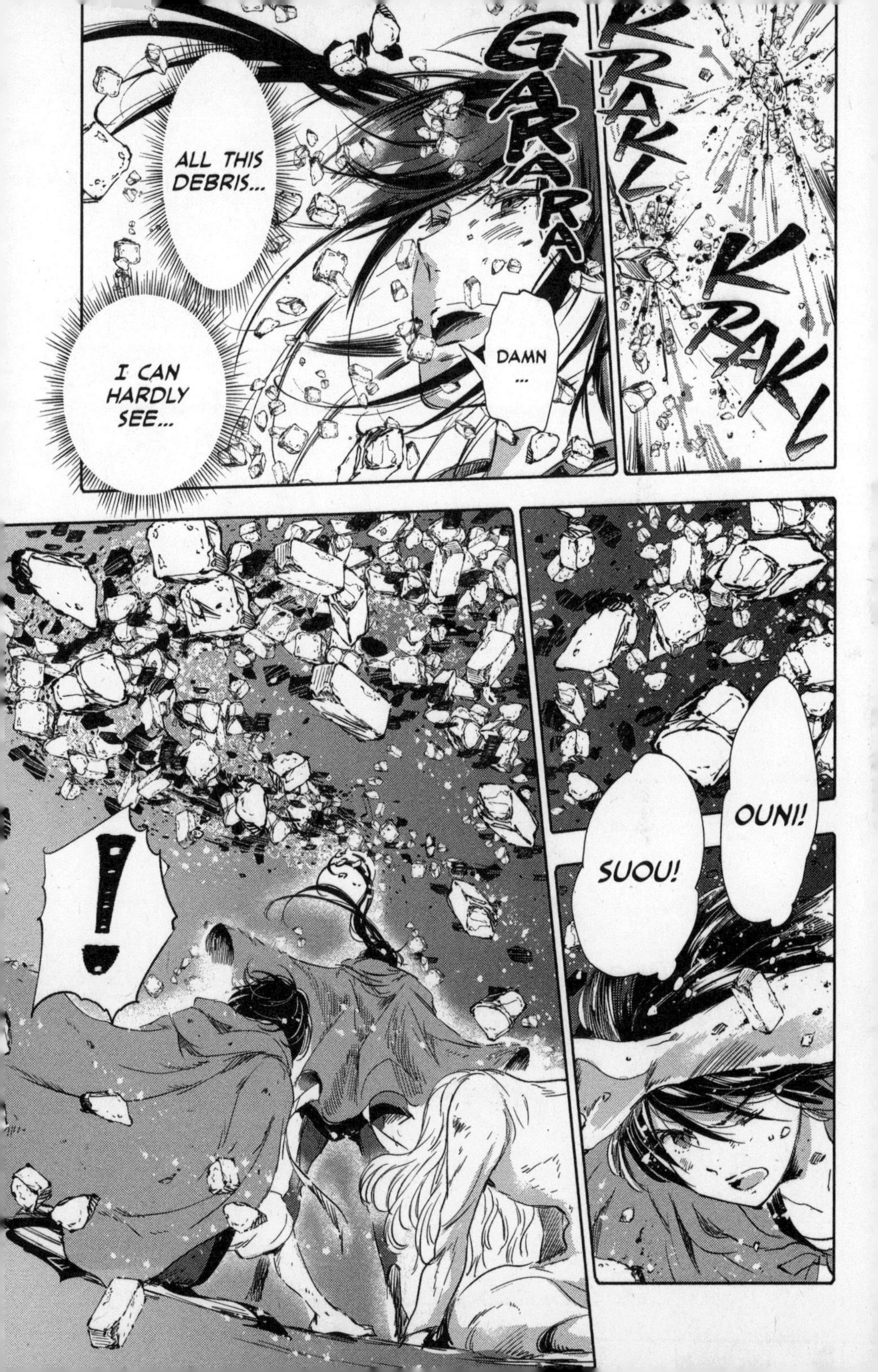
KRAKL
KRAKL
GARARA
ALL THIS DEBRIS...
DAMN ...
I CAN HARDLY SEE...
OUNI!
SUOU!
!

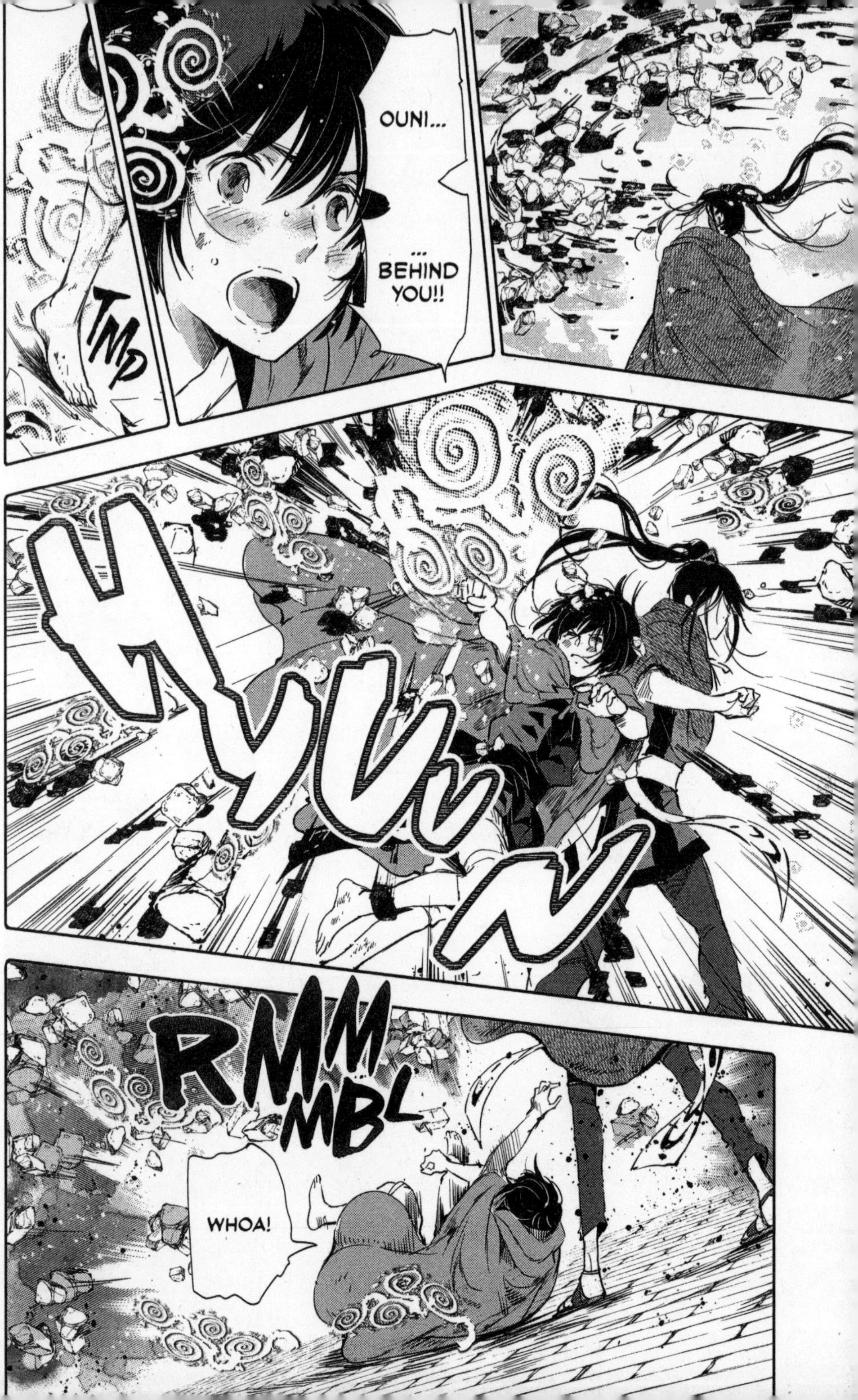
OUNI...
... BEHIND YOU!!
TMP
HYUUUN
RMMMMBL
WHOA!

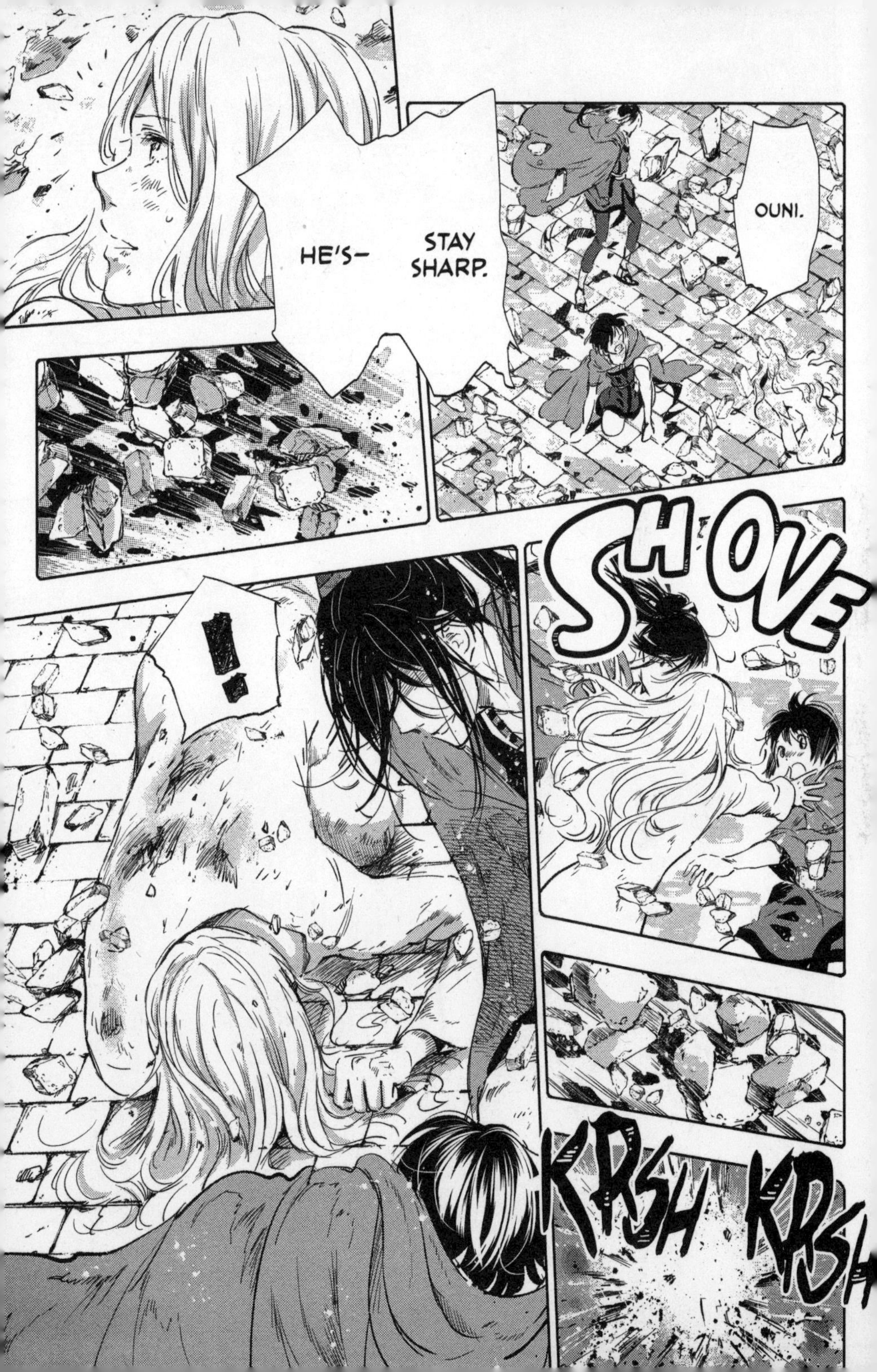
OUNI.
STAY SHARP.
HE'S—
SHOVE
!
KRSH KRSH

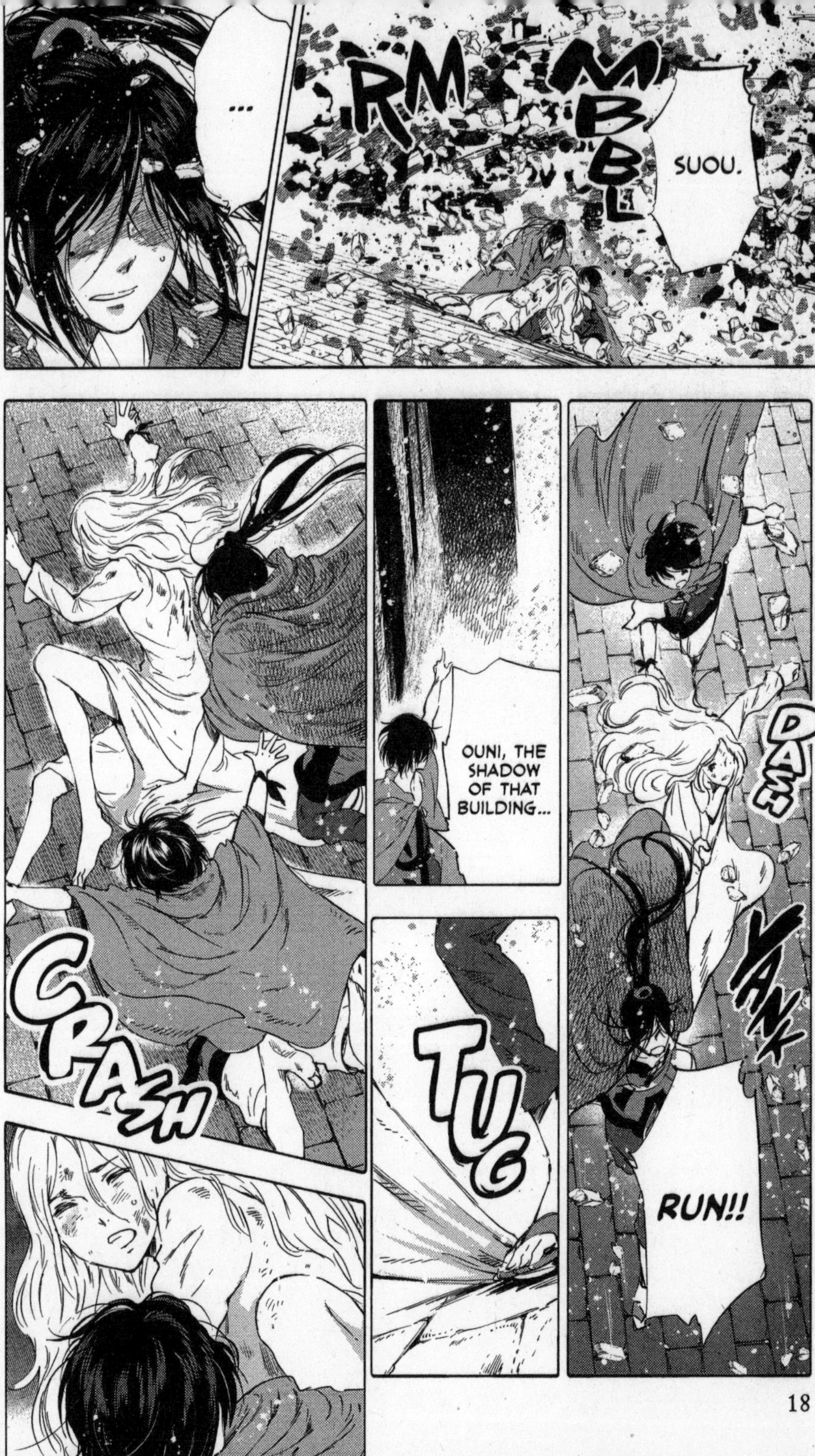
RMMBBL
SUOU.
...
DASH
YANK
RUN!!
OUNI, THE SHADOW OF THAT BUILDING...
TUG
CRASH

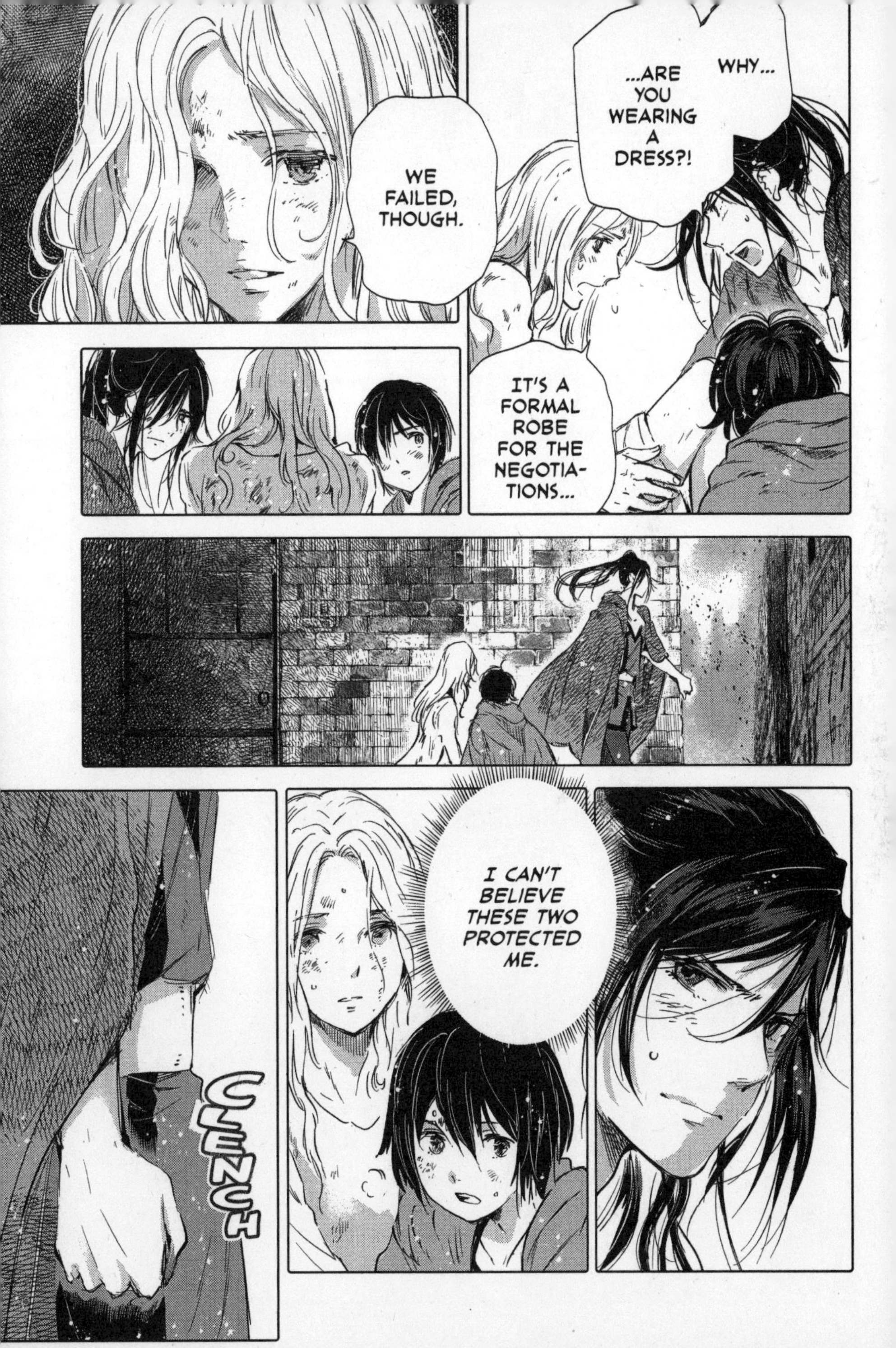
WHY...
...ARE YOU WEARING A DRESS?!
IT'S A FORMAL ROBE FOR THE NEGOTIATIONS...
WE FAILED, THOUGH.
I CAN'T BELIEVE THESE TWO PROTECTED ME.
CLENCH

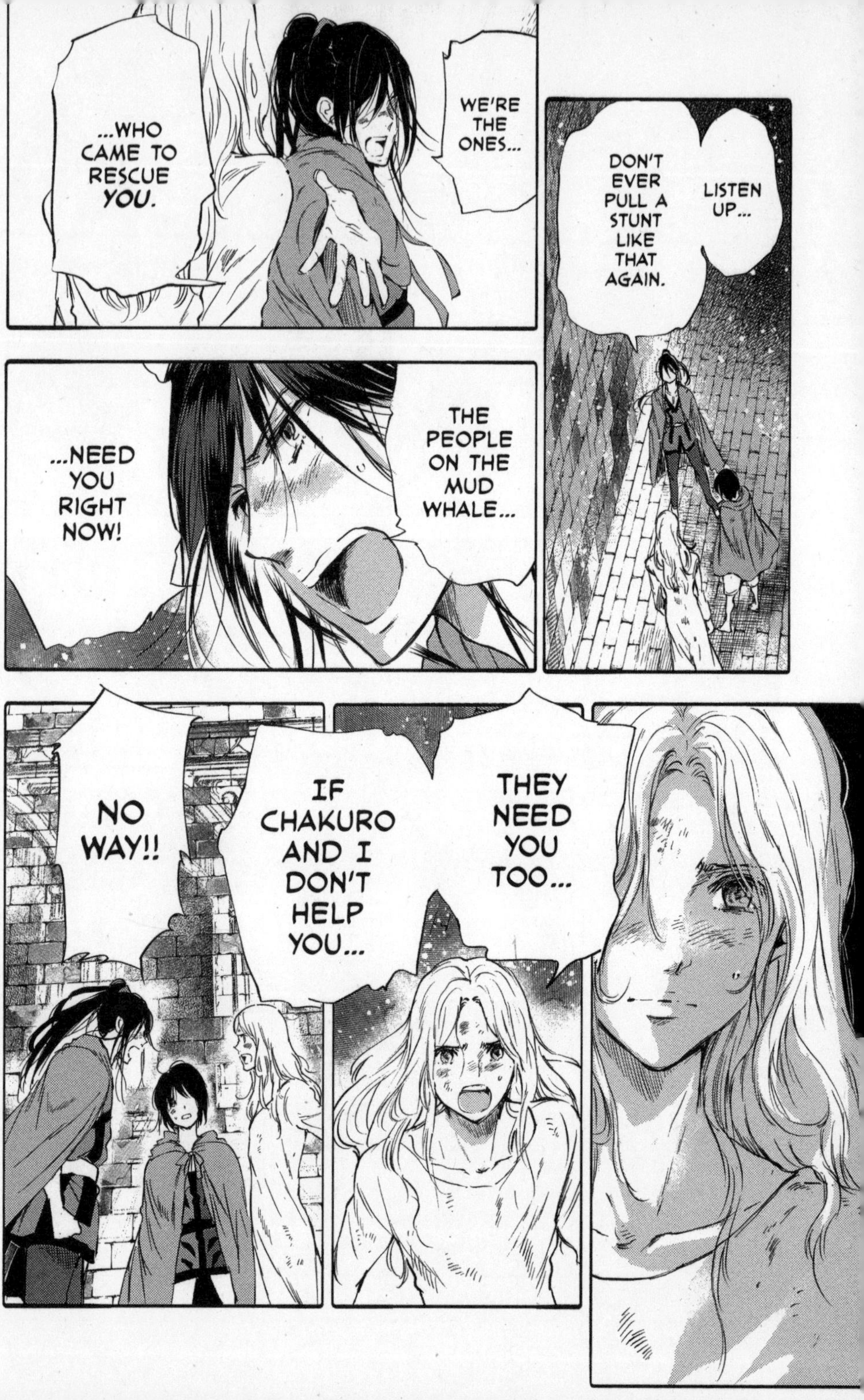
LISTEN UP...
DON'T EVER PULL A STUNT LIKE THAT AGAIN.
WE'RE THE ONES...
...WHO CAME TO RESCUE *YOU*.
THE PEOPLE ON THE MUD WHALE...
...NEED YOU RIGHT NOW!
THEY NEED YOU TOO...
IF CHAKURO AND I DON'T HELP YOU...
NO WAY!!

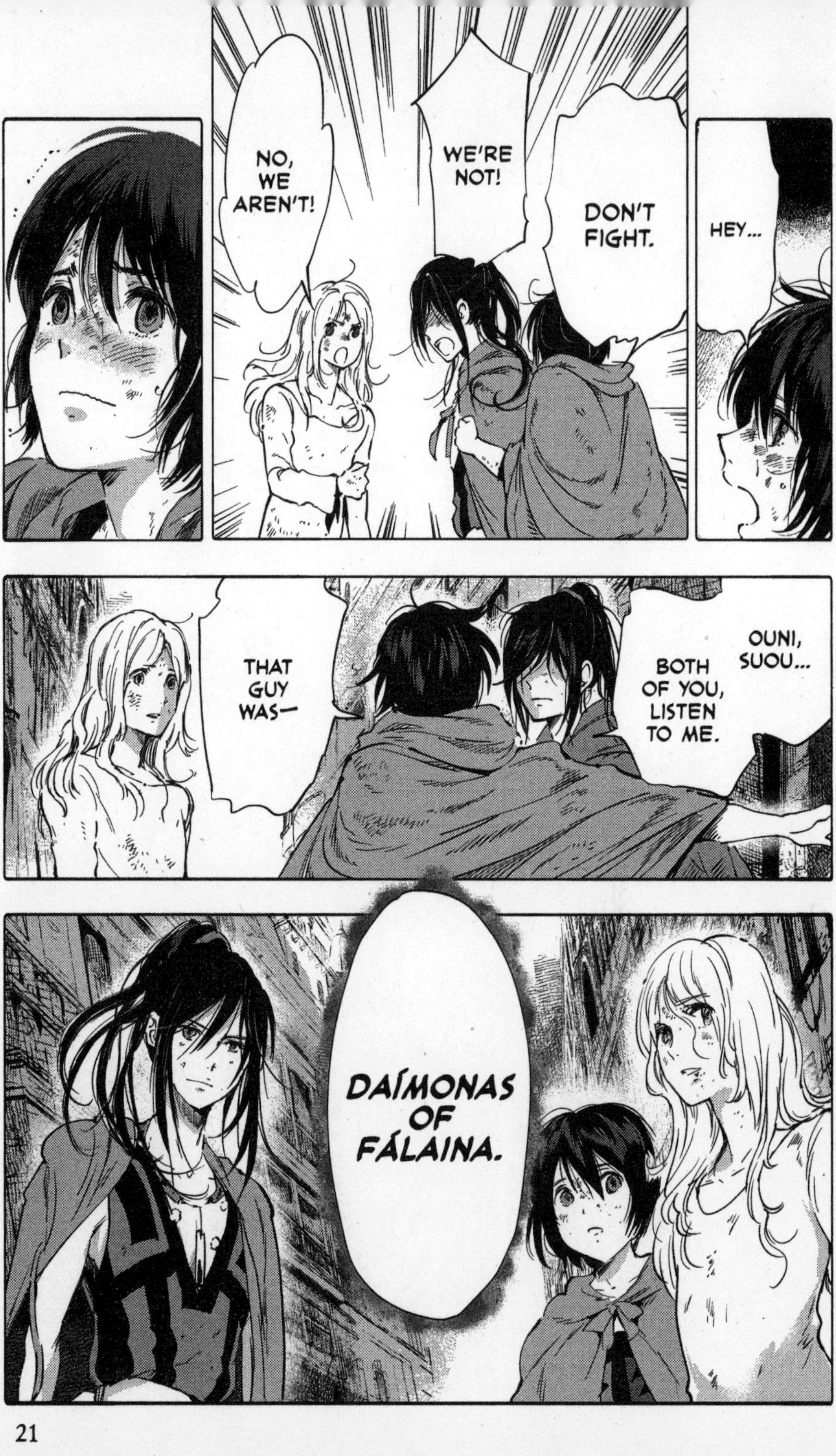
HEY...
DON'T FIGHT.
WE'RE NOT!
NO, WE AREN'T!
OUNI, SUOU... BOTH OF YOU, LISTEN TO ME.
THAT GUY WAS—
DAÍMONAS OF FÁLAINA.

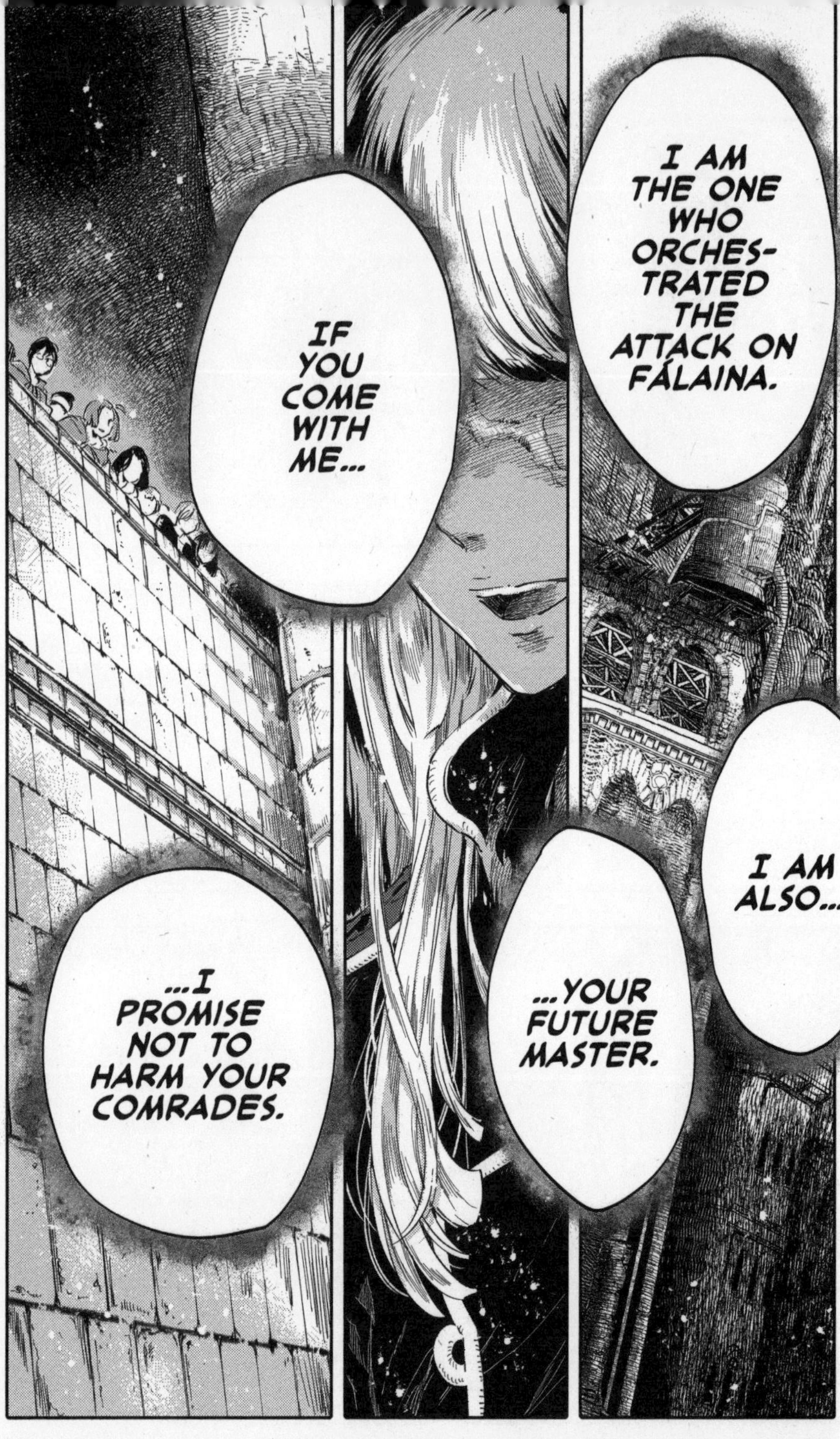
I AM THE ONE WHO ORCHES-TRATED THE ATTACK ON FÁLAINA.
I AM ALSO...
...YOUR FUTURE MASTER.
IF YOU COME WITH ME...
...I PROMISE NOT TO HARM YOUR COMRADES.

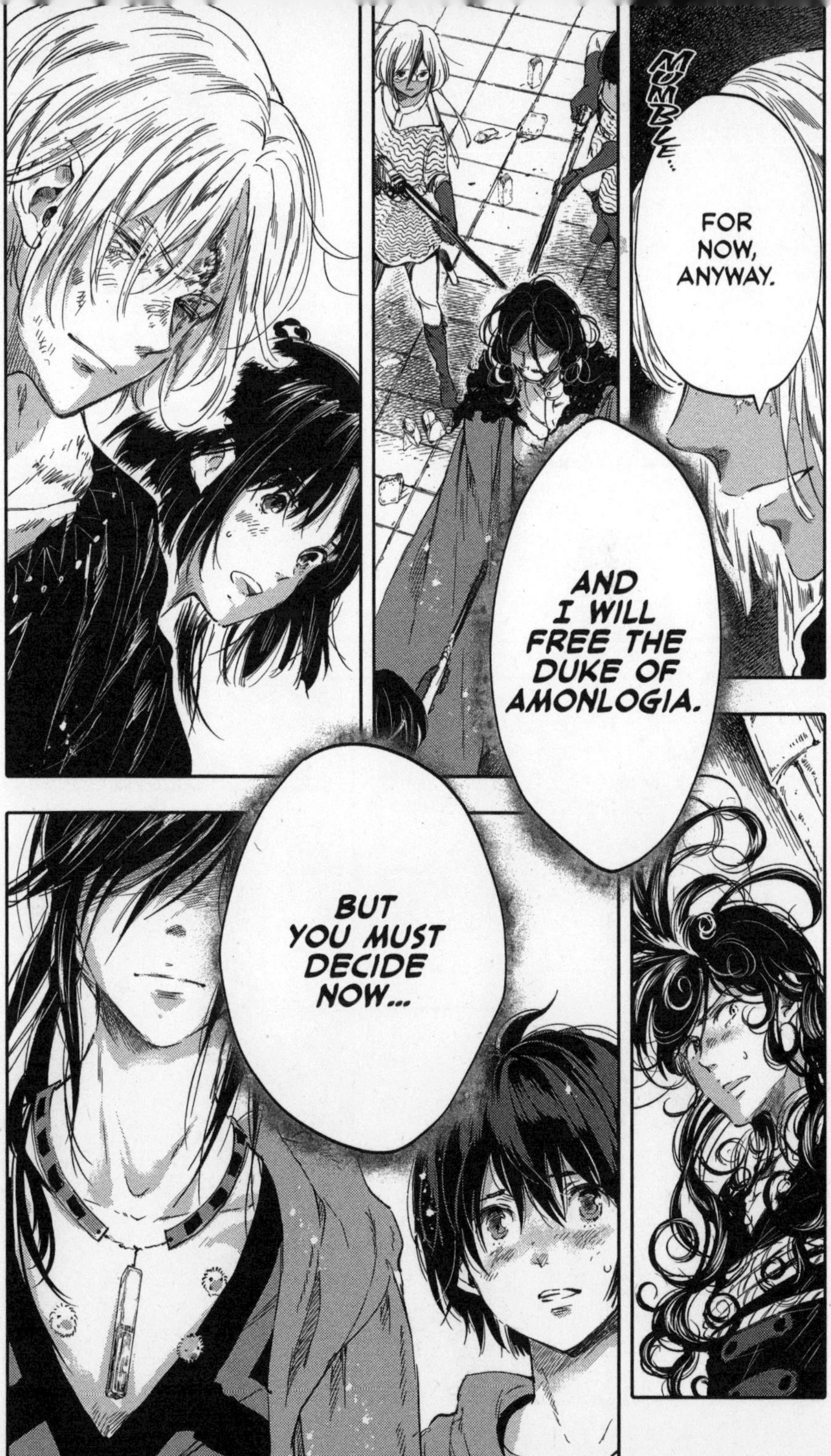
MUMBLE...
FOR NOW, ANYWAY.
AND I WILL FREE THE DUKE OF AMONLOGIA.
BUT YOU MUST DECIDE NOW...

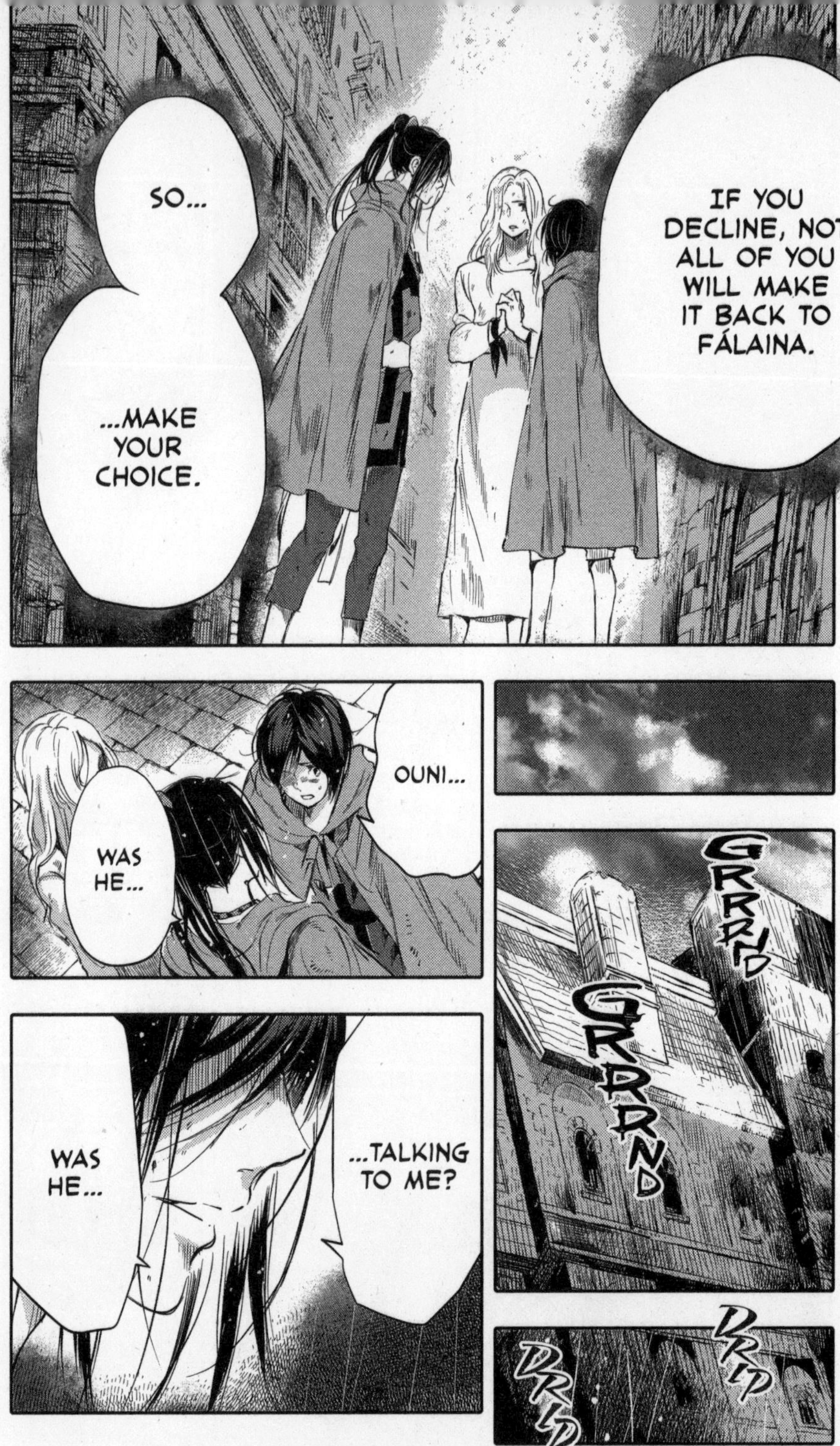
IF YOU DECLINE, NOT ALL OF YOU WILL MAKE IT BACK TO FÁLAINA.
SO...
...MAKE YOUR CHOICE.
GRRRND
GRRRND
DRIP
DRIP
OUNI...
WAS HE...
WAS HE...
...TALKING TO ME?

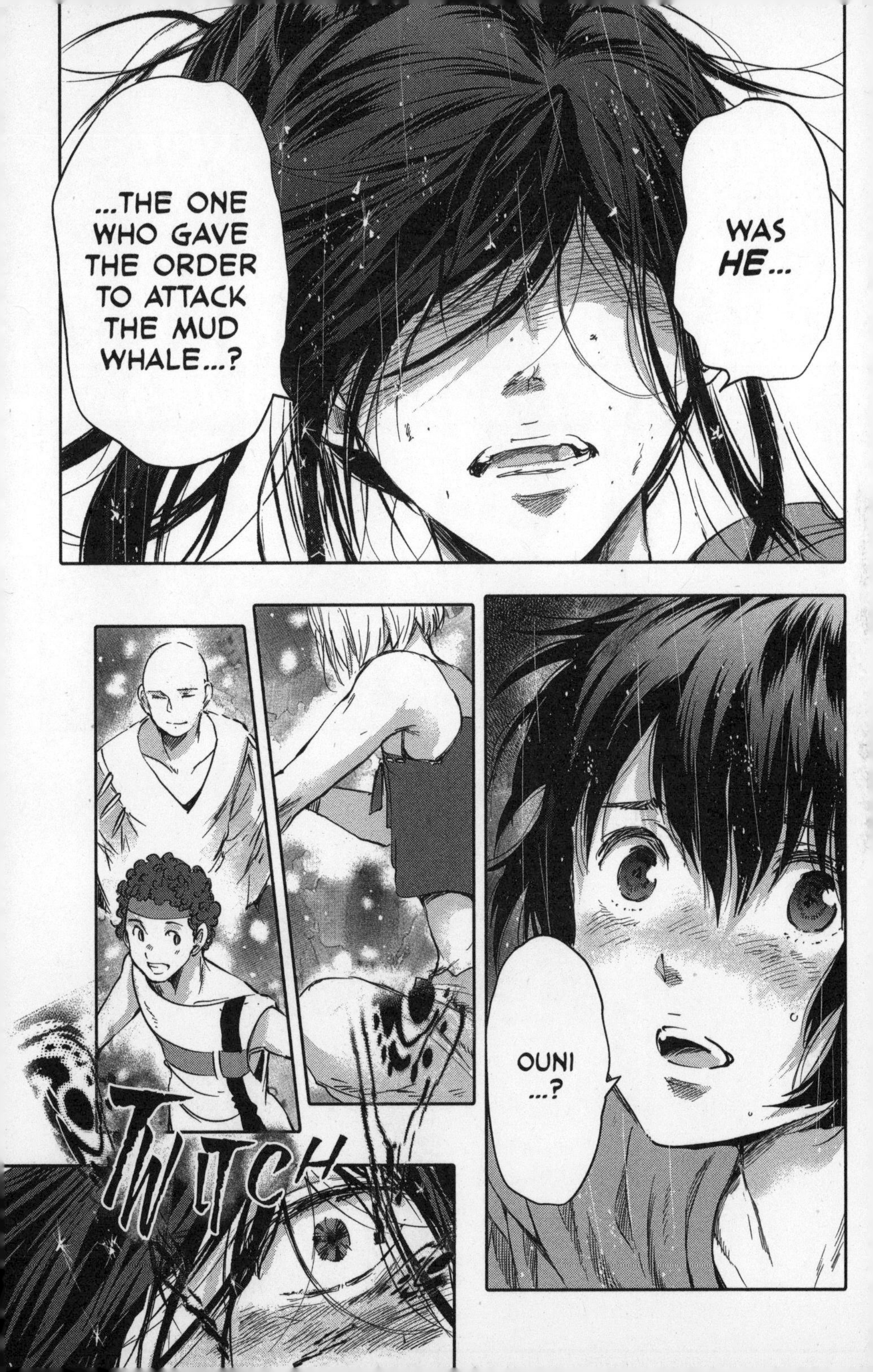
WAS HE...
...THE ONE WHO GAVE THE ORDER TO ATTACK THE MUD WHALE...?
OUNI ...?
TWITCH

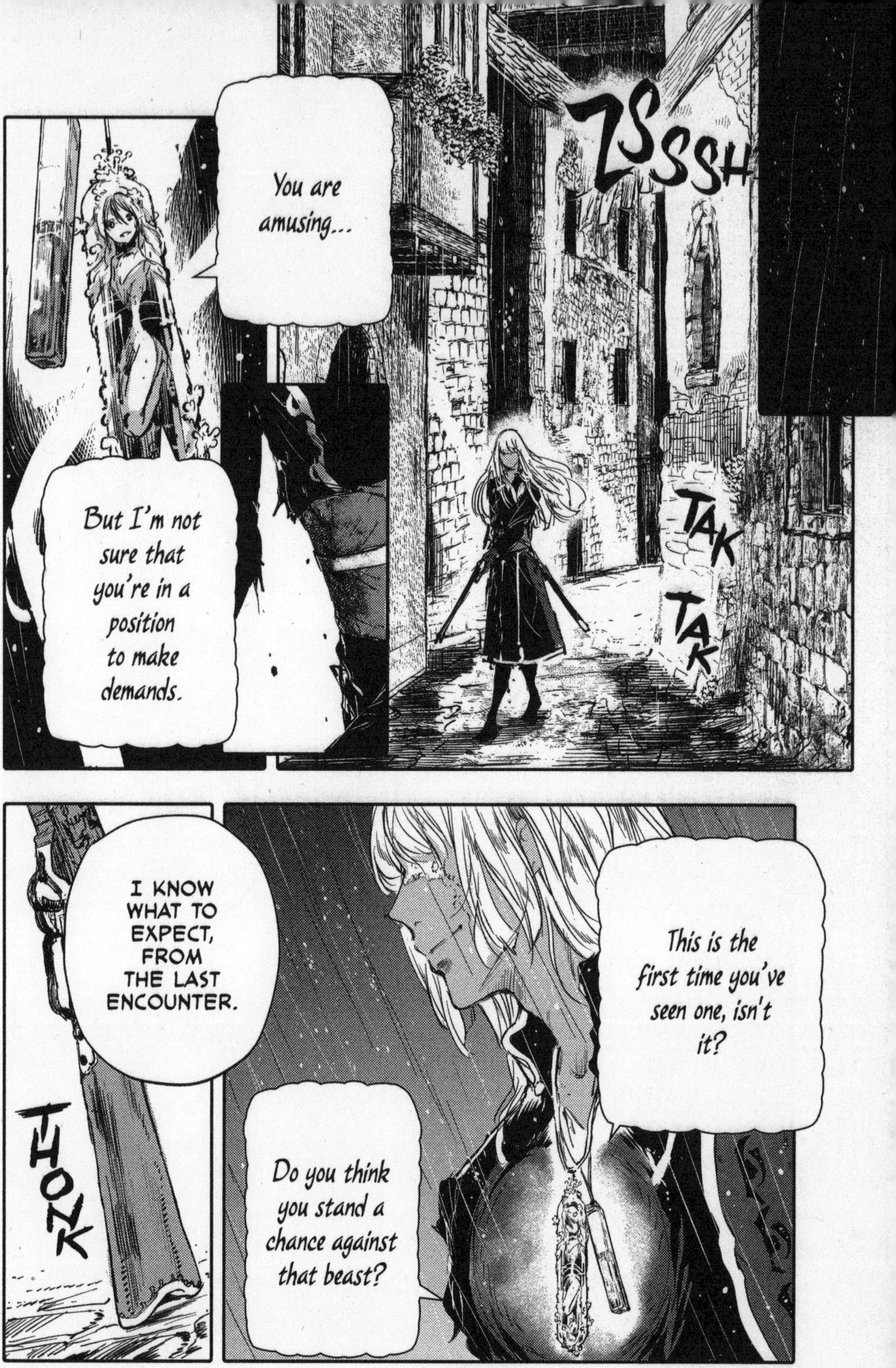
ZSSSH
TAK TAK
You are amusing...
But I'm not sure that you're in a position to make demands.
This is the first time you've seen one, isn't it?
Do you think you stand a chance against that beast?
I KNOW WHAT TO EXPECT, FROM THE LAST ENCOUNTER.
THONK

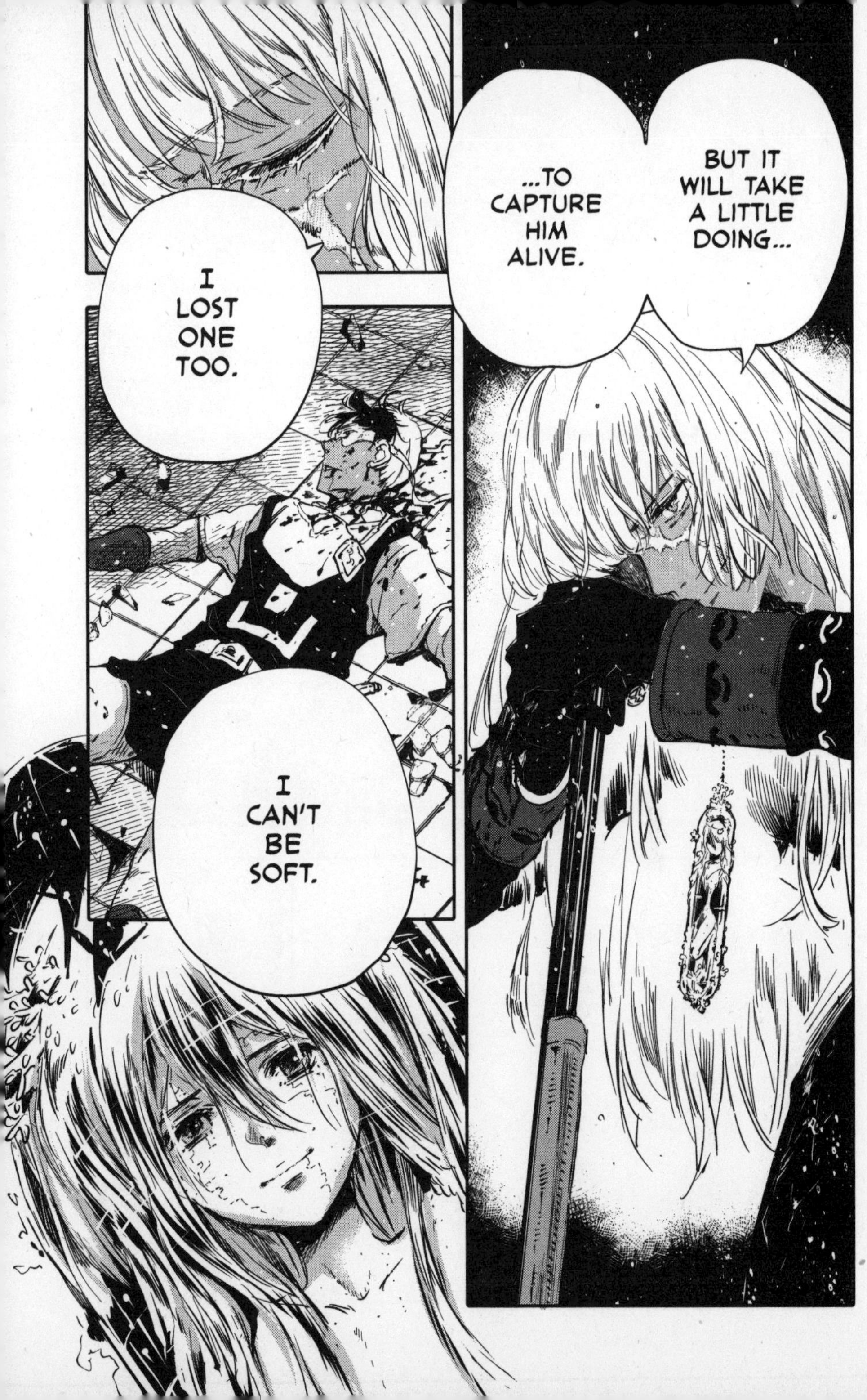
BUT IT WILL TAKE A LITTLE DOING...
...TO CAPTURE HIM ALIVE.
I LOST ONE TOO.
I CAN'T BE SOFT.

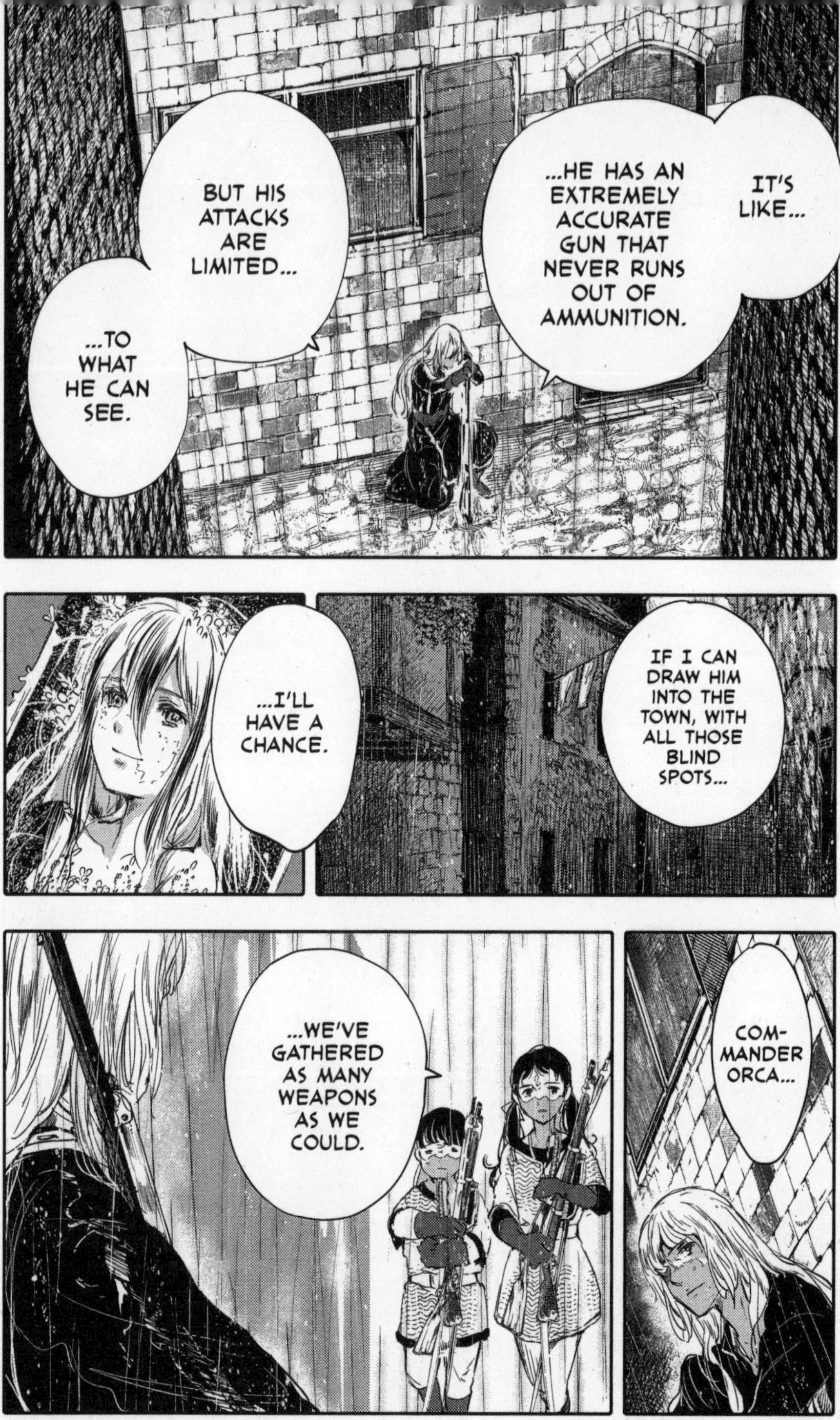
IT'S LIKE...
...HE HAS AN EXTREMELY ACCURATE GUN THAT NEVER RUNS OUT OF AMMUNITION.
BUT HIS ATTACKS ARE LIMITED...
...TO WHAT HE CAN SEE.
IF I CAN DRAW HIM INTO THE TOWN, WITH ALL THOSE BLIND SPOTS...
...I'LL HAVE A CHANCE.
COM-MANDER ORCA...
...WE'VE GATHERED AS MANY WEAPONS AS WE COULD.

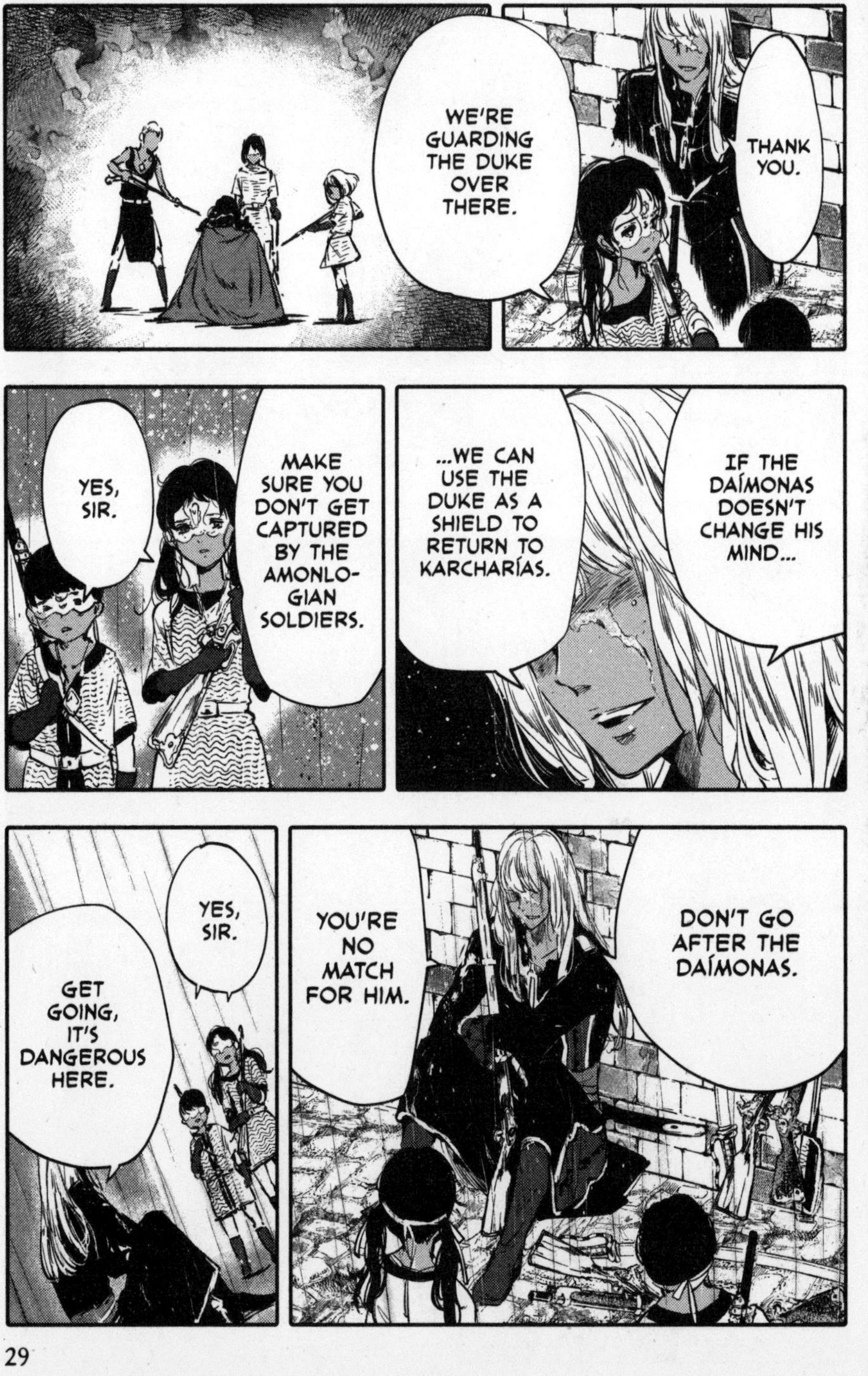
THANK YOU.
WE'RE GUARDING THE DUKE OVER THERE.
IF THE DAÍMONAS DOESN'T CHANGE HIS MIND...
...WE CAN USE THE DUKE AS A SHIELD TO RETURN TO KARCHARÍAS.
MAKE SURE YOU DON'T GET CAPTURED BY THE AMONLOGIAN SOLDIERS.
YES, SIR.
DON'T GO AFTER THE DAÍMONAS.
YOU'RE NO MATCH FOR HIM.
GET GOING, IT'S DANGEROUS HERE.
YES, SIR.

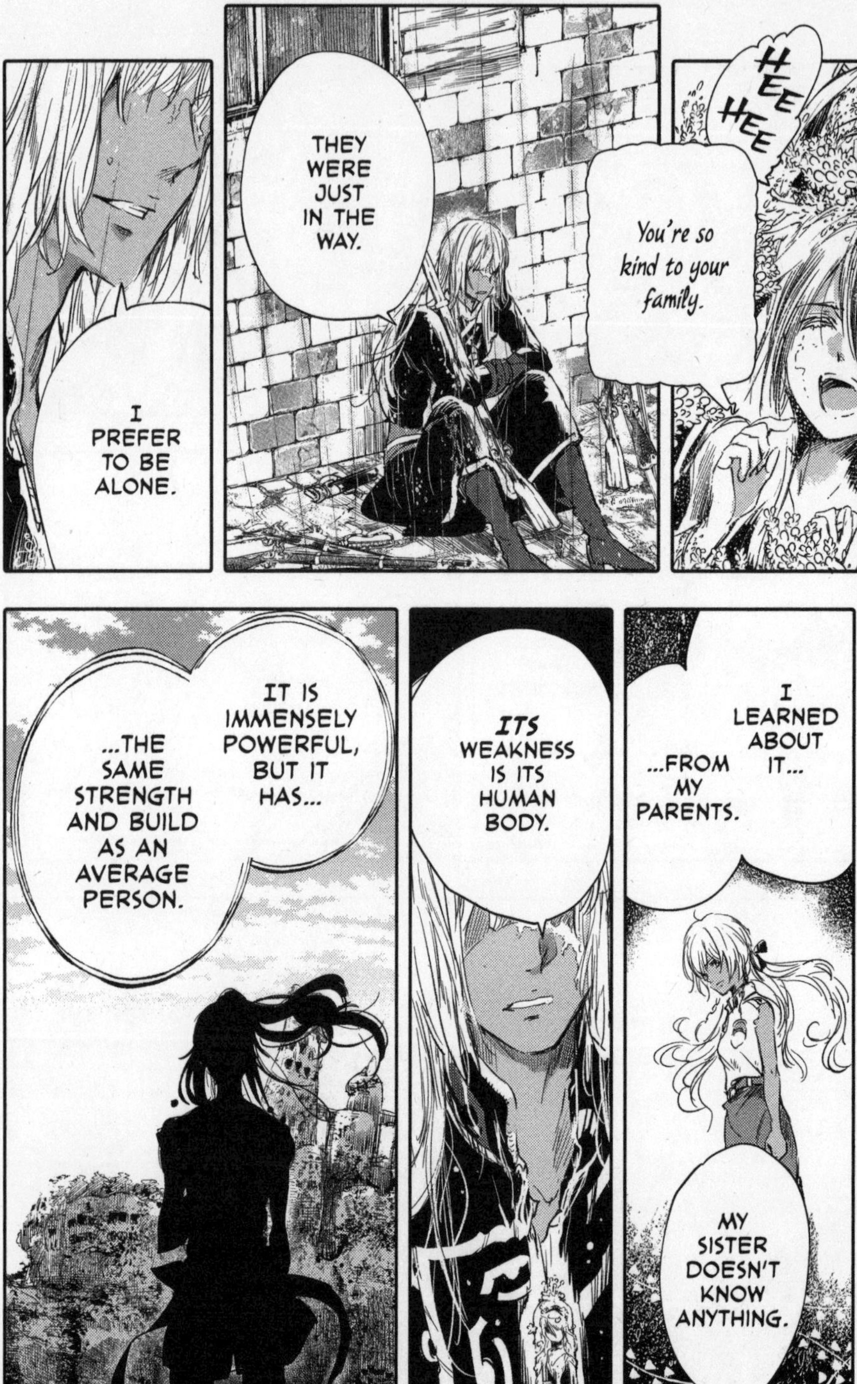
HEE HEE
You're so kind to your family.
THEY WERE JUST IN THE WAY.
I PREFER TO BE ALONE.
I LEARNED ABOUT IT...
...FROM MY PARENTS.
MY SISTER DOESN'T KNOW ANYTHING.
ITS WEAKNESS IS ITS HUMAN BODY.
IT IS IMMENSELY POWERFUL, BUT IT HAS...
...THE SAME STRENGTH AND BUILD AS AN AVERAGE PERSON.

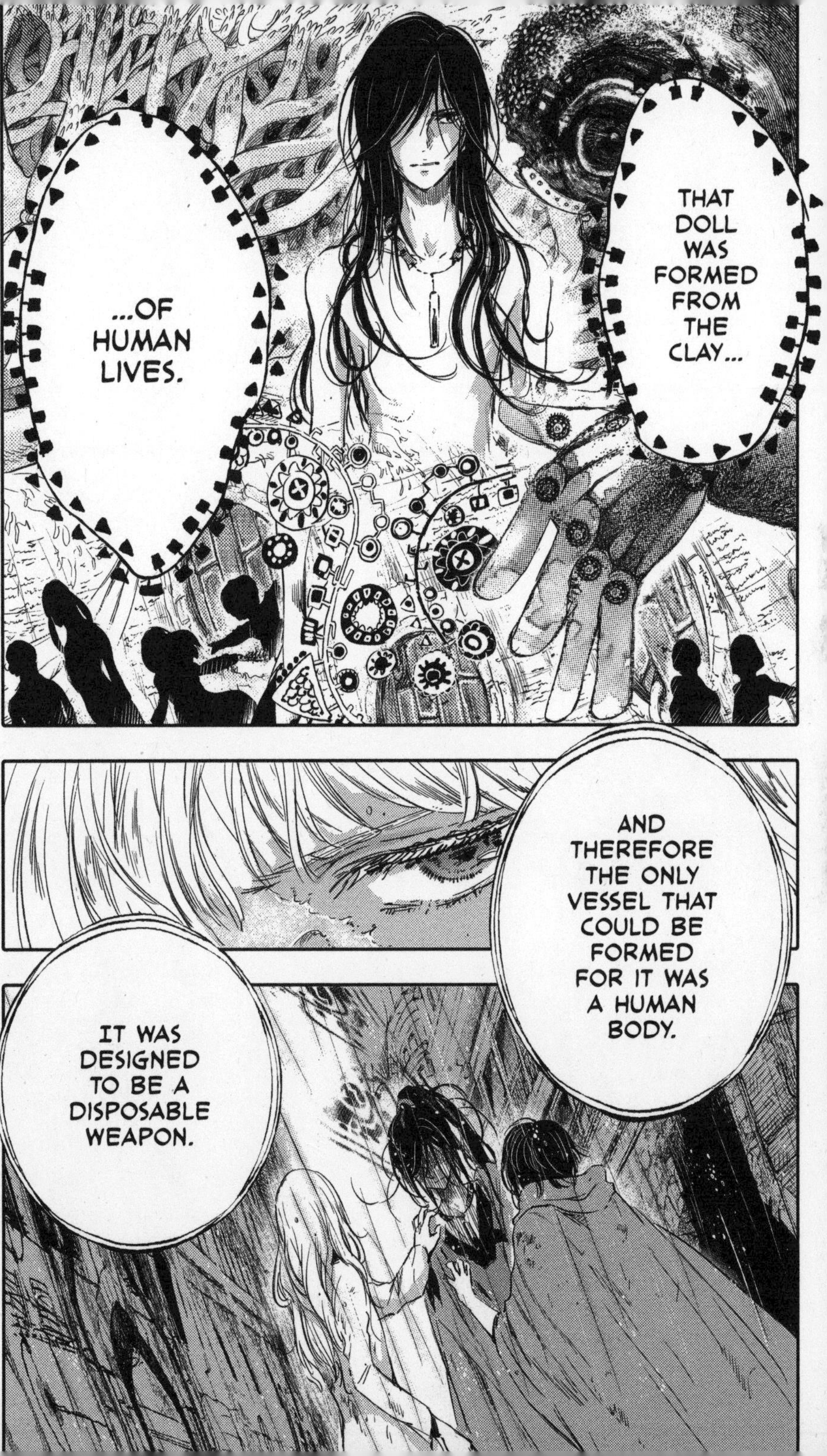
THAT DOLL WAS FORMED FROM THE CLAY...
...OF HUMAN LIVES.
AND THEREFORE THE ONLY VESSEL THAT COULD BE FORMED FOR IT WAS A HUMAN BODY.
IT WAS DESIGNED TO BE A DISPOSABLE WEAPON.

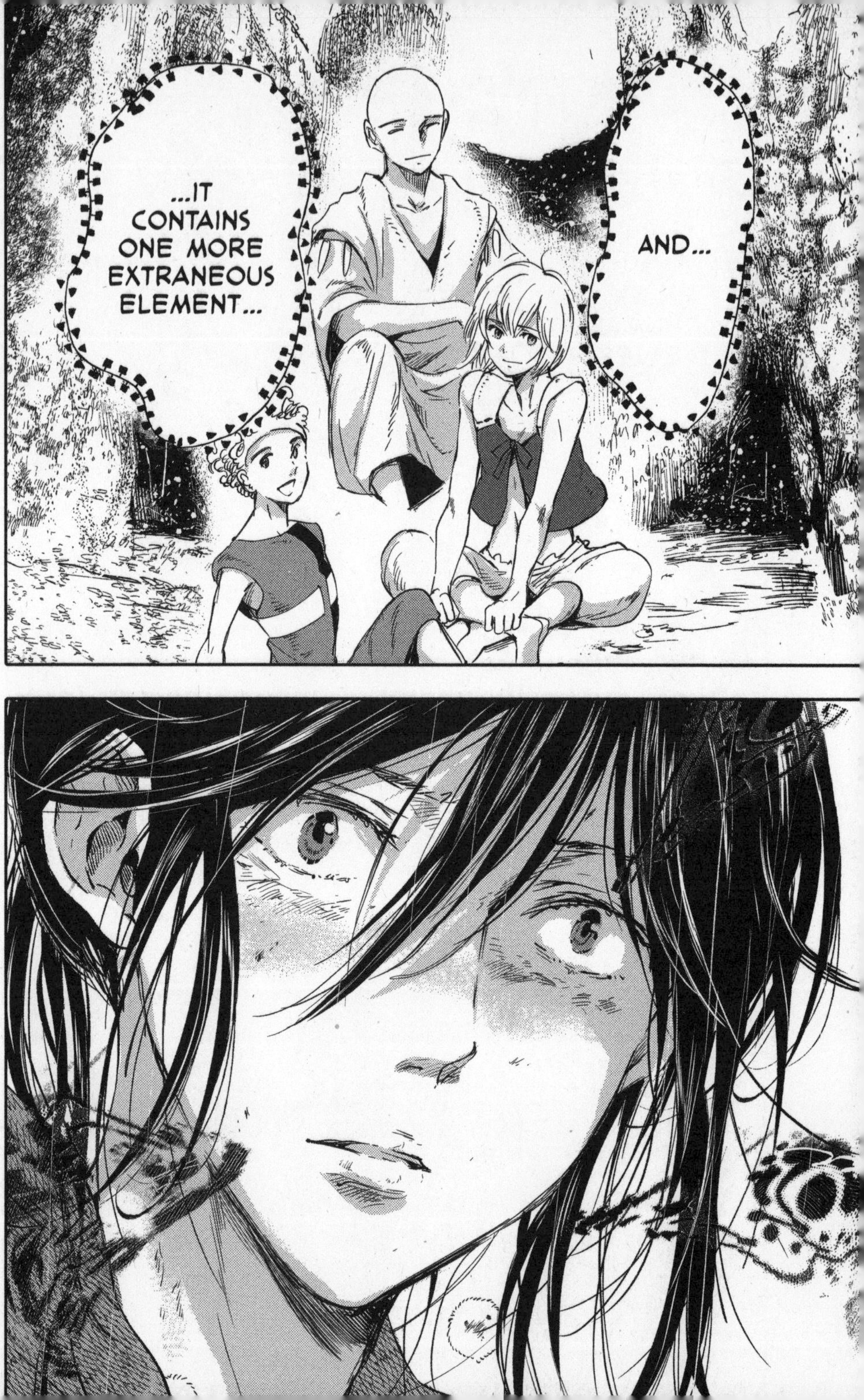
AND...
...IT CONTAINS ONE MORE EXTRANEOUS ELEMENT...

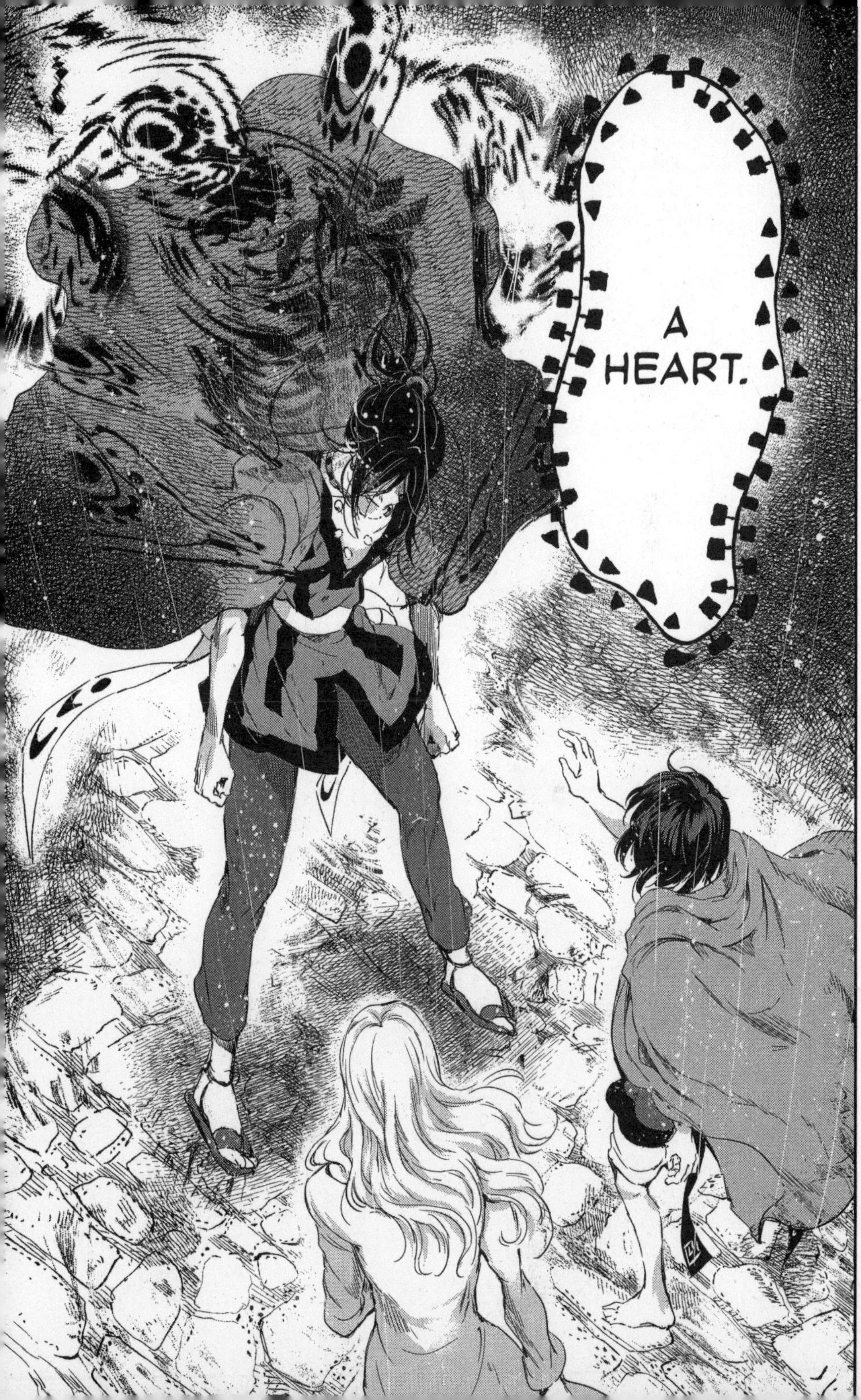
A HEART.

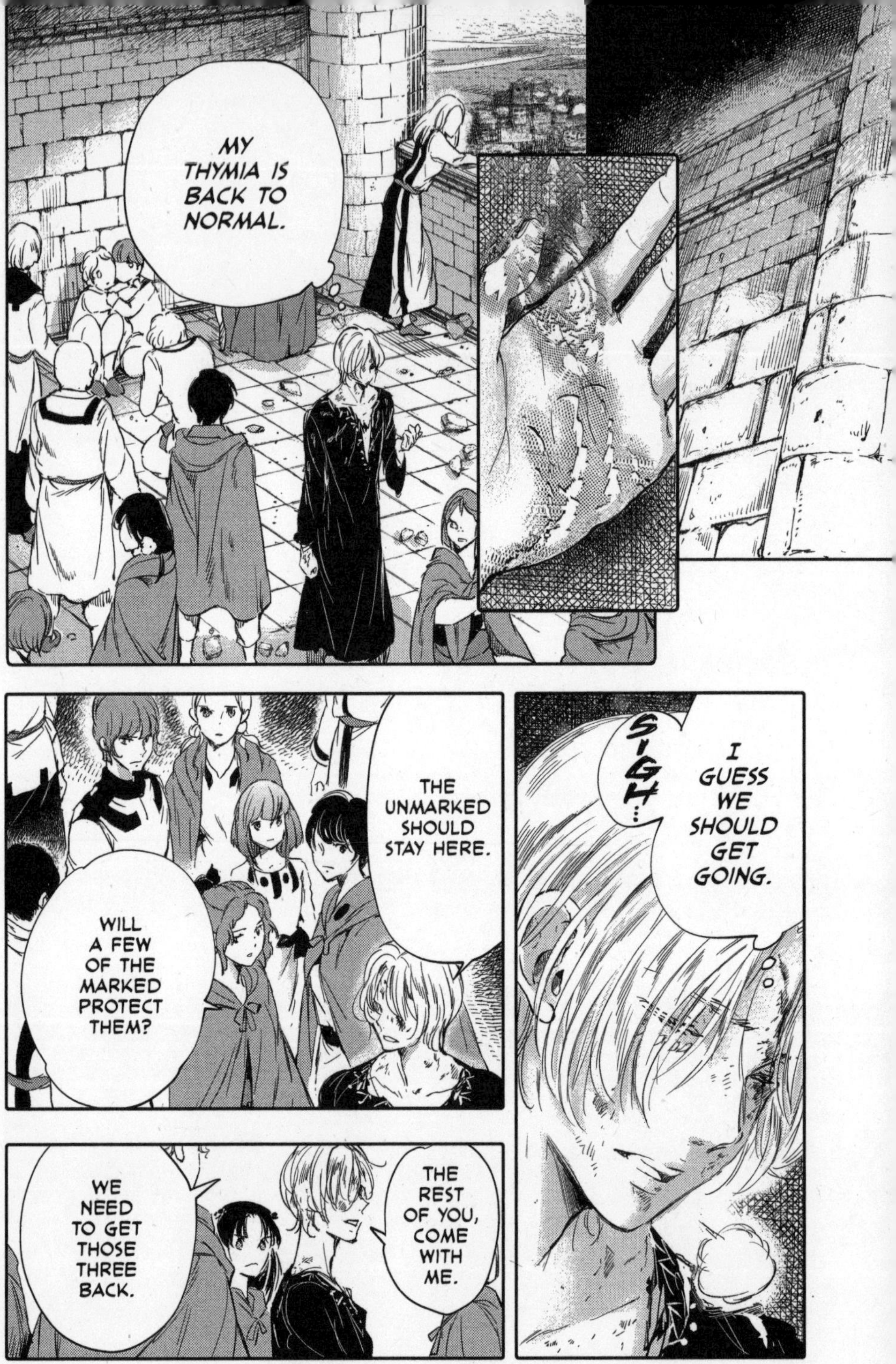
MY THYMIA IS BACK TO NORMAL.
SIGH...
I GUESS WE SHOULD GET GOING.
THE UNMARKED SHOULD STAY HERE.
WILL A FEW OF THE MARKED PROTECT THEM?
THE REST OF YOU, COME WITH ME.
WE NEED TO GET THOSE THREE BACK.

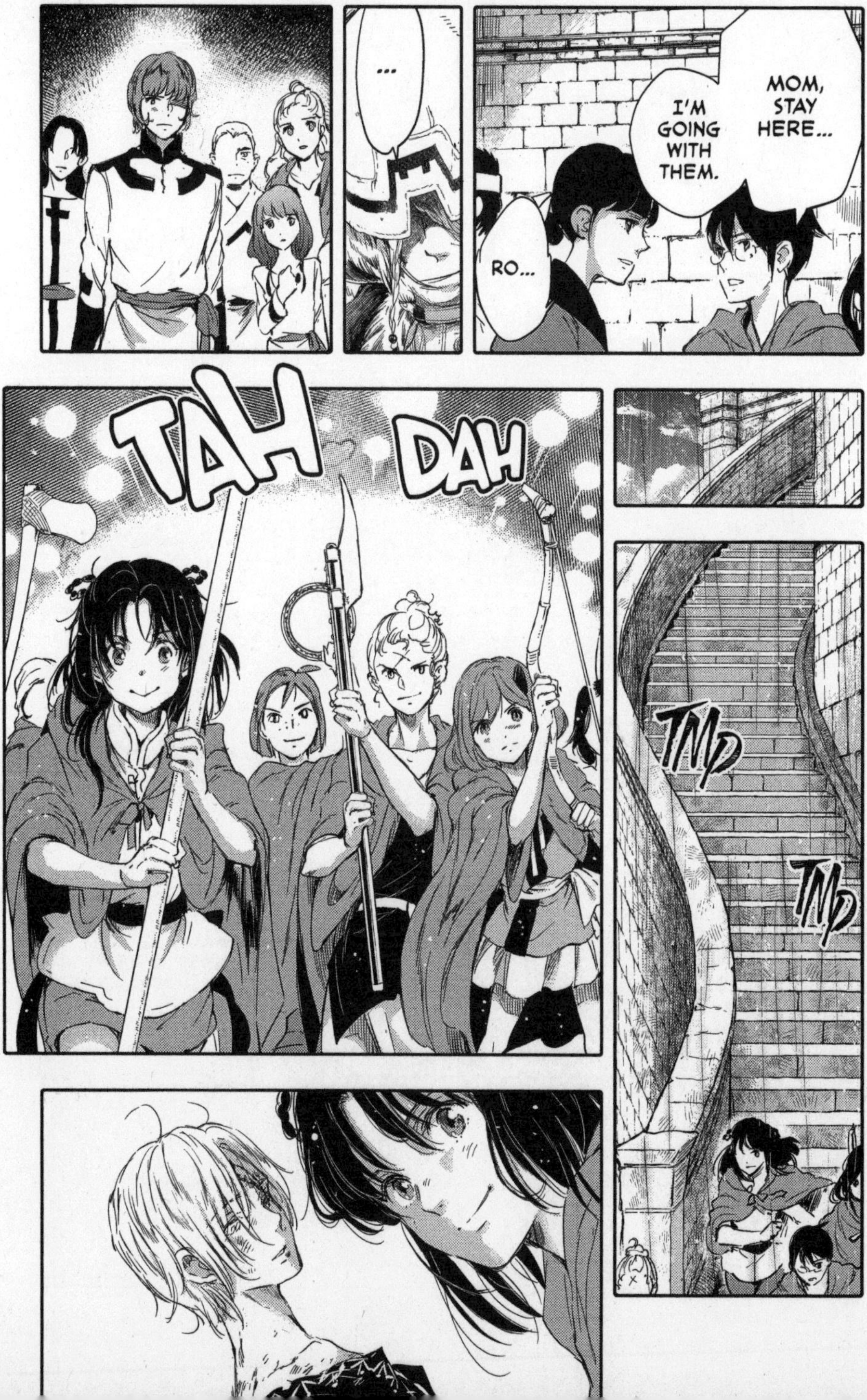
MOM, STAY HERE...
I'M GOING WITH THEM.
RO...
...
TMP
TMP
TAH
DAH

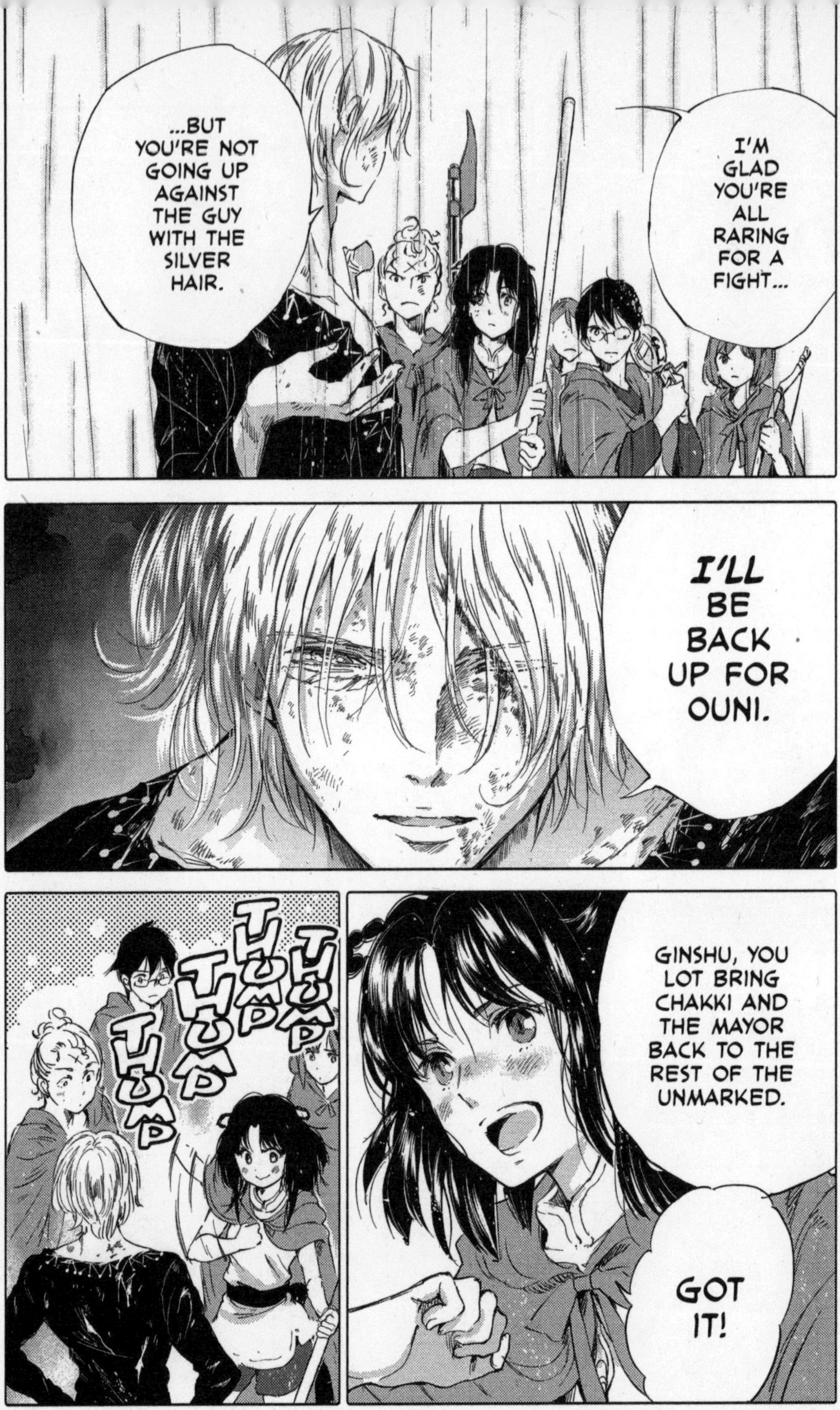
I'M GLAD YOU'RE ALL RARING FOR A FIGHT...
...BUT YOU'RE NOT GOING UP AGAINST THE GUY WITH THE SILVER HAIR.
I'LL BE BACK UP FOR OUNI.
GINSHU, YOU LOT BRING CHAKKI AND THE MAYOR BACK TO THE REST OF THE UNMARKED.
GOT IT!
THUMP
THUMP
THUMP
THUMP

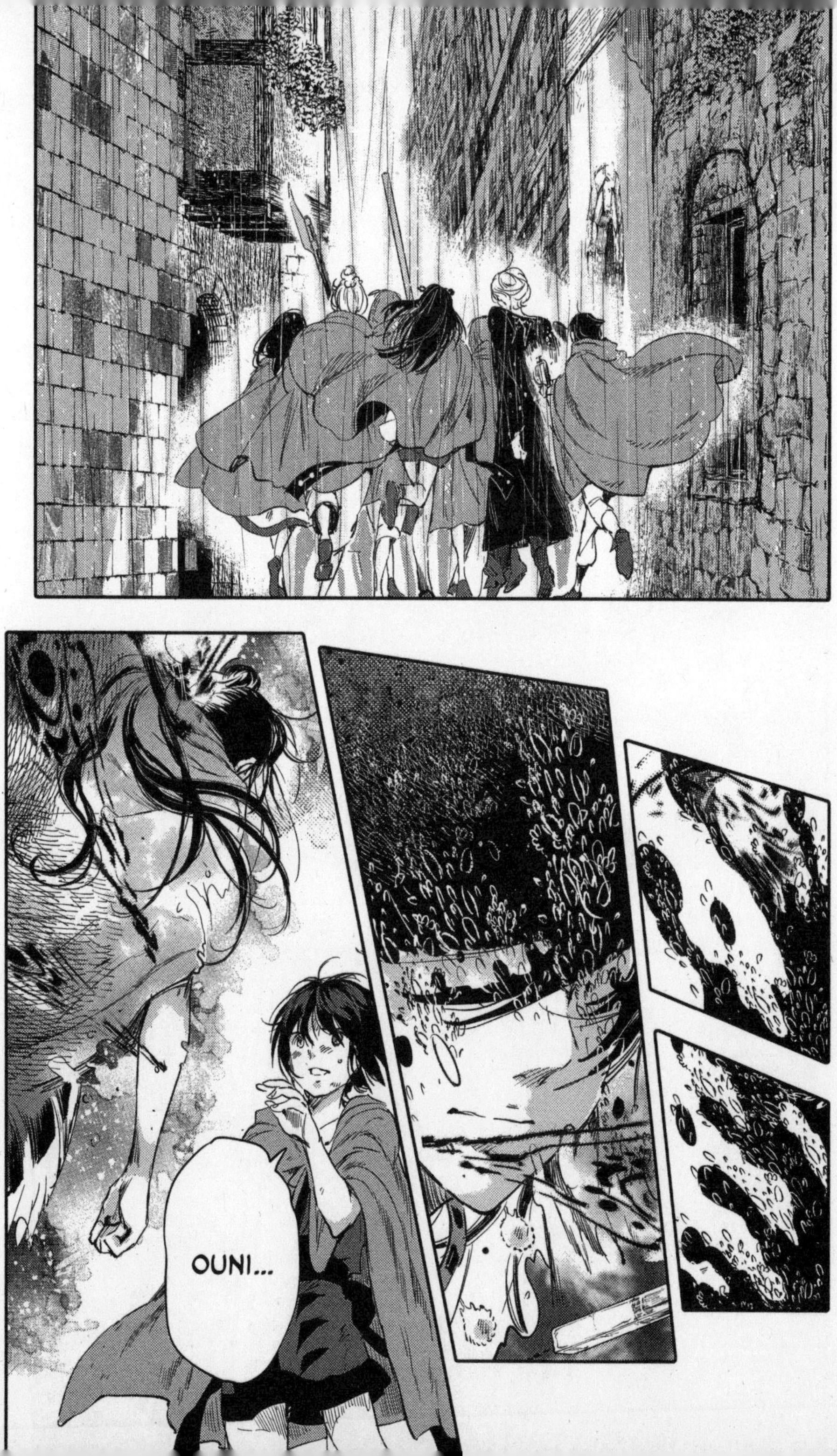
OUNI...

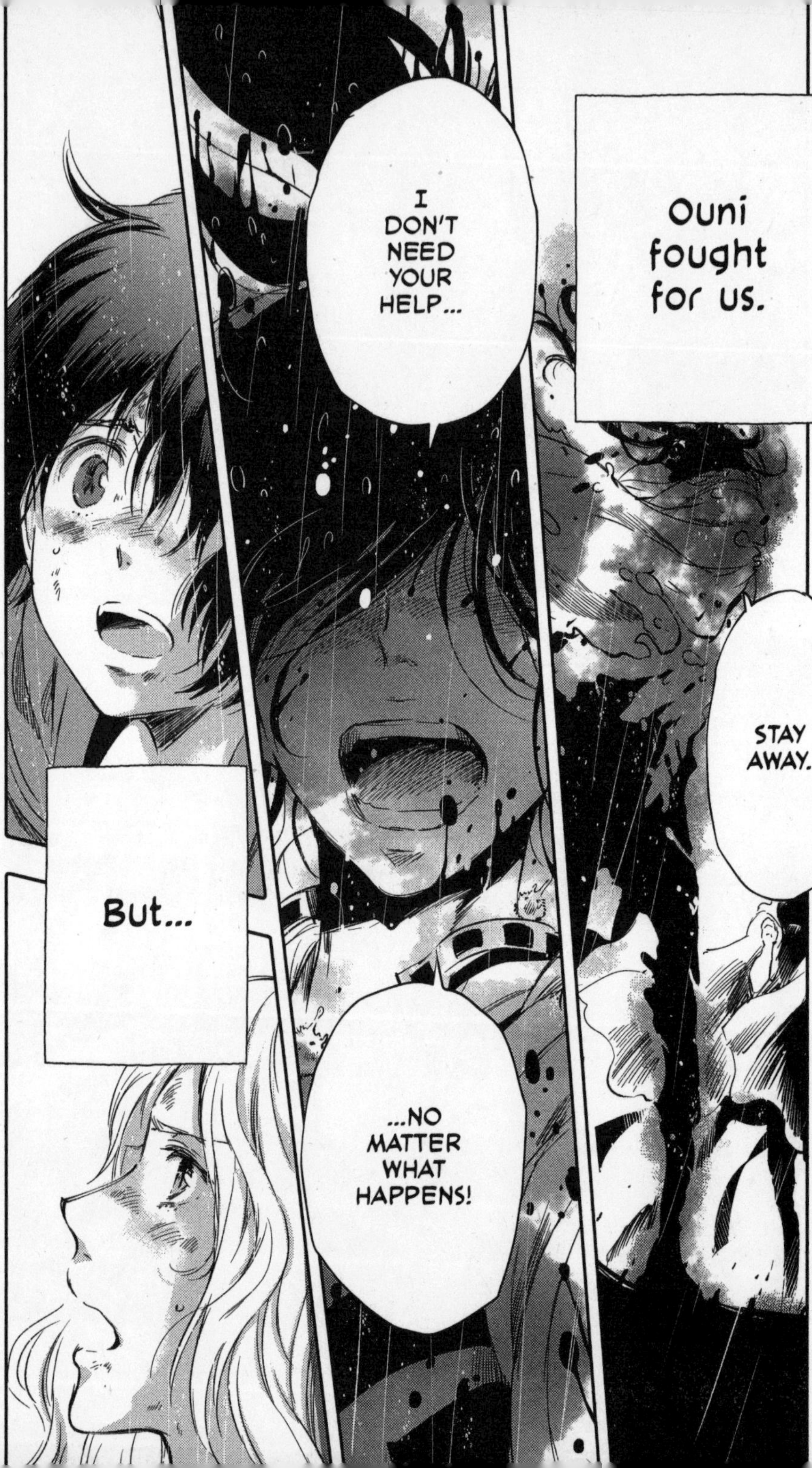
Ouni fought for us.
STAY AWAY.
I DON'T NEED YOUR HELP...
...NO MATTER WHAT HAPPENS!
But...

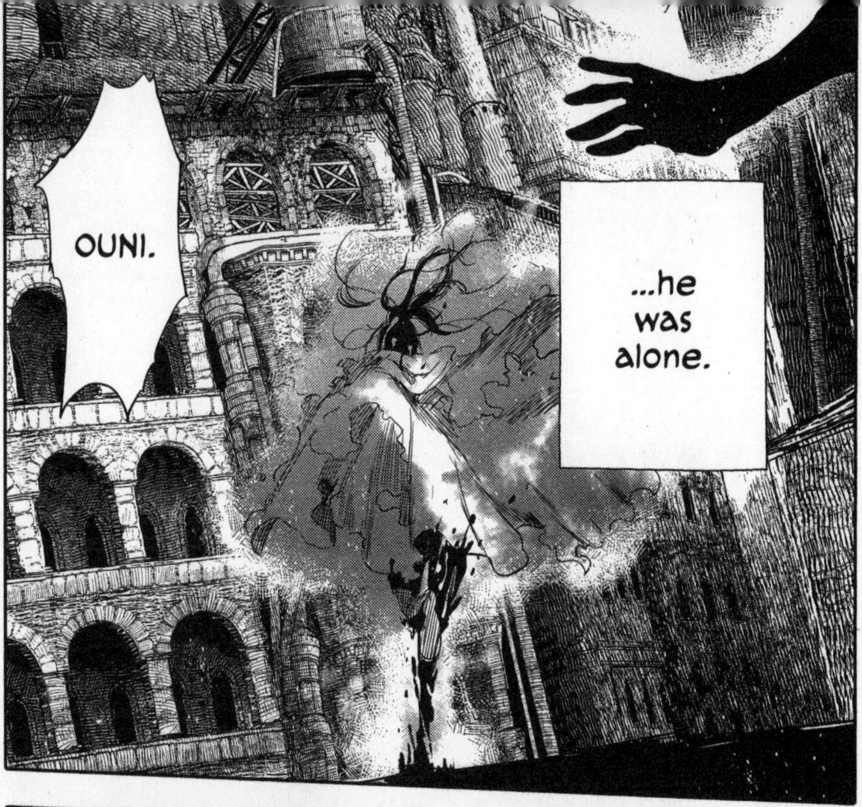
...he was alone.
OUNI.
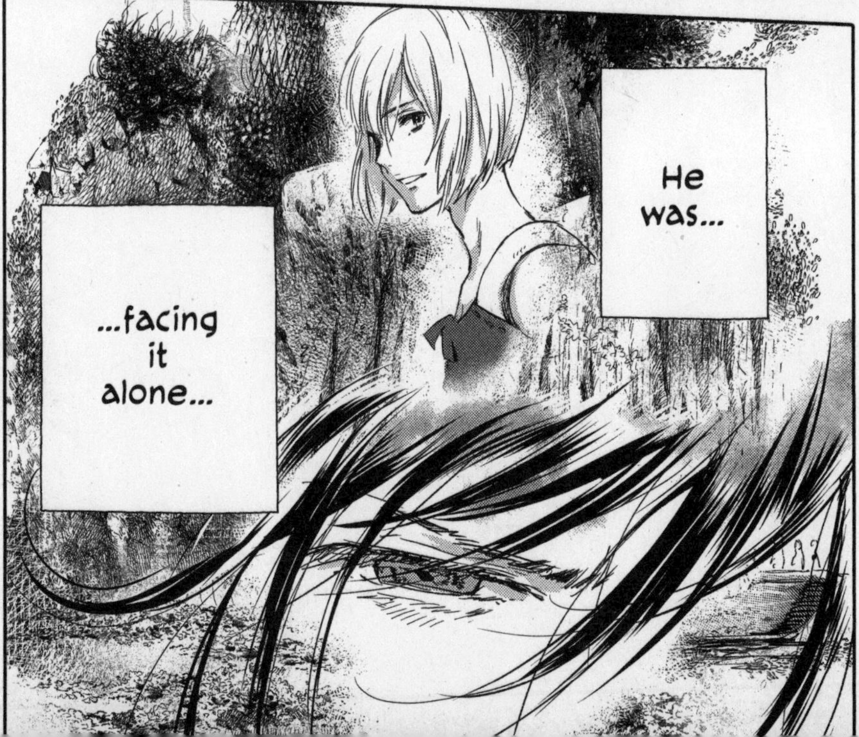
He was...
...facing it alone...

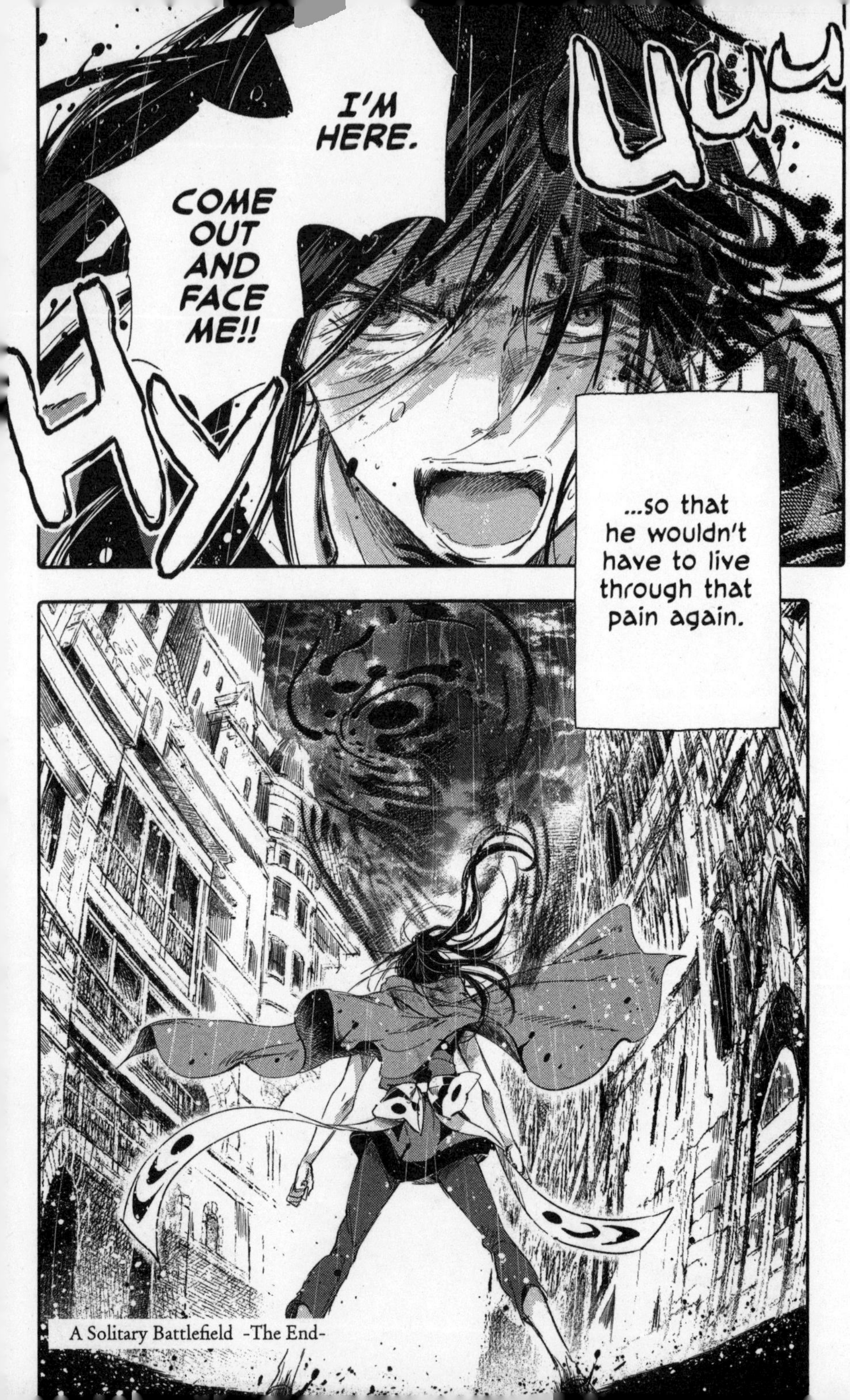
I'M HERE.
COME OUT AND FACE ME!!
...so that he wouldn't have to live through that pain again.
A Solitary Battlefield -The End-

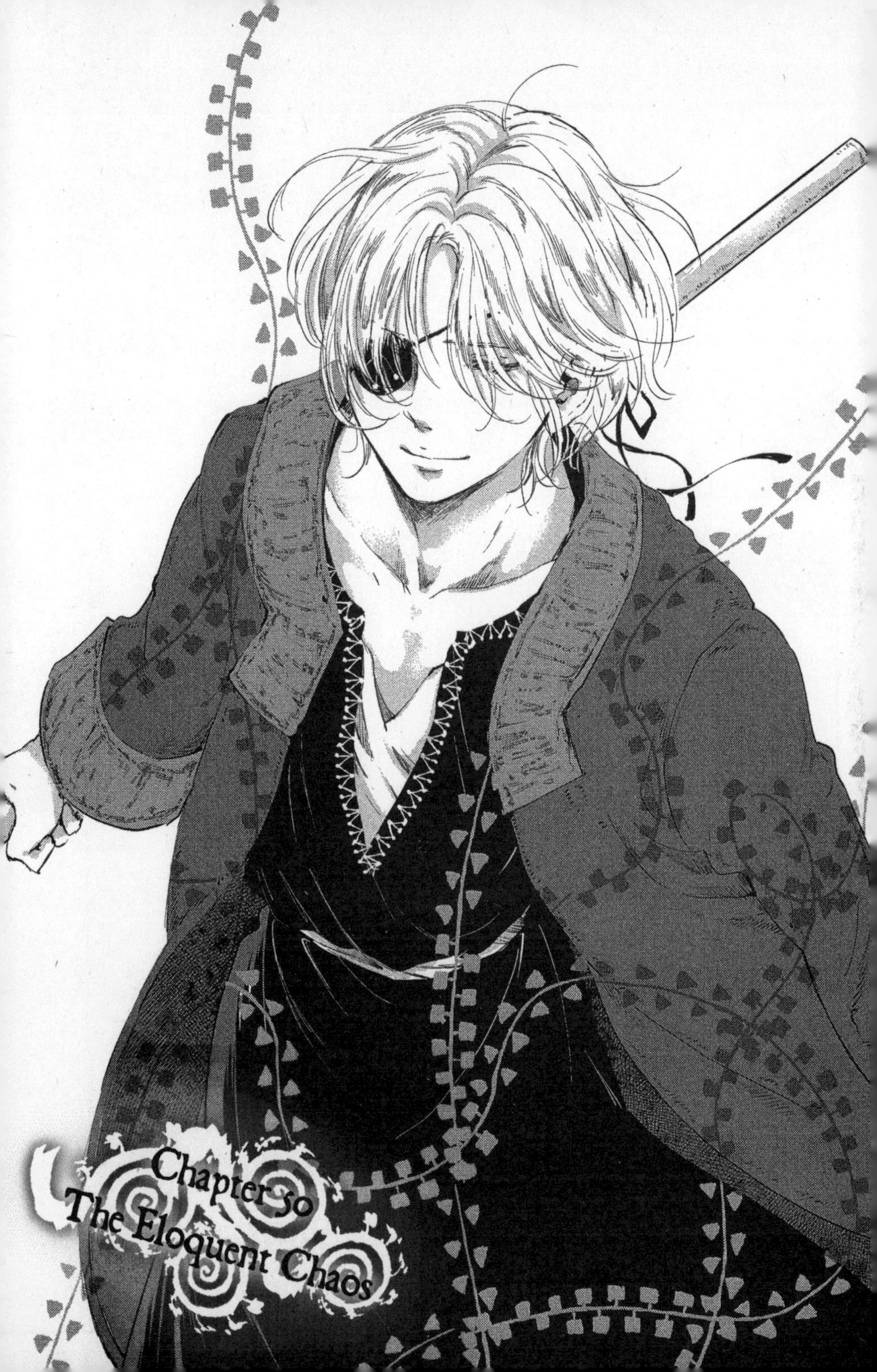
Chapter 50
The Eloquent Chaos

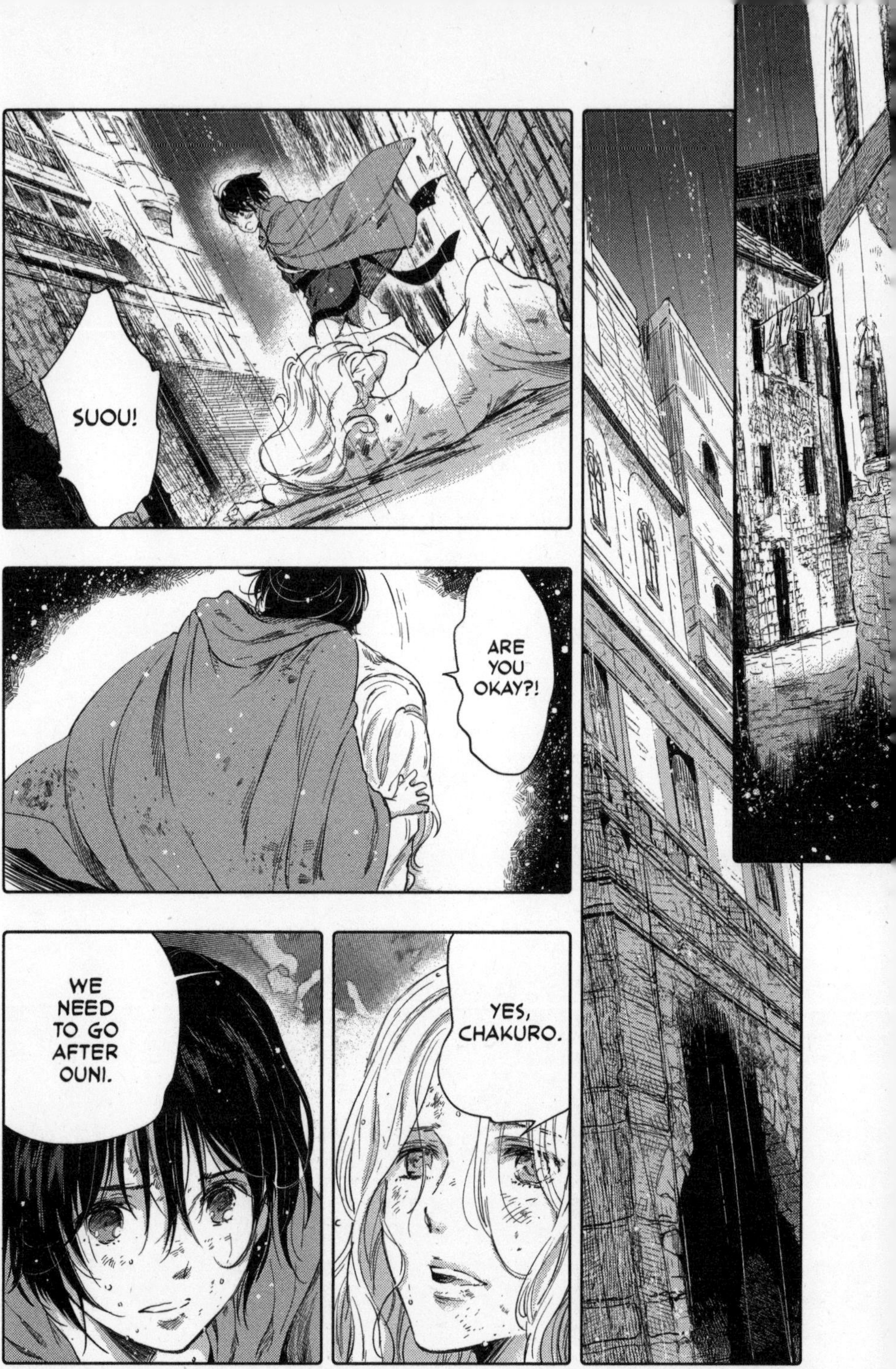
SUOU!
ARE YOU OKAY?!
YES, CHAKURO.
WE NEED TO GO AFTER OUNI.

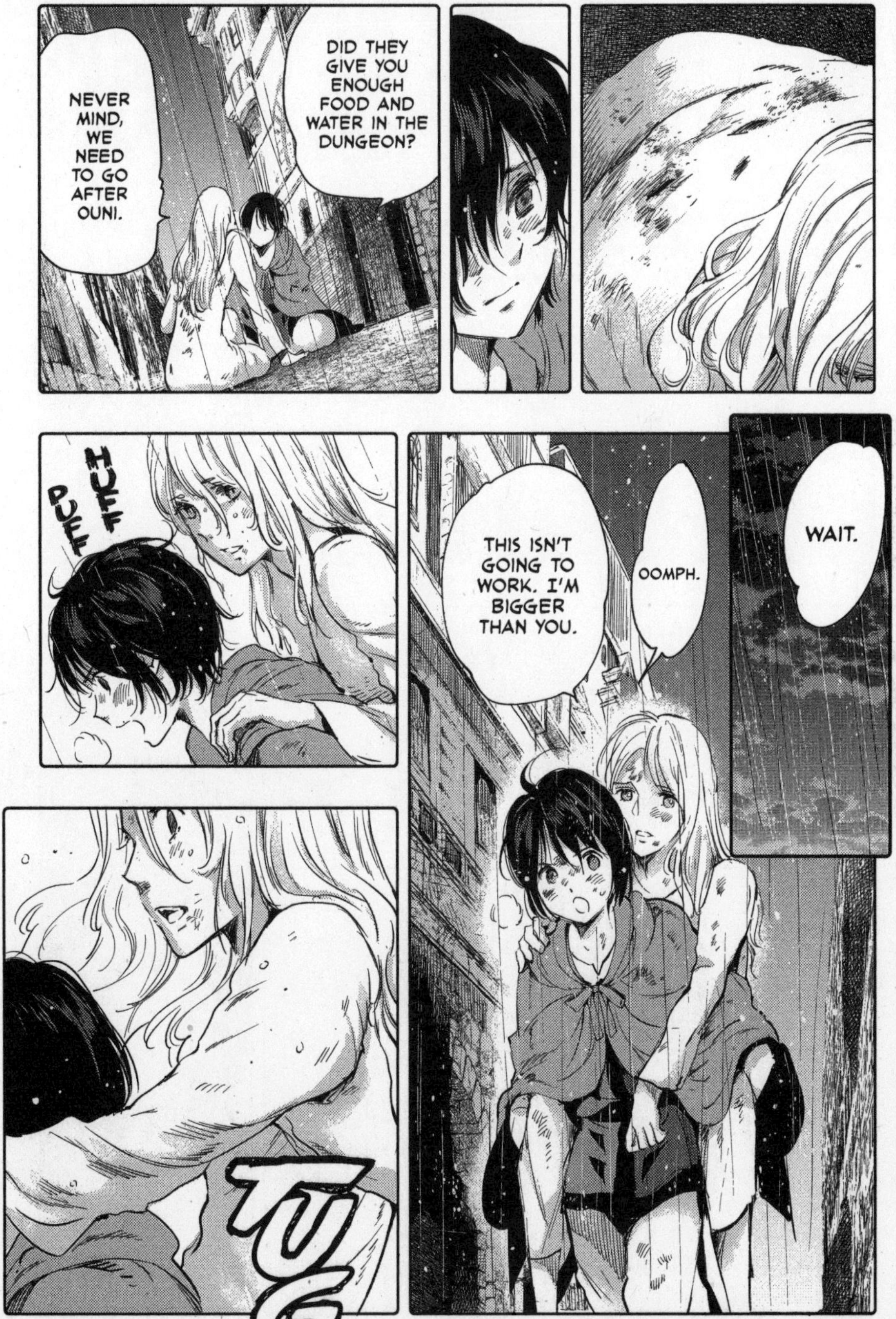

DID THEY GIVE YOU ENOUGH FOOD AND WATER IN THE DUNGEON?
NEVER MIND, WE NEED TO GO AFTER OUNI.
WAIT.
OOMPH.
THIS ISN'T GOING TO WORK. I'M BIGGER THAN YOU.
HUFF PUFF
TUG

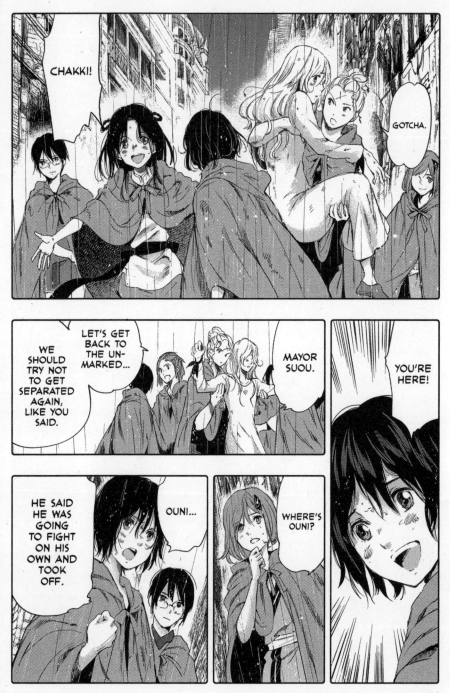

GOTCHA.
CHAKKI!
YOU'RE HERE!
MAYOR SUOU.
LET'S GET BACK TO THE UN-MARKED...
WE SHOULD TRY NOT TO GET SEPARATED AGAIN, LIKE YOU SAID.
WHERE'S OUNI?
OUNI...
HE SAID HE WAS GOING TO FIGHT ON HIS OWN AND TOOK OFF.

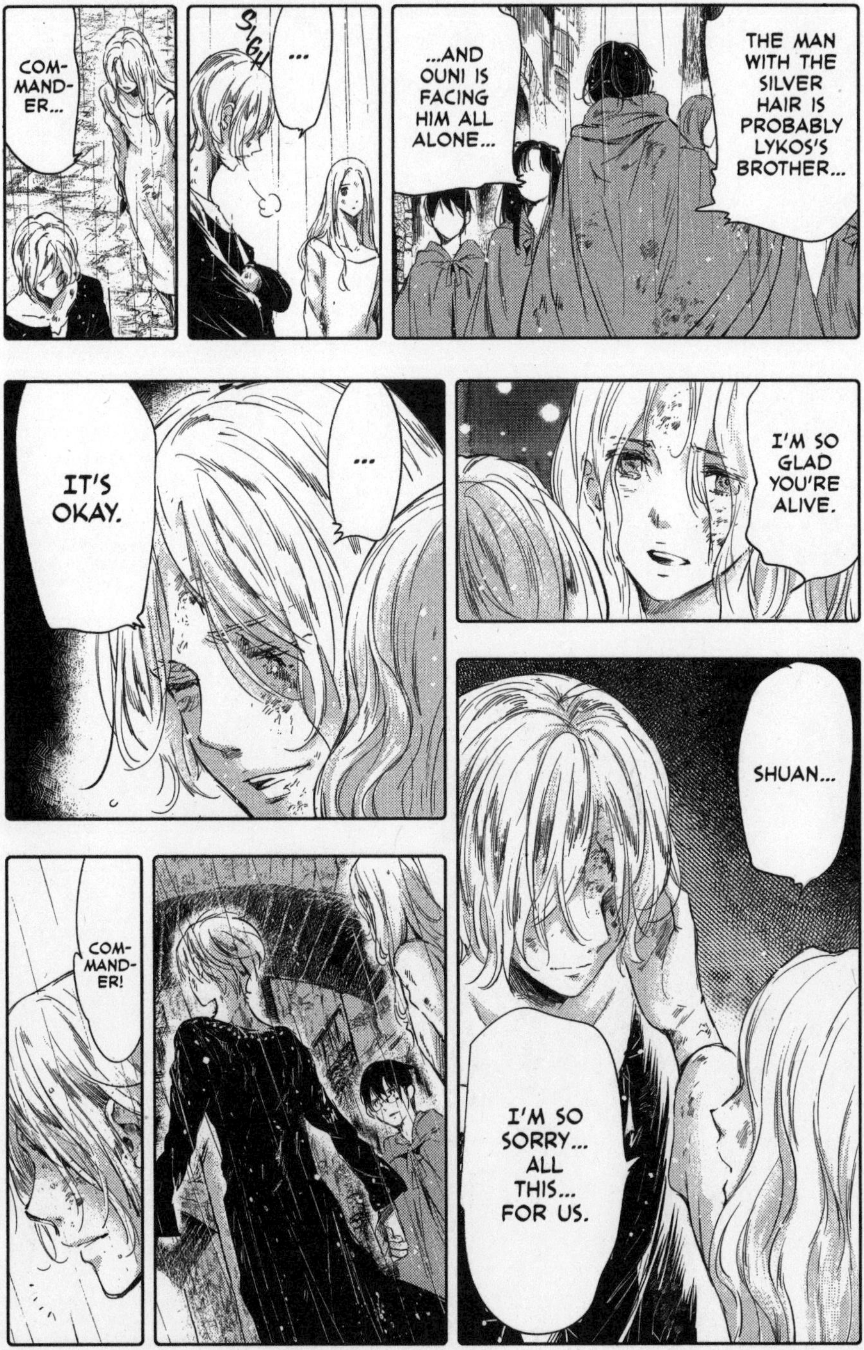
THE MAN WITH THE SILVER HAIR IS PROBABLY LYKOS'S BROTHER...
...AND OUNI IS FACING HIM ALL ALONE...
SIGH
...
COM-MANDER-ER...
I'M SO GLAD YOU'RE ALIVE.
...
IT'S OKAY.
SHUAN...
I'M SO SORRY... ALL THIS... FOR US.
COM-MAND-ER!

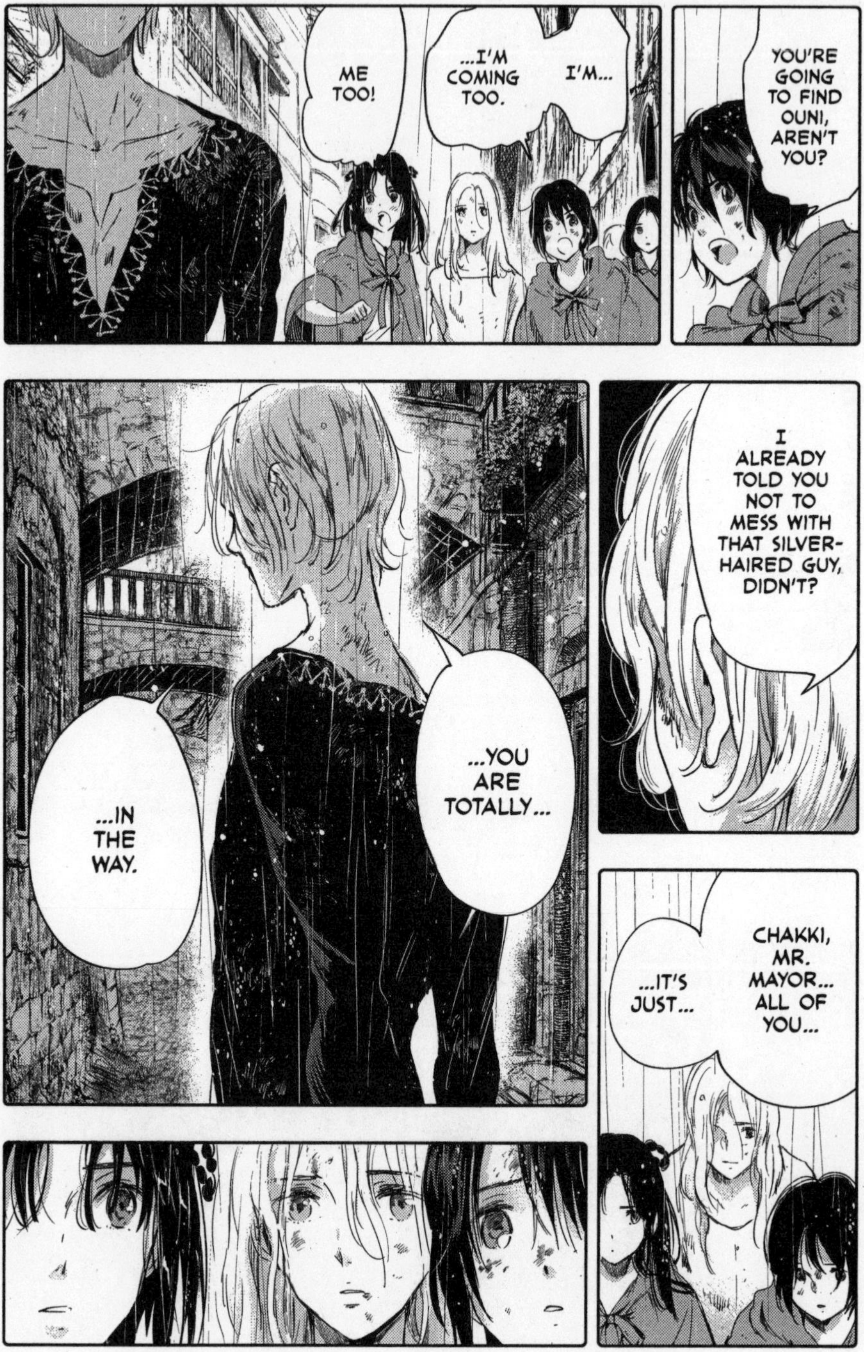
YOU'RE GOING TO FIND OUNI, AREN'T YOU?
I'M...
...I'M COMING TOO.
ME TOO!
I ALREADY TOLD YOU NOT TO MESS WITH THAT SILVER-HAIRED GUY, DIDN'T?
CHAKKI, MR. MAYOR... ALL OF YOU...
...IT'S JUST...
...YOU ARE TOTALLY...
...IN THE WAY.

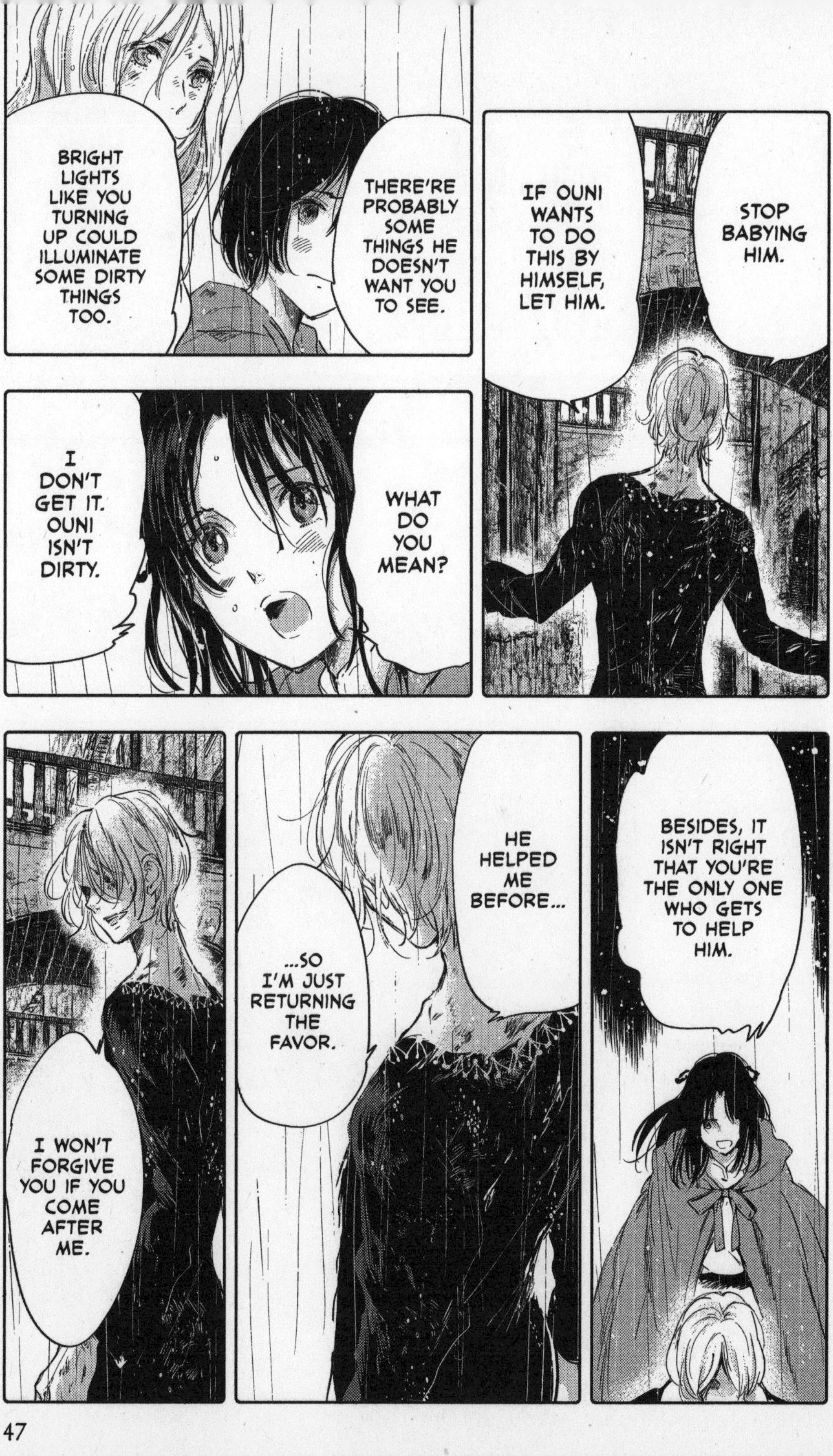
STOP BABYING HIM.
IF OUNI WANTS TO DO THIS BY HIMSELF, LET HIM.
THERE'RE PROBABLY SOME THINGS HE DOESN'T WANT YOU TO SEE.
BRIGHT LIGHTS LIKE YOU TURNING UP COULD ILLUMINATE SOME DIRTY THINGS TOO.
WHAT DO YOU MEAN?
I DON'T GET IT. OUNI ISN'T DIRTY.
BESIDES, IT ISN'T RIGHT THAT YOU'RE THE ONLY ONE WHO GETS TO HELP HIM.
HE HELPED ME BEFORE...
...SO I'M JUST RETURNING THE FAVOR.
I WON'T FORGIVE YOU IF YOU COME AFTER ME.

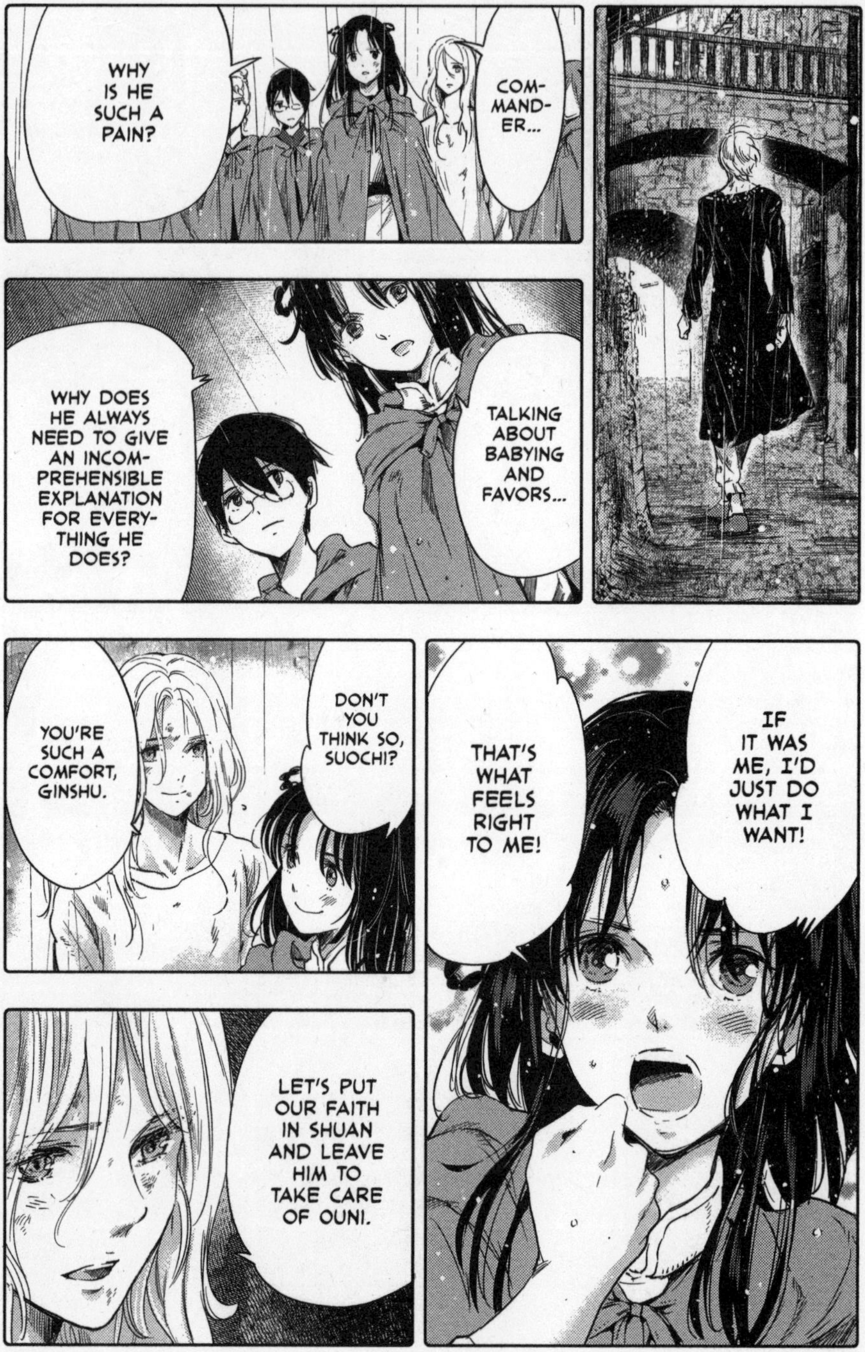
COM-MANDER...
WHY IS HE SUCH A PAIN?
TALKING ABOUT BABYING AND FAVORS...
WHY DOES HE ALWAYS NEED TO GIVE AN INCOM-PREHENSIBLE EXPLANATION FOR EVERY-THING HE DOES?
IF IT WAS ME, I'D JUST DO WHAT I WANT!
THAT'S WHAT FEELS RIGHT TO ME!
DON'T YOU THINK SO, SUOCHI?
YOU'RE SUCH A COMFORT, GINSHU.
LET'S PUT OUR FAITH IN SHUAN AND LEAVE HIM TO TAKE CARE OF OUNI.

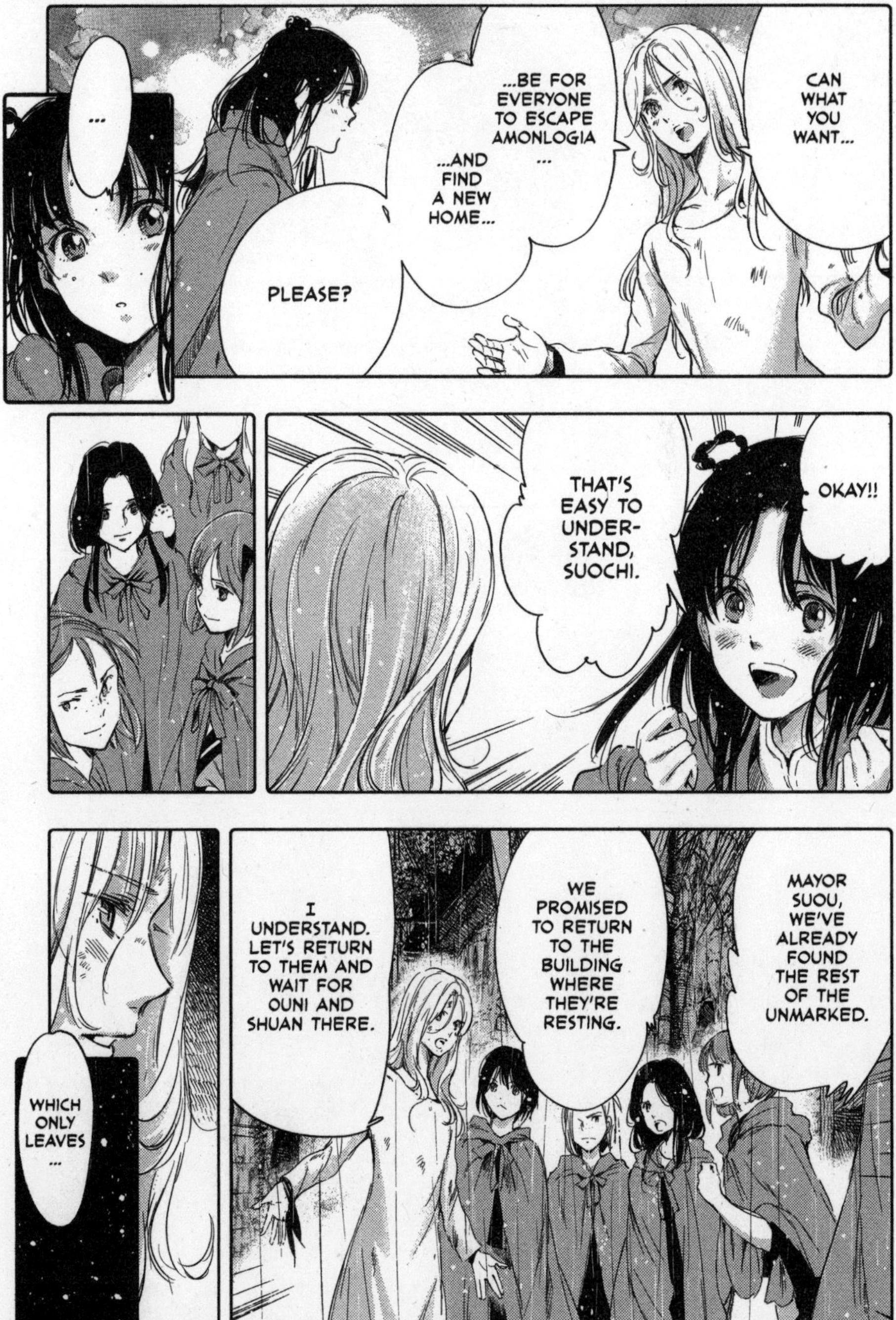
CAN WHAT YOU WANT...
...BE FOR EVERYONE TO ESCAPE AMONLOGIA ...
...AND FIND A NEW HOME...
PLEASE?
...
OKAY!!
THAT'S EASY TO UNDER-STAND, SUOCHI.
MAYOR SUOU, WE'VE ALREADY FOUND THE REST OF THE UNMARKED.
WE PROMISED TO RETURN TO THE BUILDING WHERE THEY'RE RESTING.
I UNDERSTAND. LET'S RETURN TO THEM AND WAIT FOR OUNI AND SHUAN THERE.
WHICH ONLY LEAVES ...

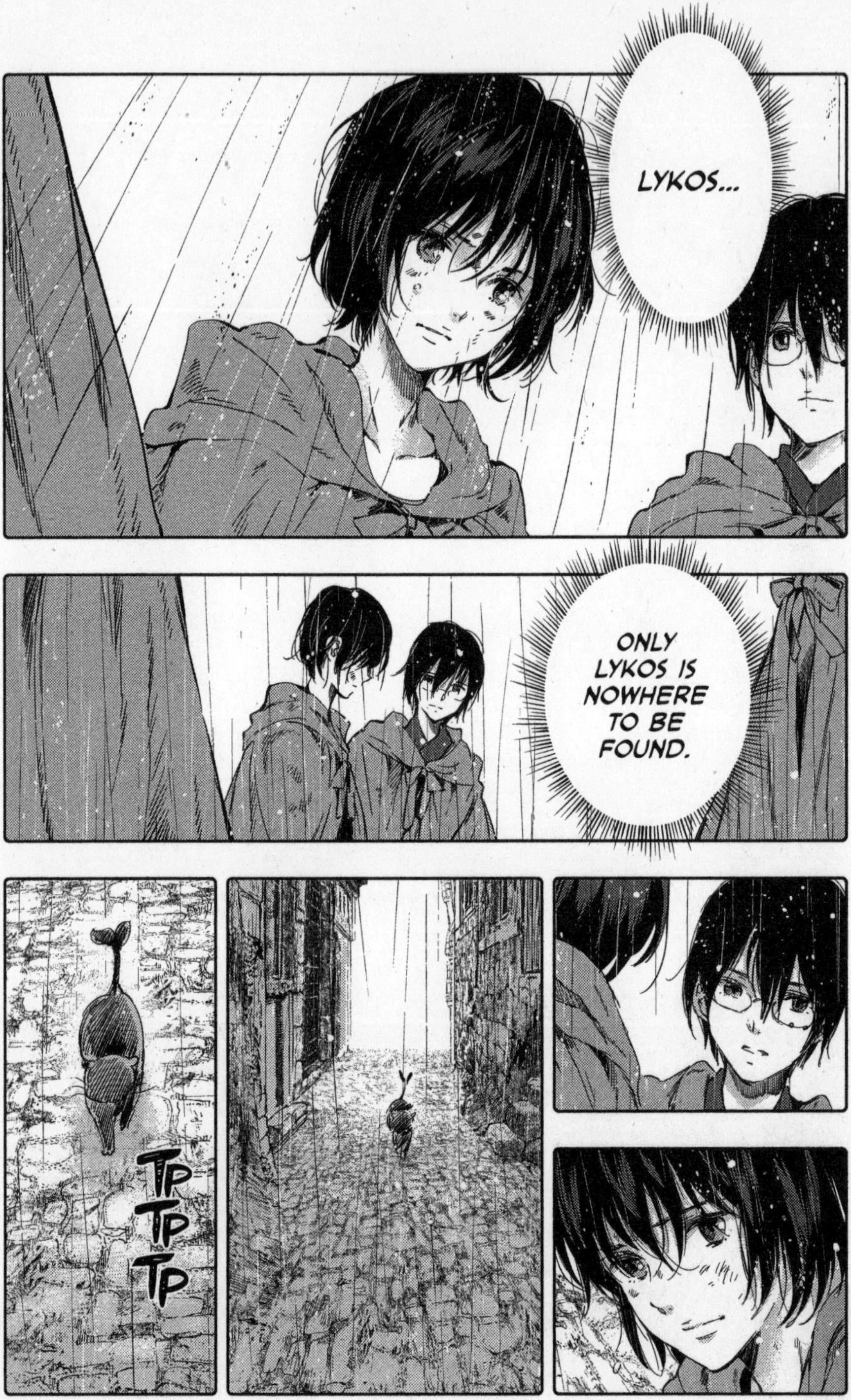
LYKOS...
ONLY LYKOS IS NOWHERE TO BE FOUND.
TP TP TP

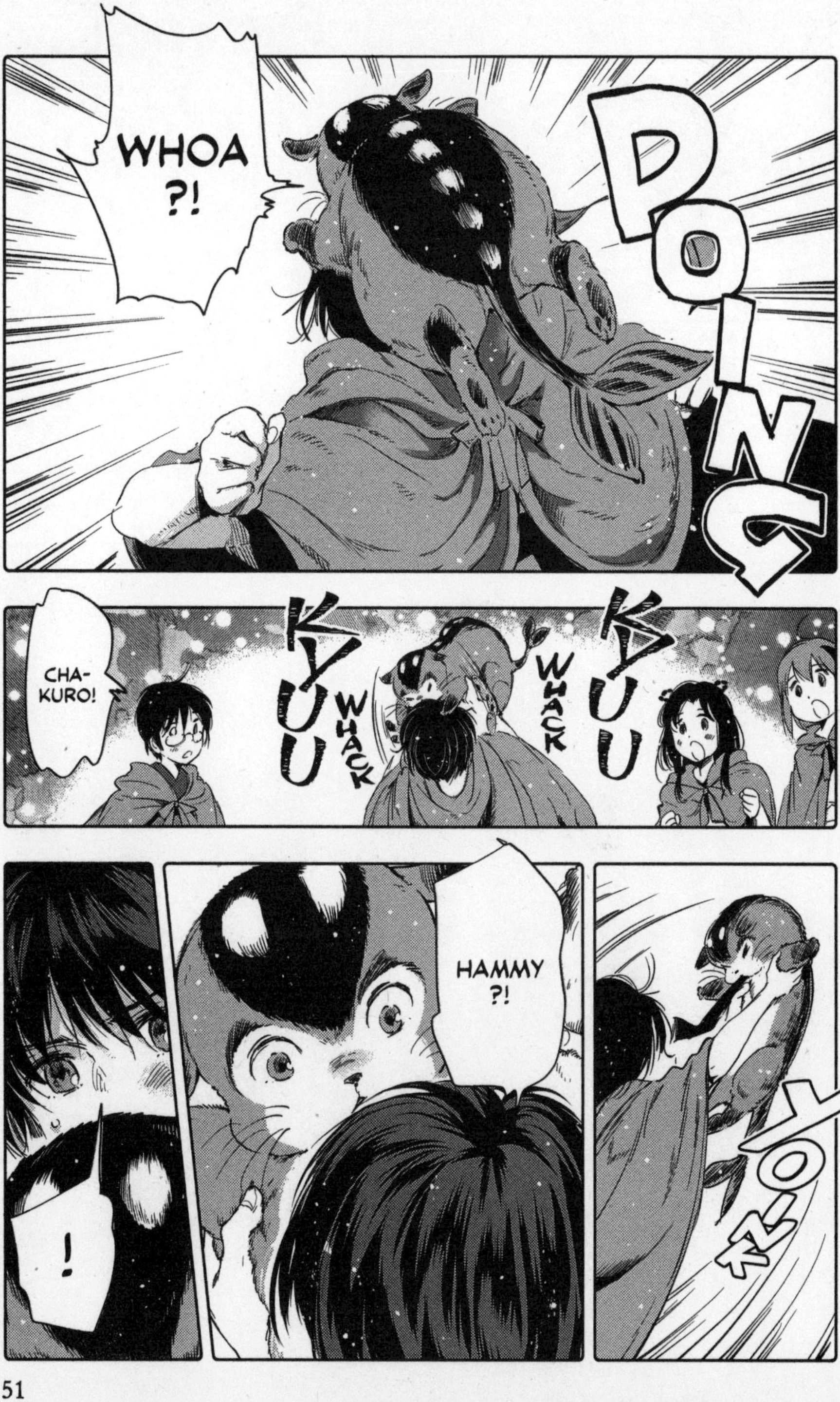
WHOA ?!
DOING
KYUUU
WHACK
KYUUU
WHACK
CHA-KURO!
YOINK
HAMMY ?!
!

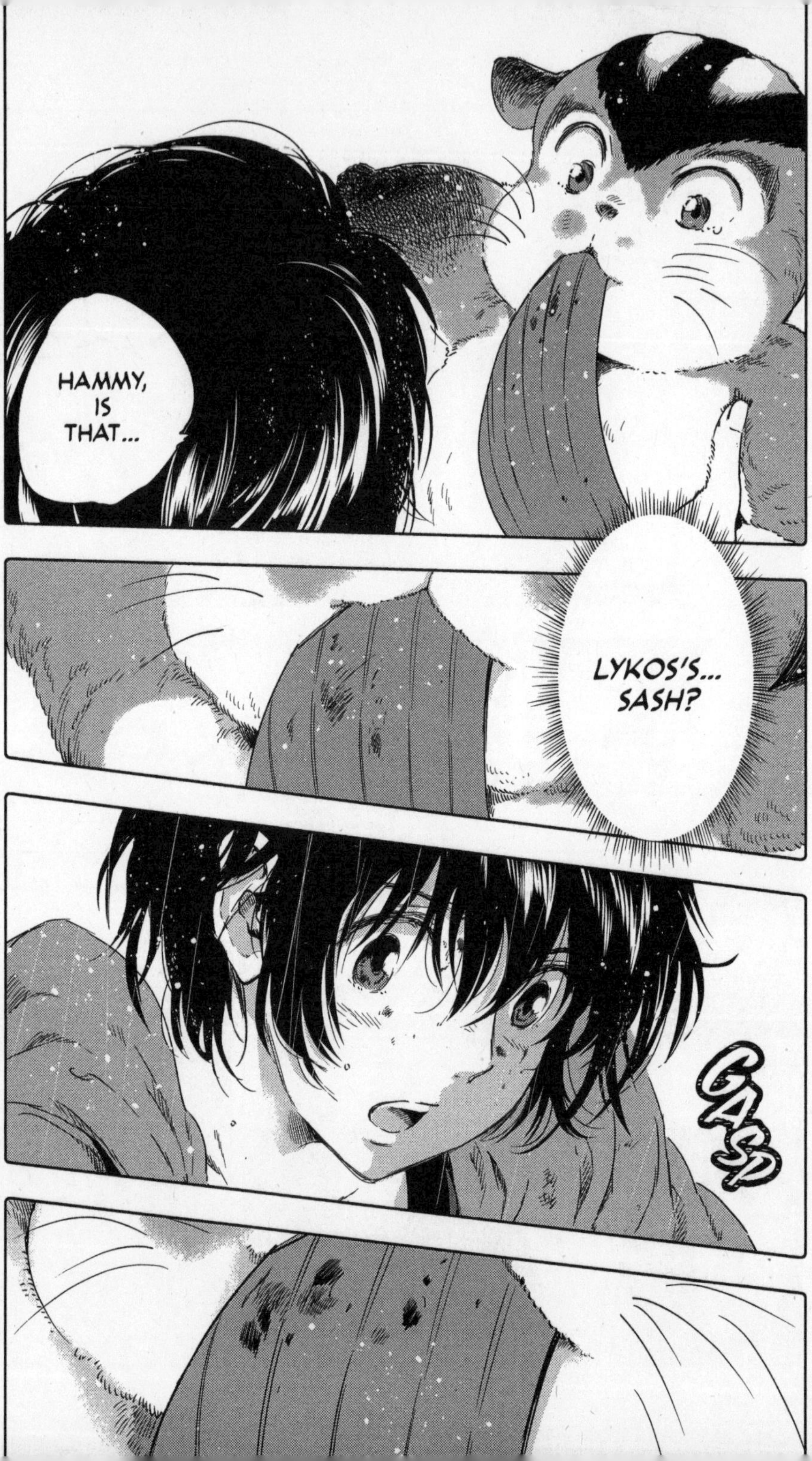
HAMMY, IS THAT...
LYKOS'S... SASH?
GASP

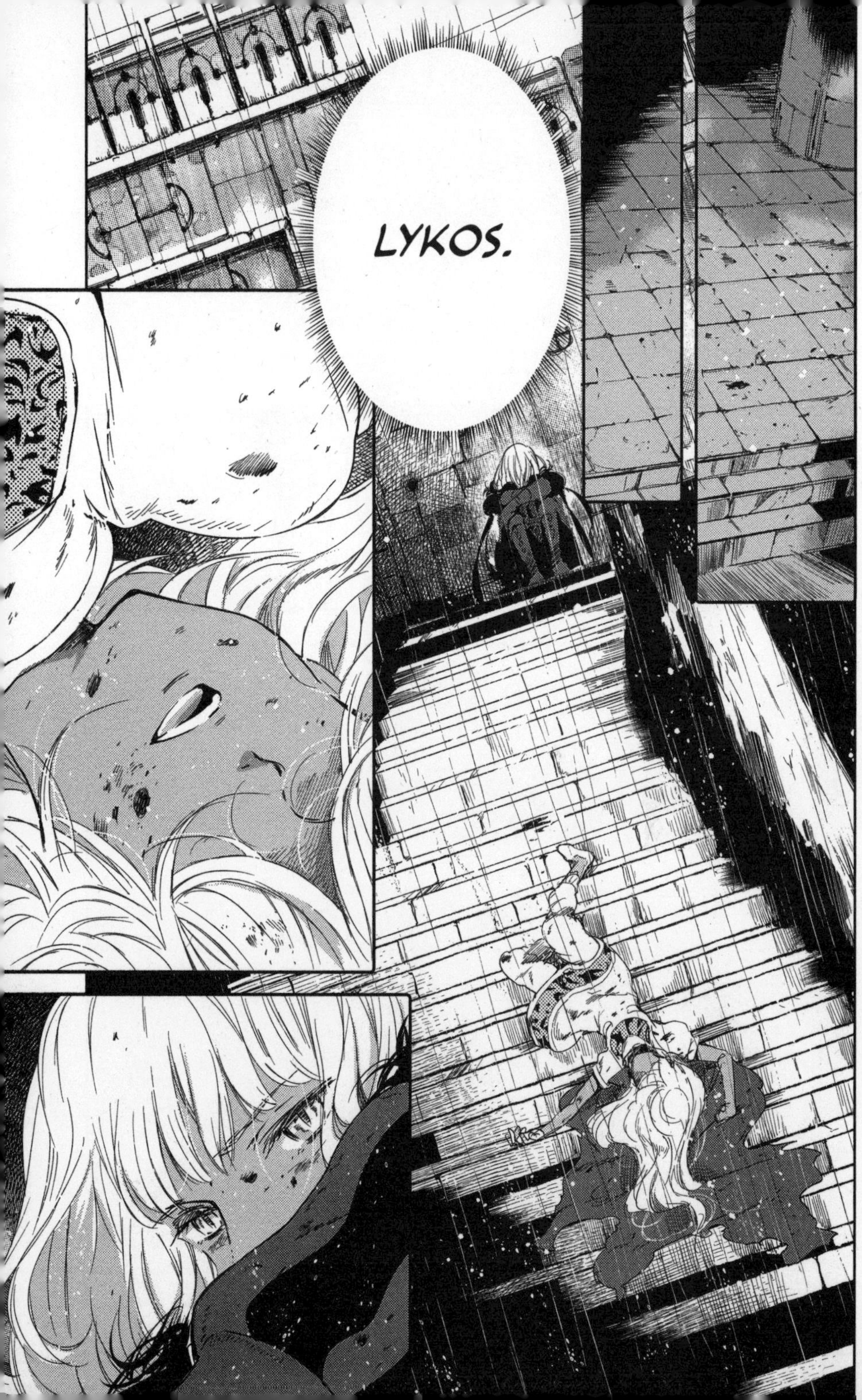
LYKOS.

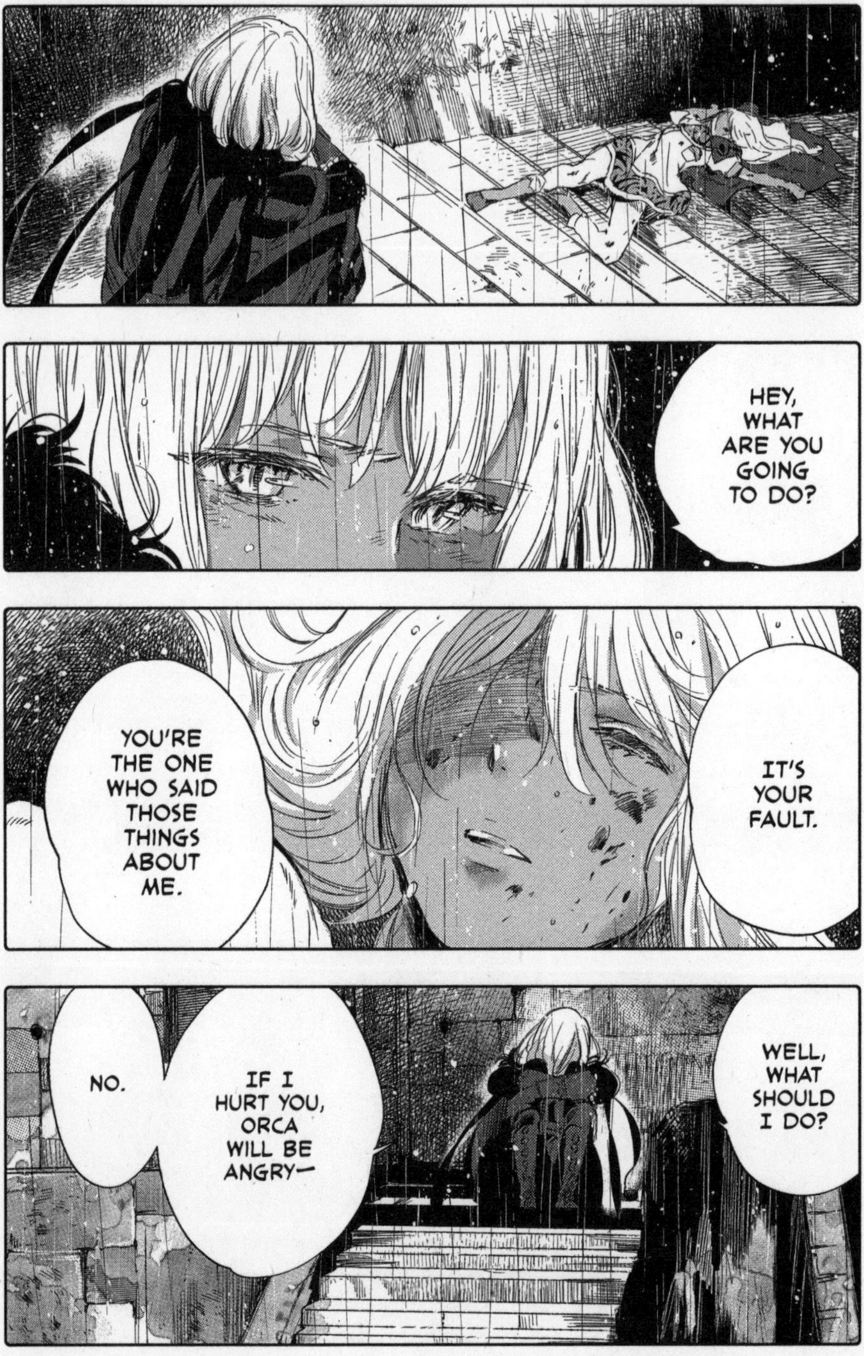
HEY, WHAT ARE YOU GOING TO DO?
IT'S YOUR FAULT.
YOU'RE THE ONE WHO SAID THOSE THINGS ABOUT ME.
WELL, WHAT SHOULD I DO?
IF I HURT YOU, ORCA WILL BE ANGRY—
NO.

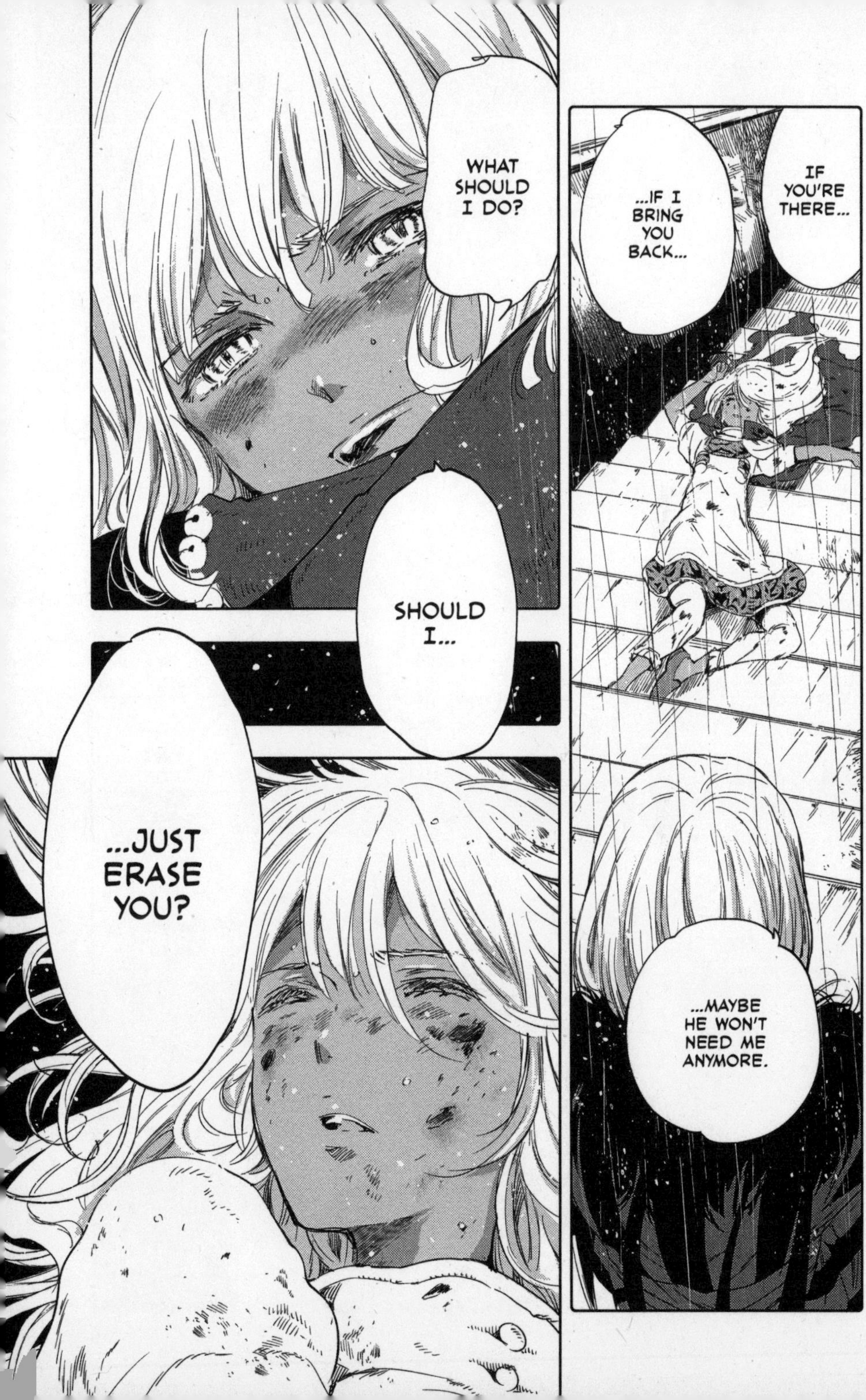
IF YOU'RE THERE...
...IF I BRING YOU BACK...
...MAYBE HE WON'T NEED ME ANYMORE.
WHAT SHOULD I DO?
SHOULD I...
...JUST ERASE YOU?

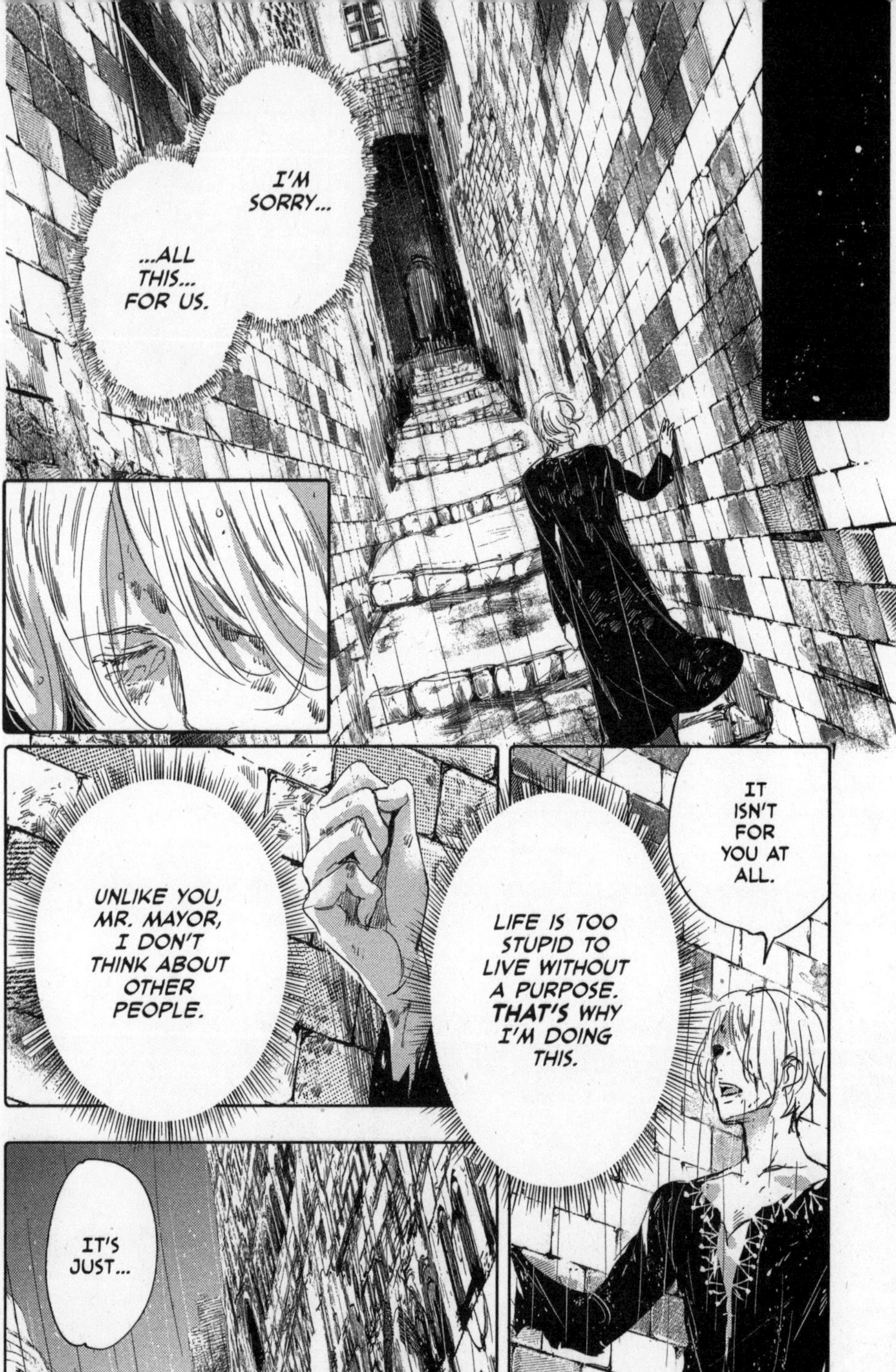
I'M SORRY...
...ALL THIS... FOR US.
IT ISN'T FOR YOU AT ALL.
LIFE IS TOO STUPID TO LIVE WITHOUT A PURPOSE. THAT'S WHY I'M DOING THIS.
UNLIKE YOU, MR. MAYOR, I DON'T THINK ABOUT OTHER PEOPLE.
IT'S JUST...

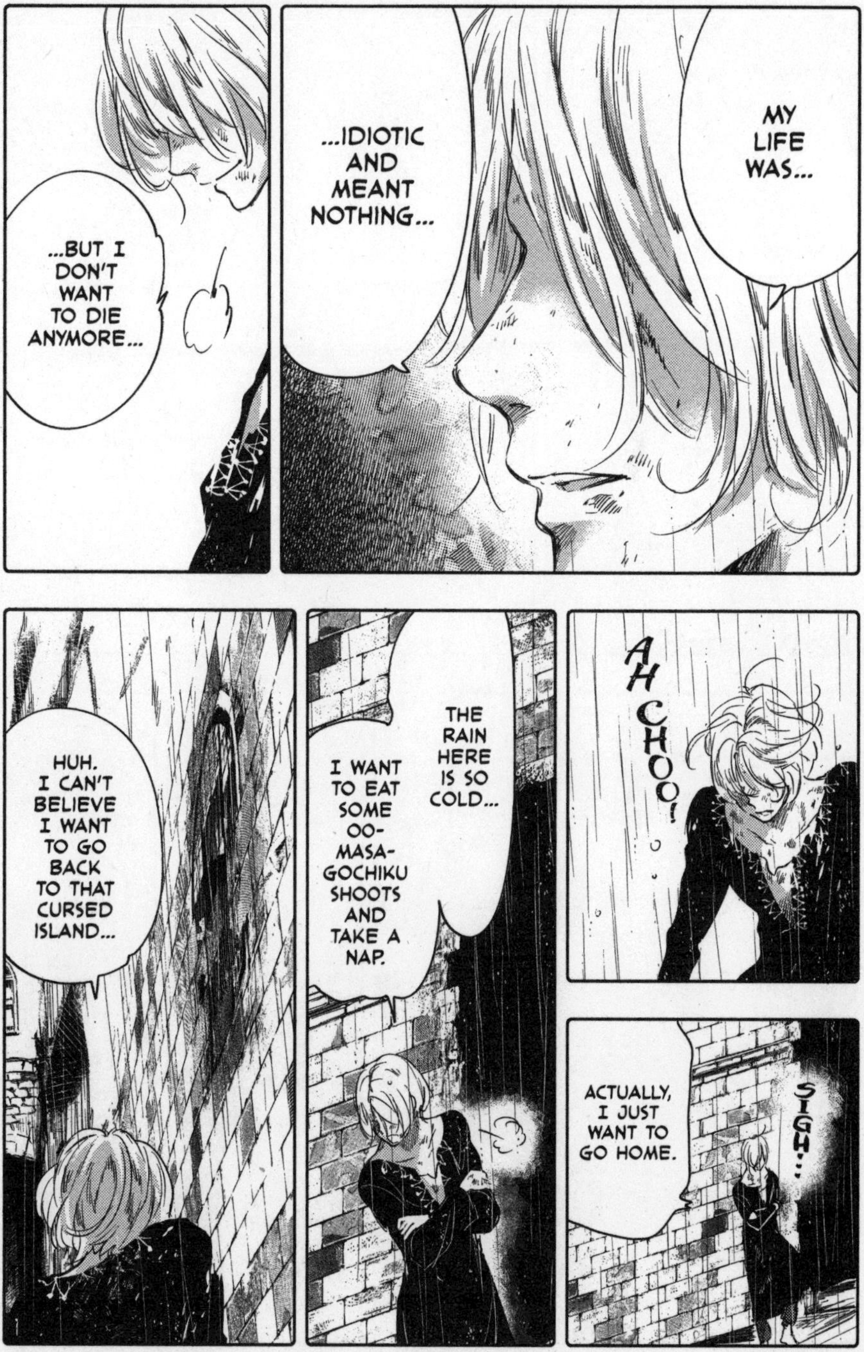
MY LIFE WAS...
...IDIOTIC AND MEANT NOTHING...
...BUT I DON'T WANT TO DIE ANYMORE...
AH CHOO!
ACTUALLY, I JUST WANT TO GO HOME.
SIGH...
THE RAIN HERE IS SO COLD...
I WANT TO EAT SOME OO-MASA-GOCHIKU SHOOTS AND TAKE A NAP.
HUH. I CAN'T BELIEVE I WANT TO GO BACK TO THAT CURSED ISLAND...

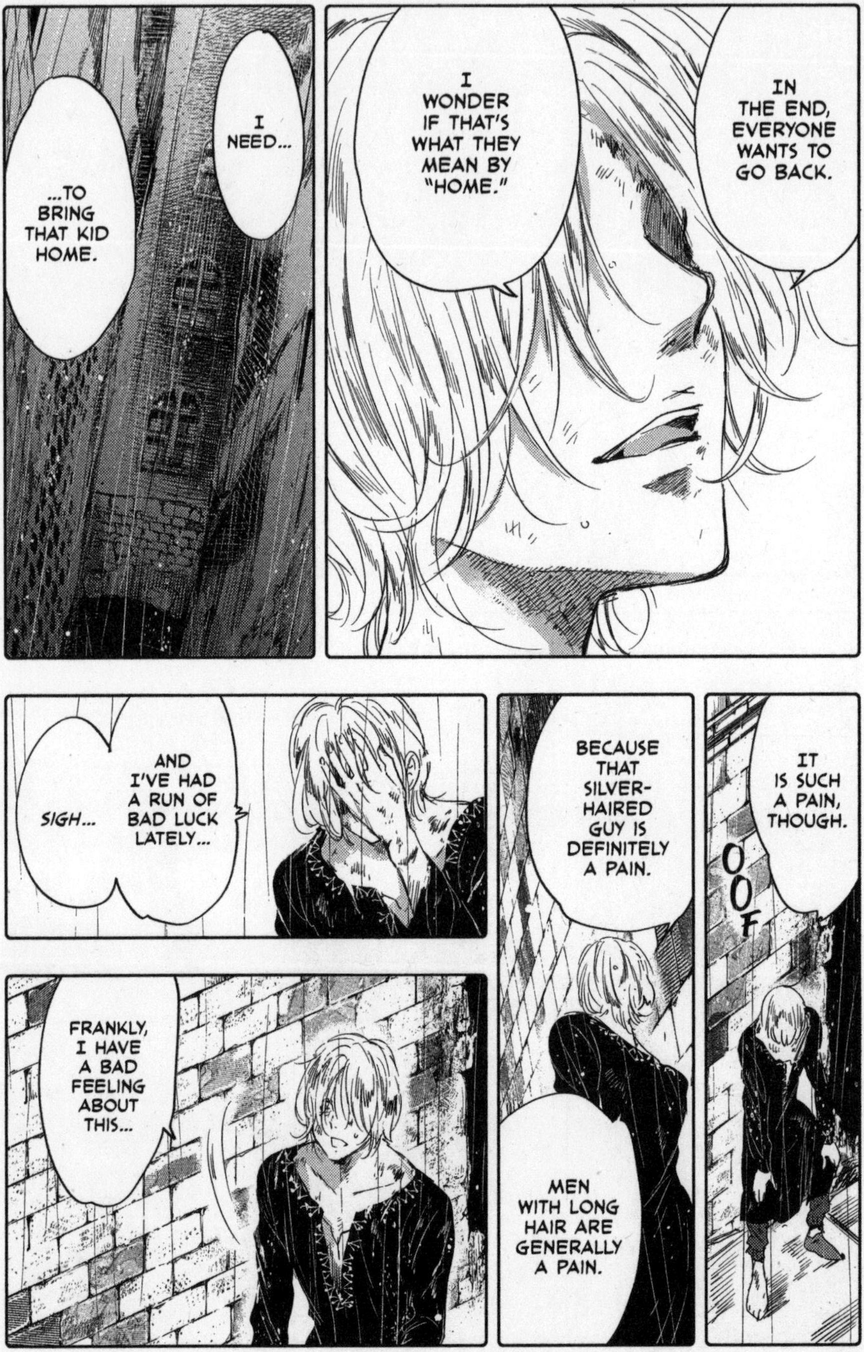
IN THE END, EVERYONE WANTS TO GO BACK.
I WONDER IF THAT'S WHAT THEY MEAN BY "HOME."
I NEED...
...TO BRING THAT KID HOME.
IT IS SUCH A PAIN, THOUGH.
OOF
BECAUSE THAT SILVER-HAIRED GUY IS DEFINITELY A PAIN.
MEN WITH LONG HAIR ARE GENERALLY A PAIN.
AND I'VE HAD A RUN OF BAD LUCK LATELY...
SIGH...
FRANKLY, I HAVE A BAD FEELING ABOUT THIS...

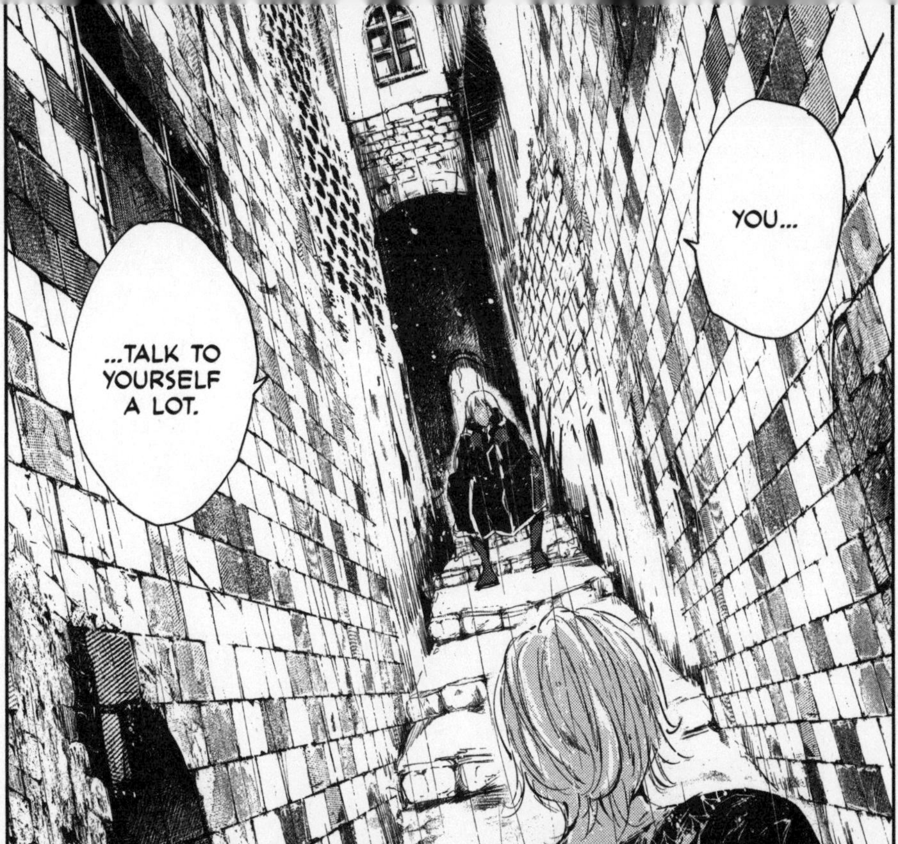
YOU...
...TALK TO YOURSELF A LOT.
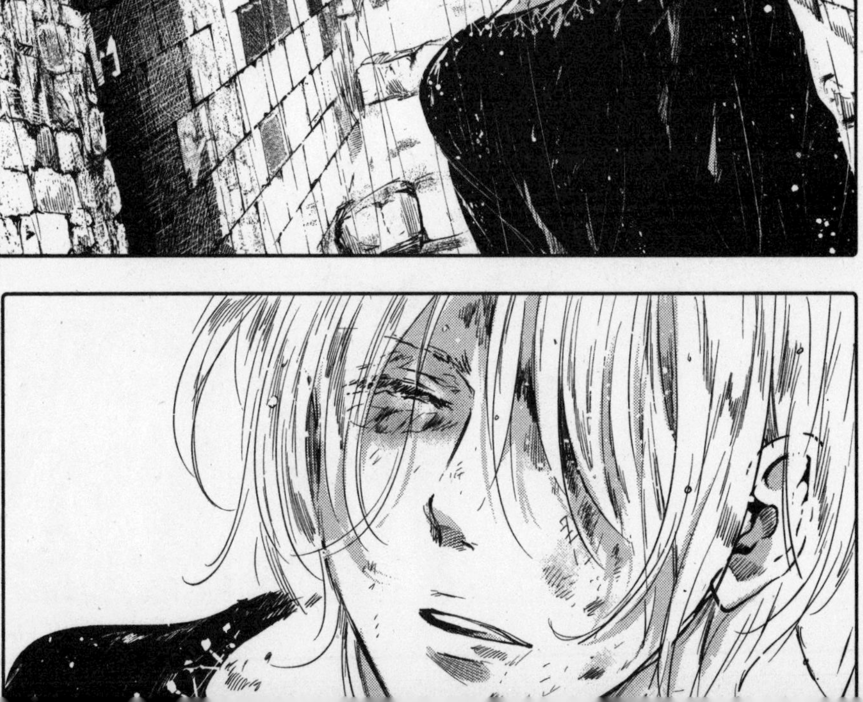

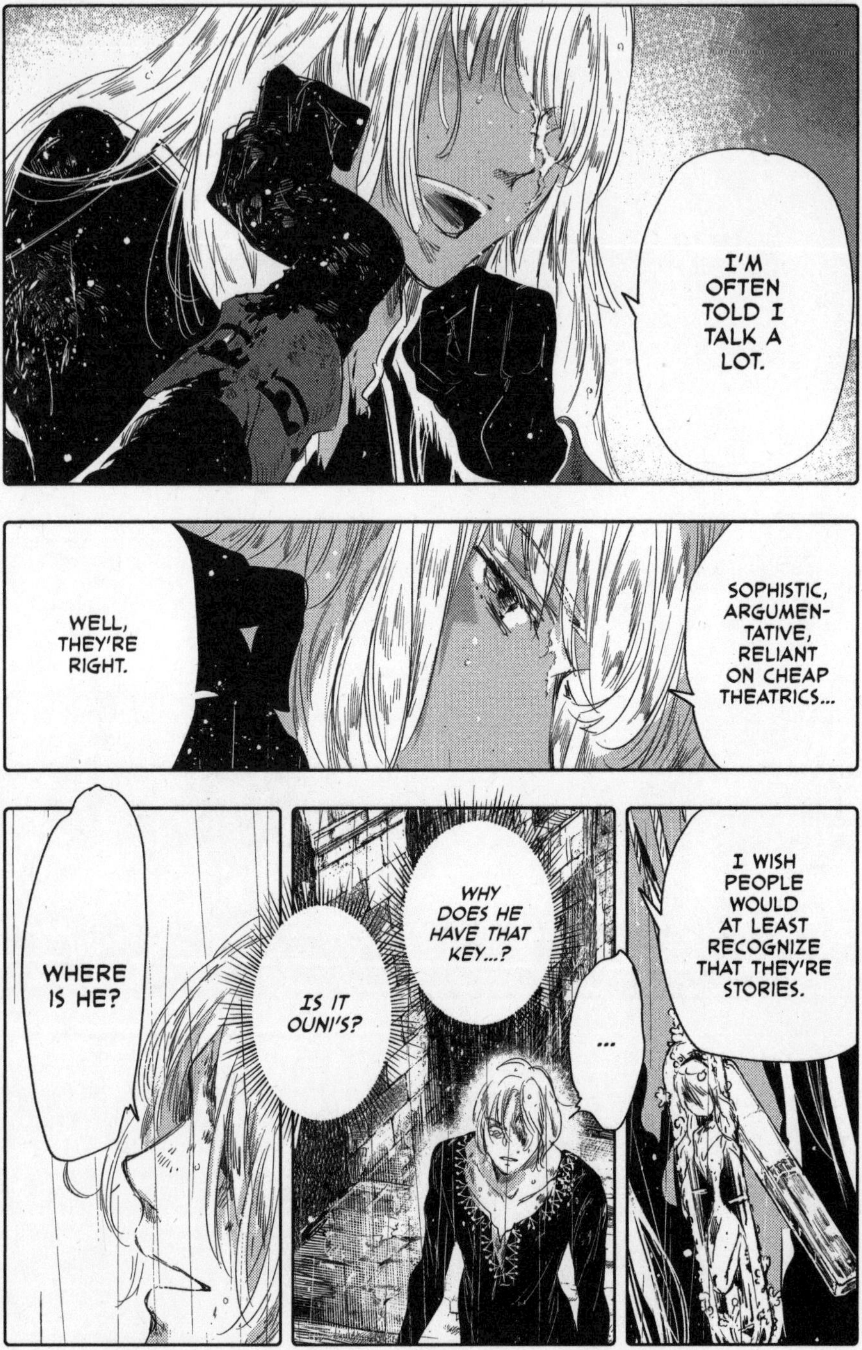
I'M OFTEN TOLD I TALK A LOT.
SOPHISTIC, ARGUMENTATIVE, RELIANT ON CHEAP THEATRICS...
WELL, THEY'RE RIGHT.
I WISH PEOPLE WOULD AT LEAST RECOGNIZE THAT THEY'RE STORIES.
WHY DOES HE HAVE THAT KEY...?
...
IS IT OUNI'S?
WHERE IS HE?

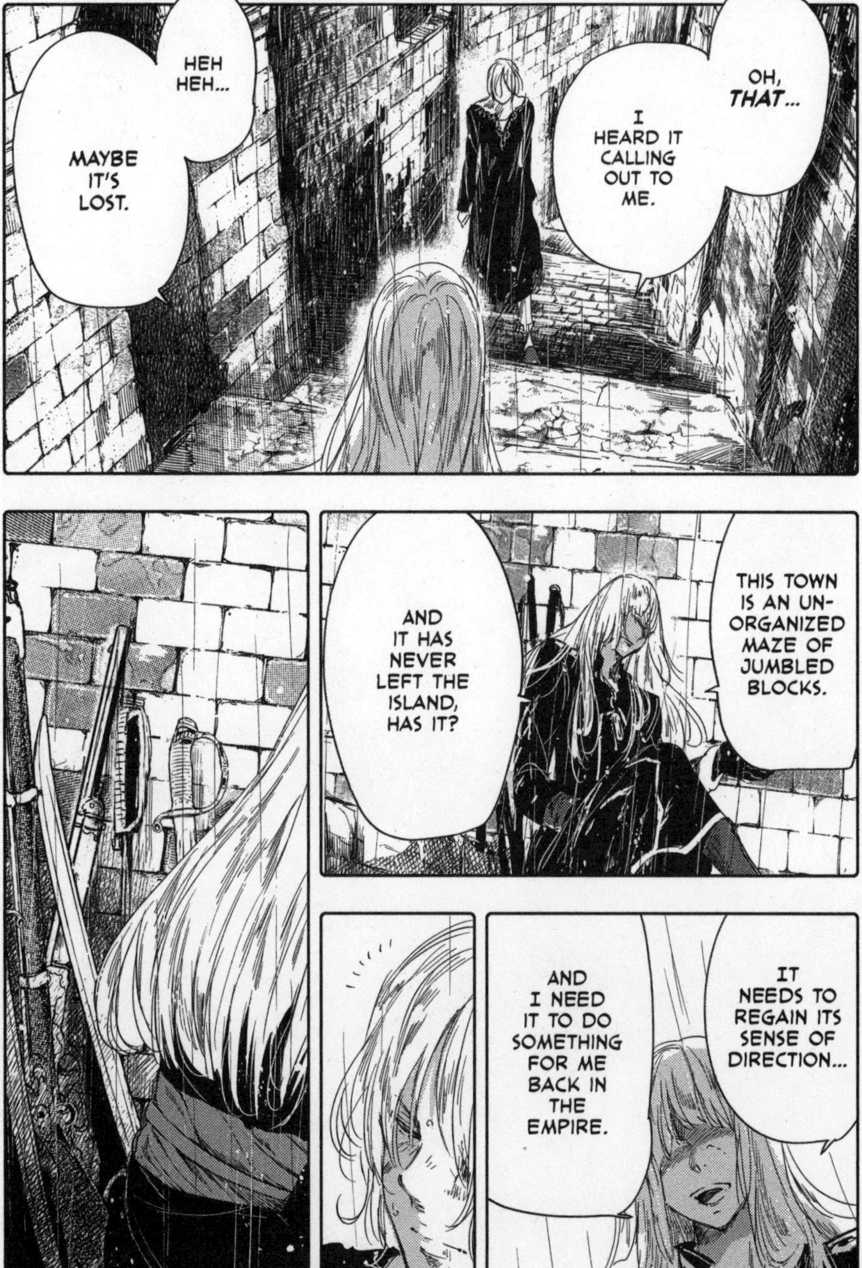
OH, *THAT*...
I HEARD IT CALLING OUT TO ME.
HEH HEH...
MAYBE IT'S LOST.
THIS TOWN IS AN UN-ORGANIZED MAZE OF JUMBLED BLOCKS.
AND IT HAS NEVER LEFT THE ISLAND, HAS IT?
IT NEEDS TO REGAIN ITS SENSE OF DIRECTION...
AND I NEED IT TO DO SOMETHING FOR ME BACK IN THE EMPIRE.

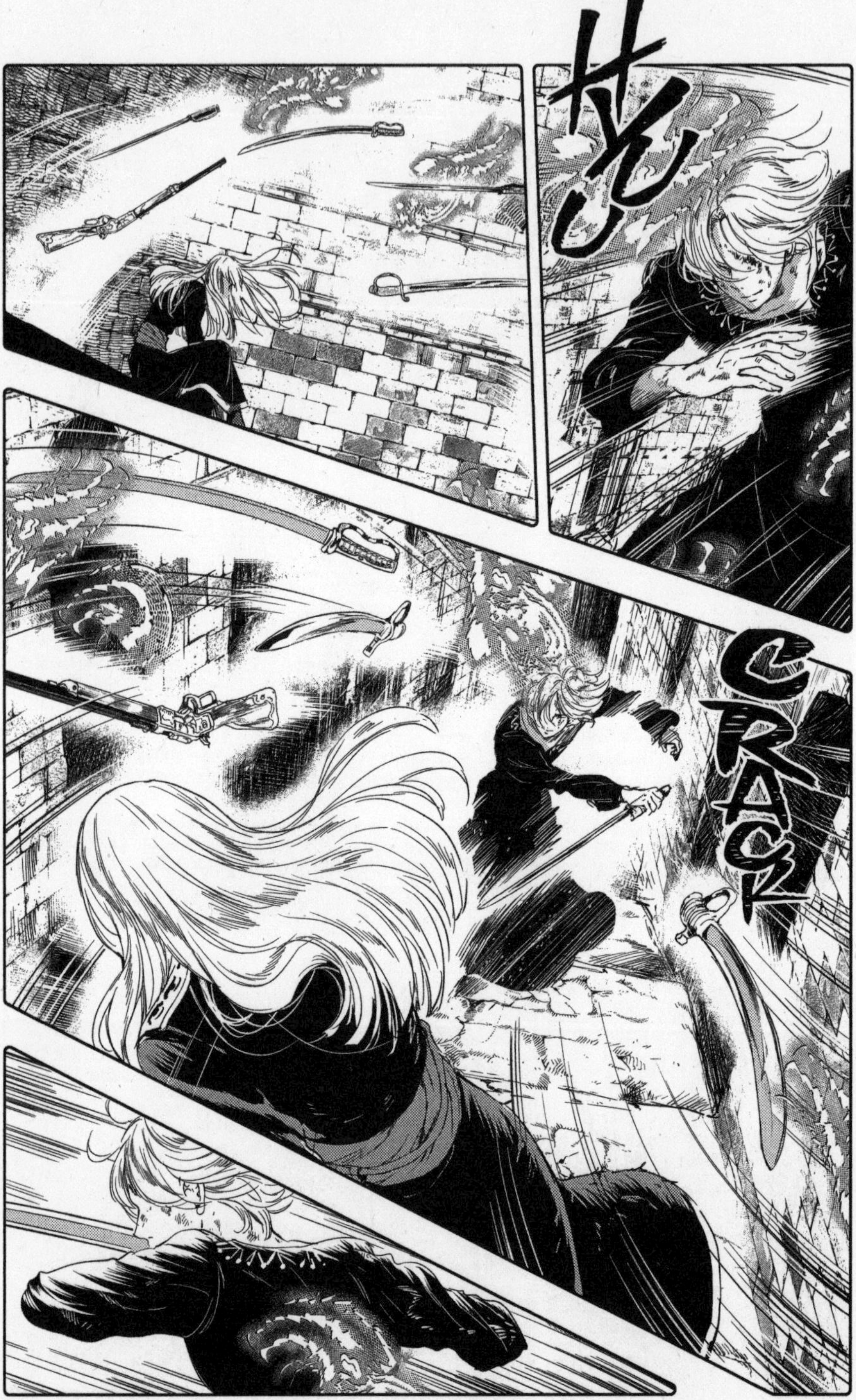
HYU
CRACK

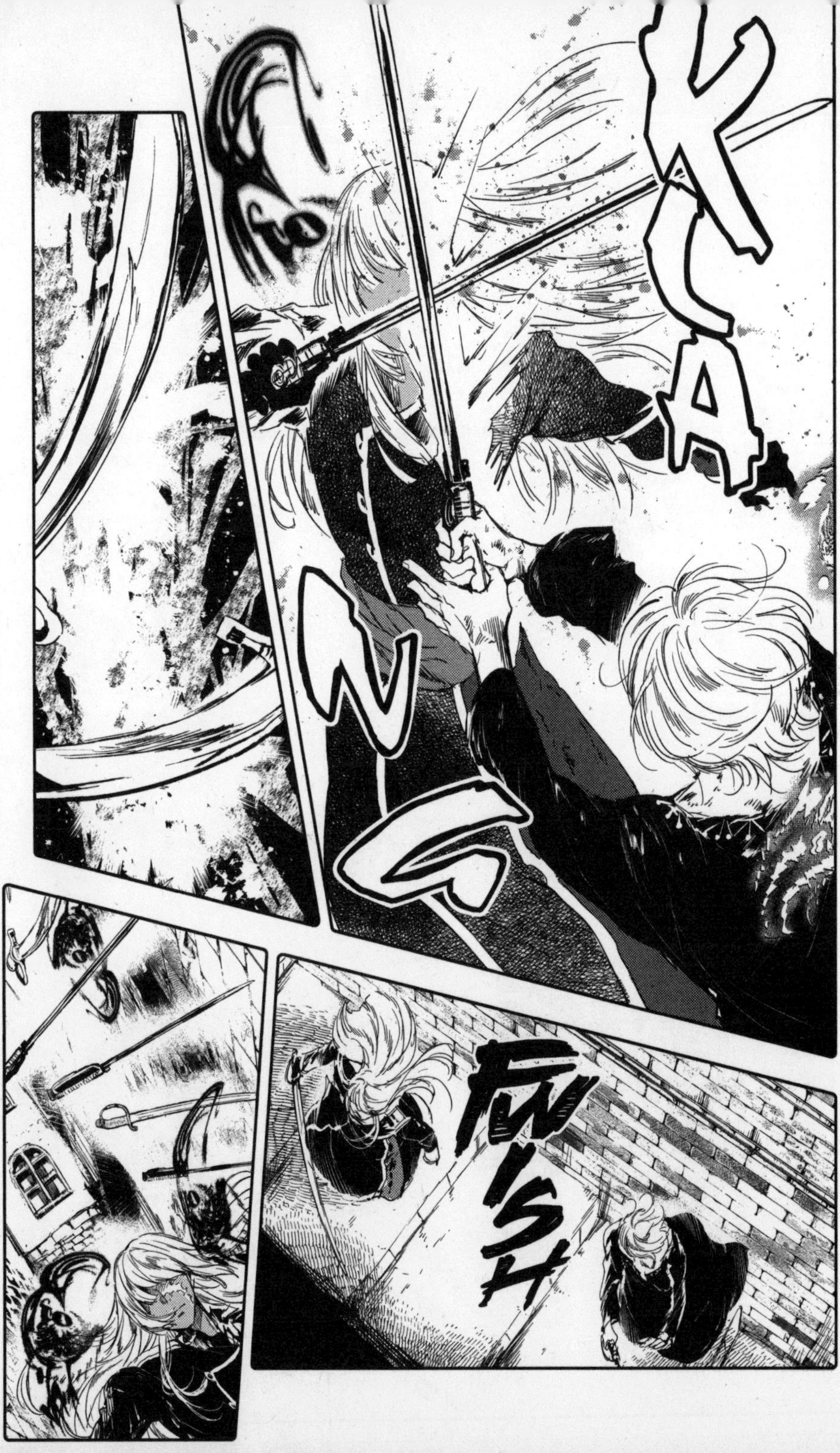
FWISH

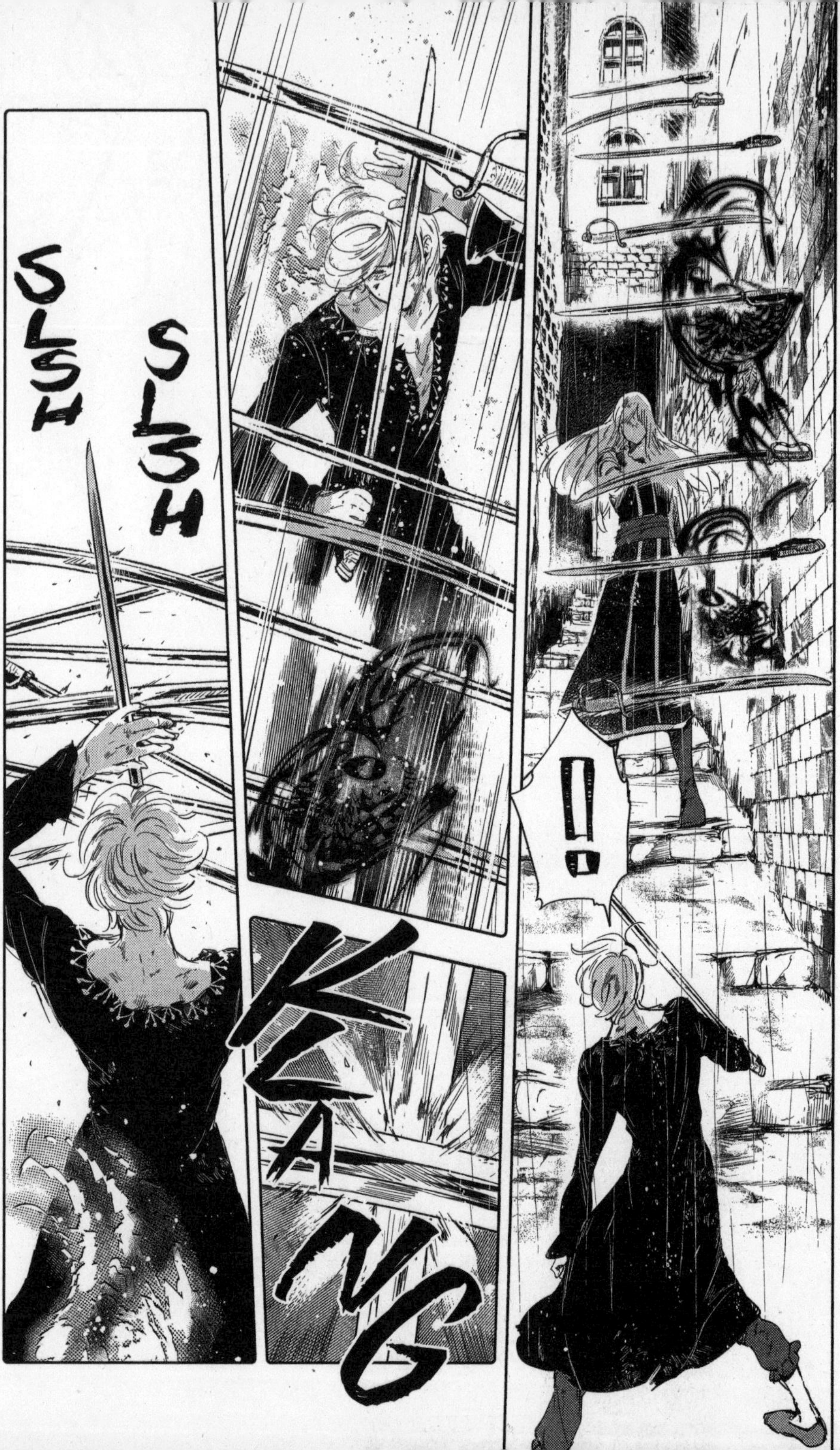
!!
KLANG
SLSH
SLSH

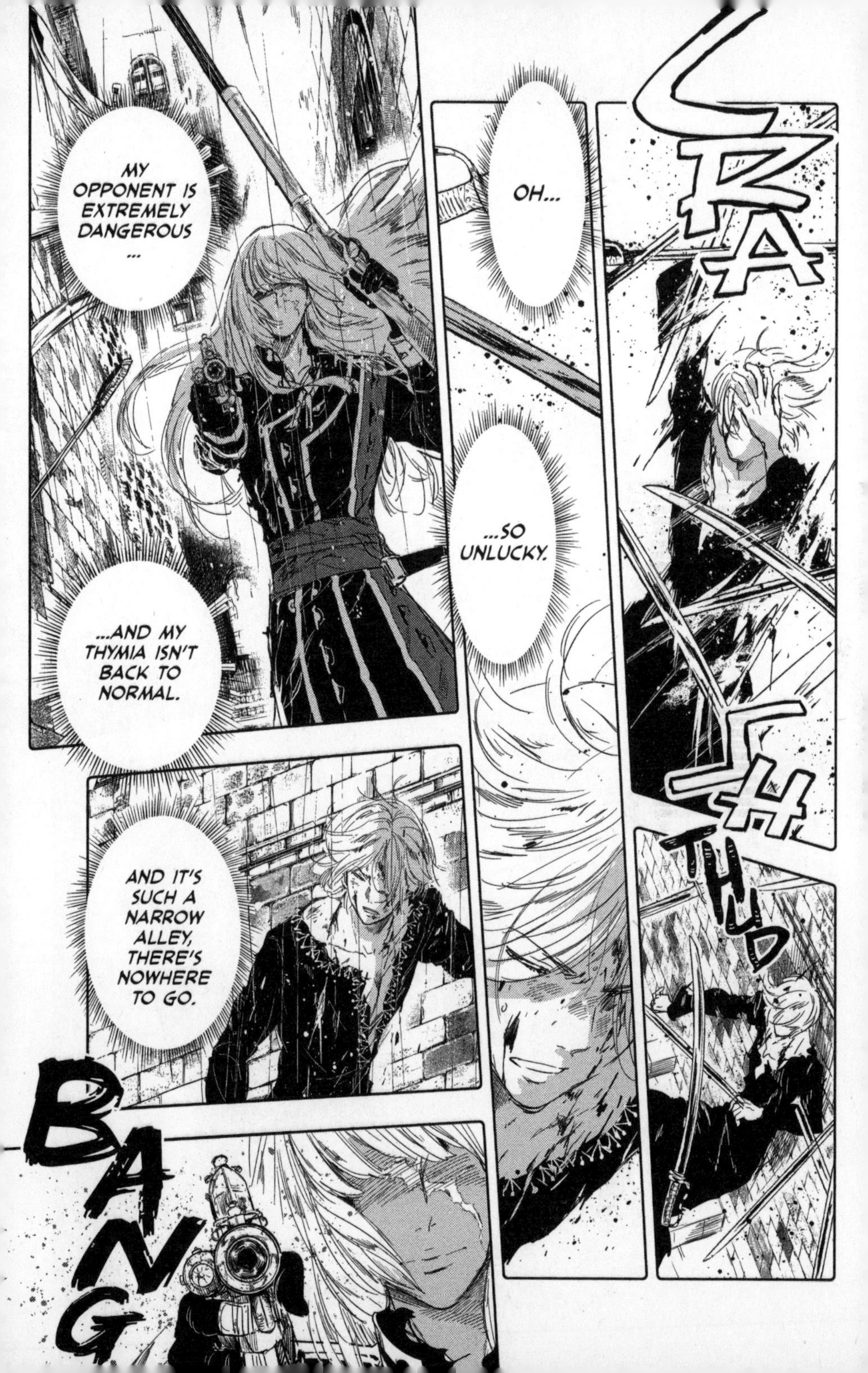

CRASH
THUD
OH...
...SO UNLUCKY.
MY OPPONENT IS EXTREMELY DANGEROUS ...
...AND MY THYMIA ISN'T BACK TO NORMAL.
AND IT'S SUCH A NARROW ALLEY, THERE'S NOWHERE TO GO.
BANG

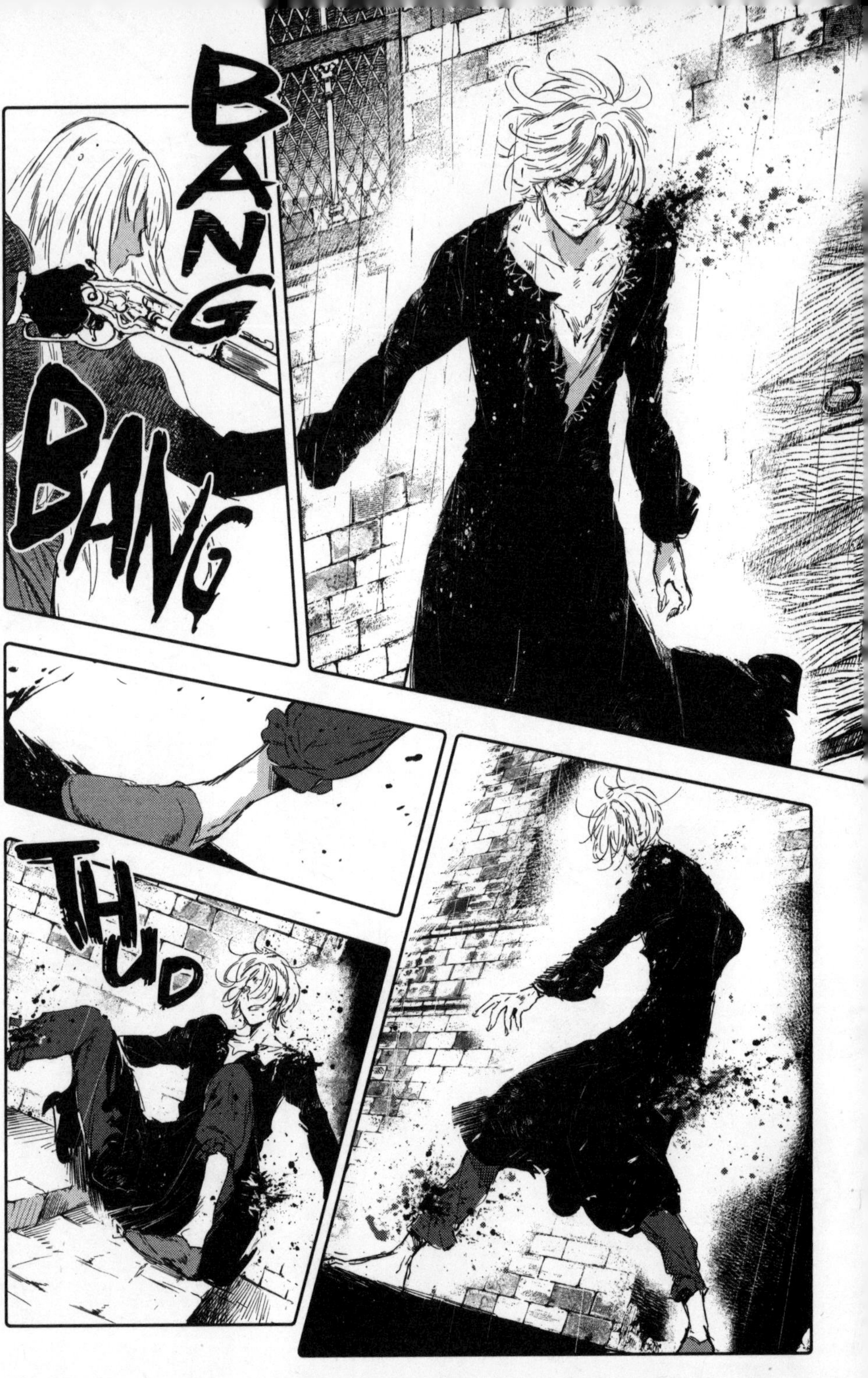
BANG
BANG
THUD

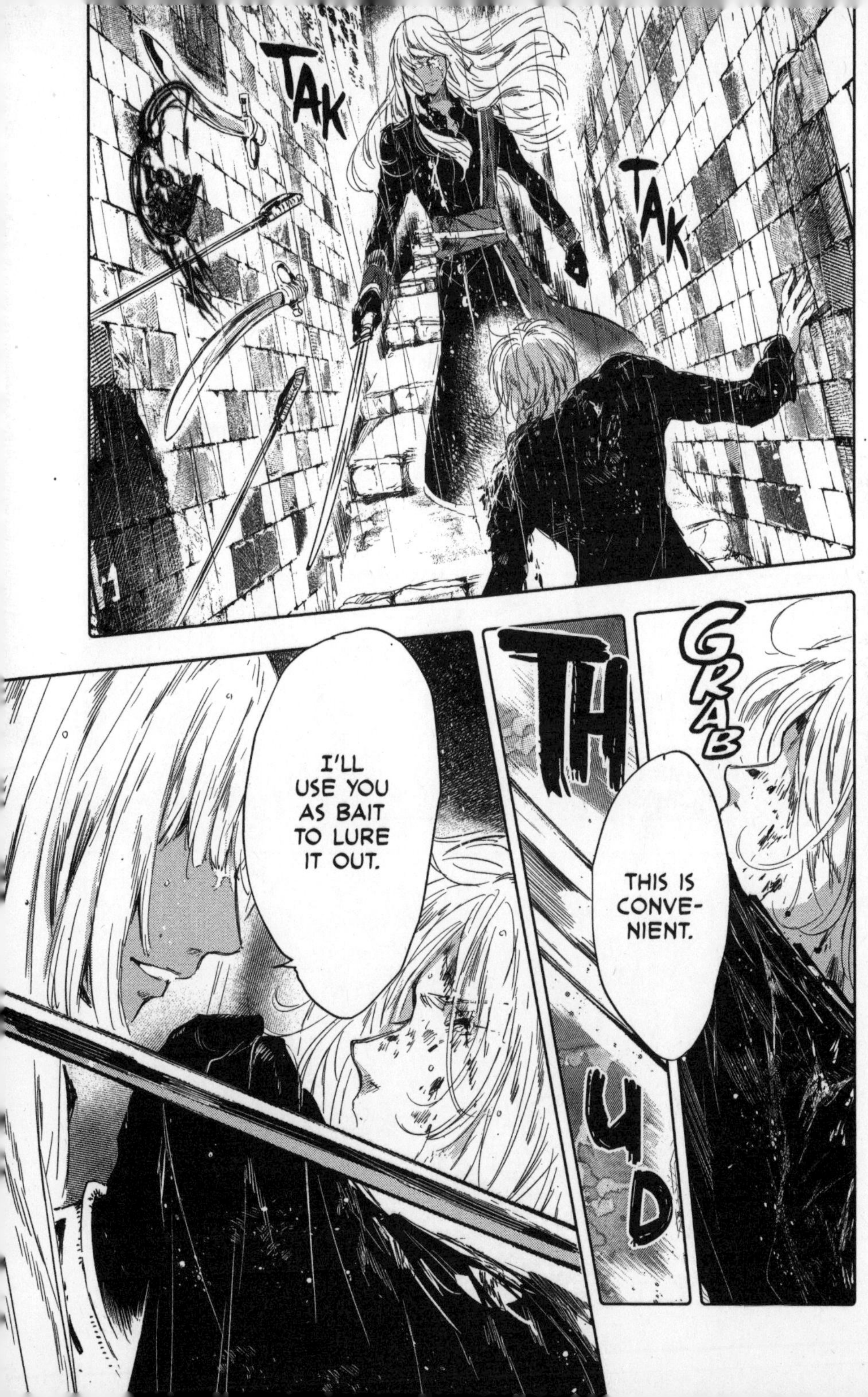
TAK
TAK
GRAB
THIS IS CONVENIENT.
THUD
I'LL USE YOU AS BAIT TO LURE IT OUT.

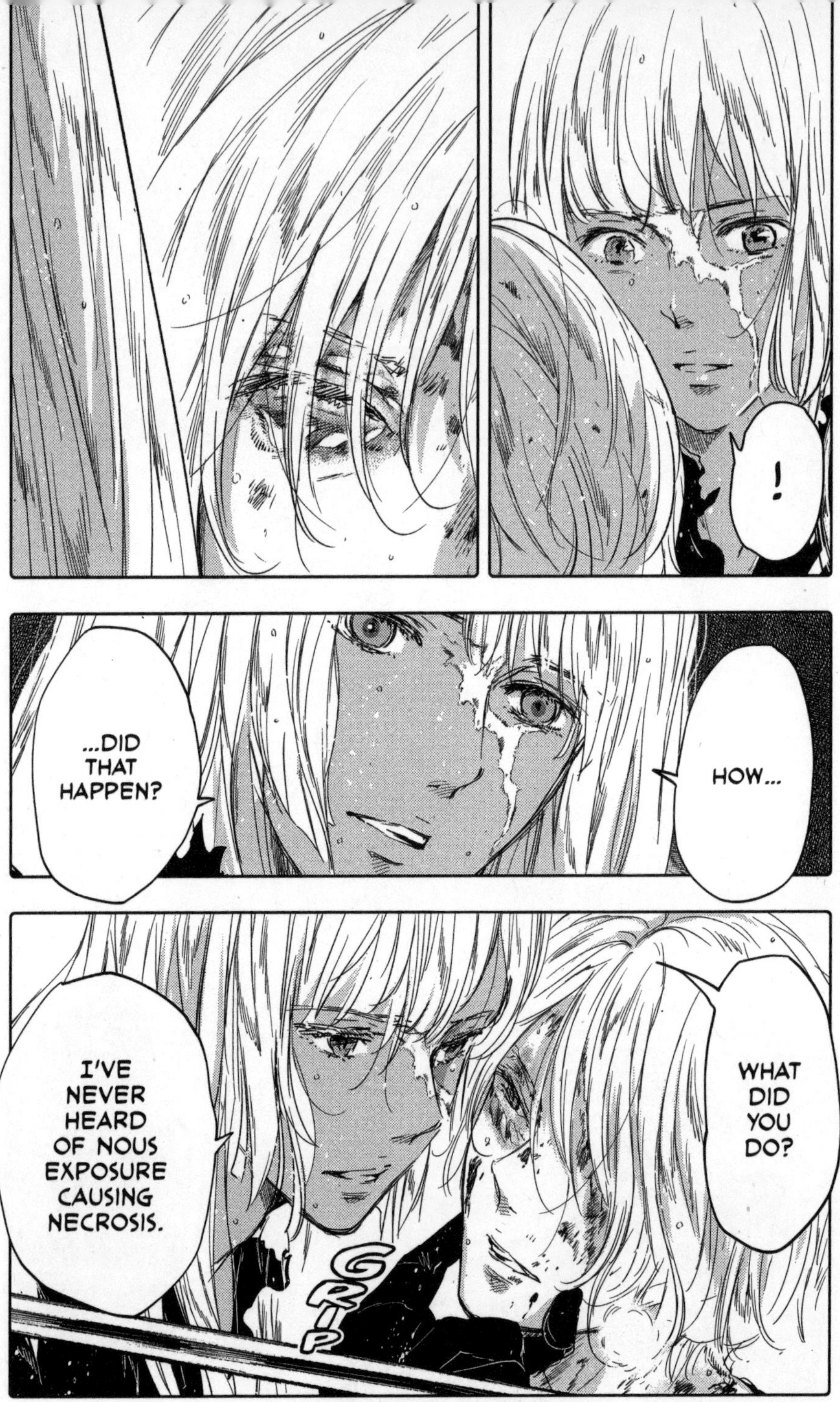
!
HOW...
...DID THAT HAPPEN?
WHAT DID YOU DO?
I'VE NEVER HEARD OF NOUS EXPOSURE CAUSING NECROSIS.
GRIP

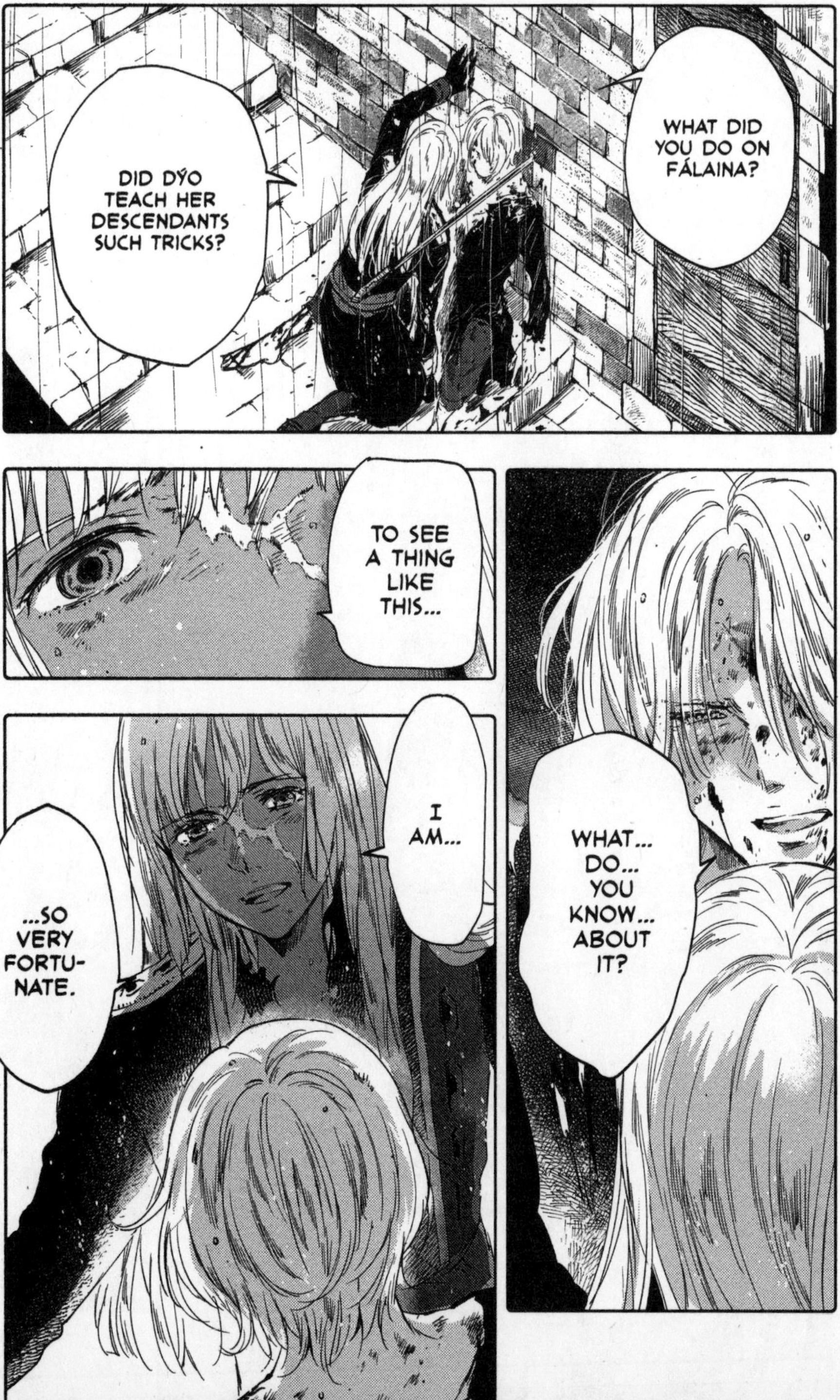
WHAT DID YOU DO ON FÁLAINA?
DID DÝO TEACH HER DESCENDANTS SUCH TRICKS?
WHAT... DO... YOU KNOW... ABOUT IT?
TO SEE A THING LIKE THIS...
I AM...
...SO VERY FORTU-NATE.

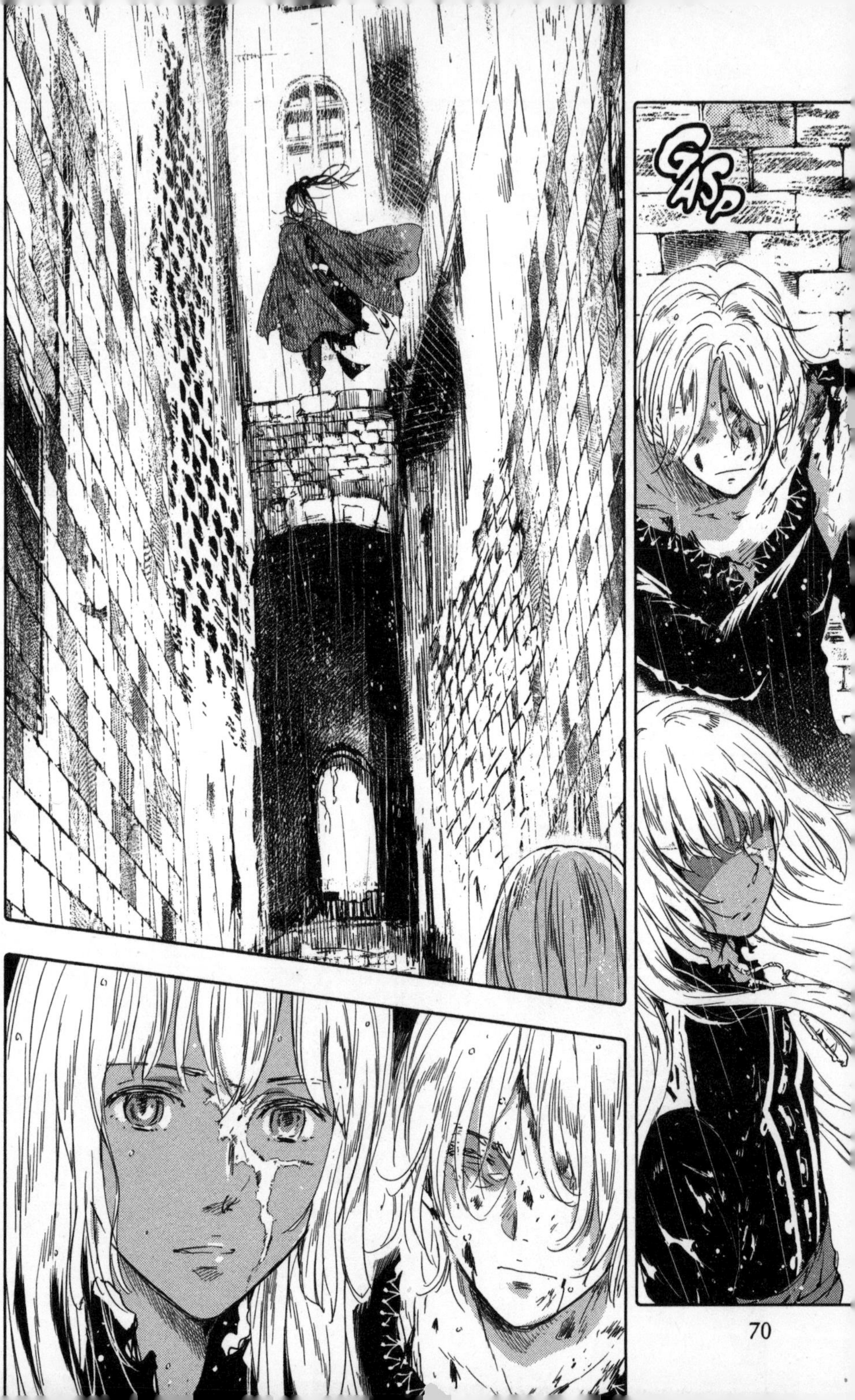
GASP

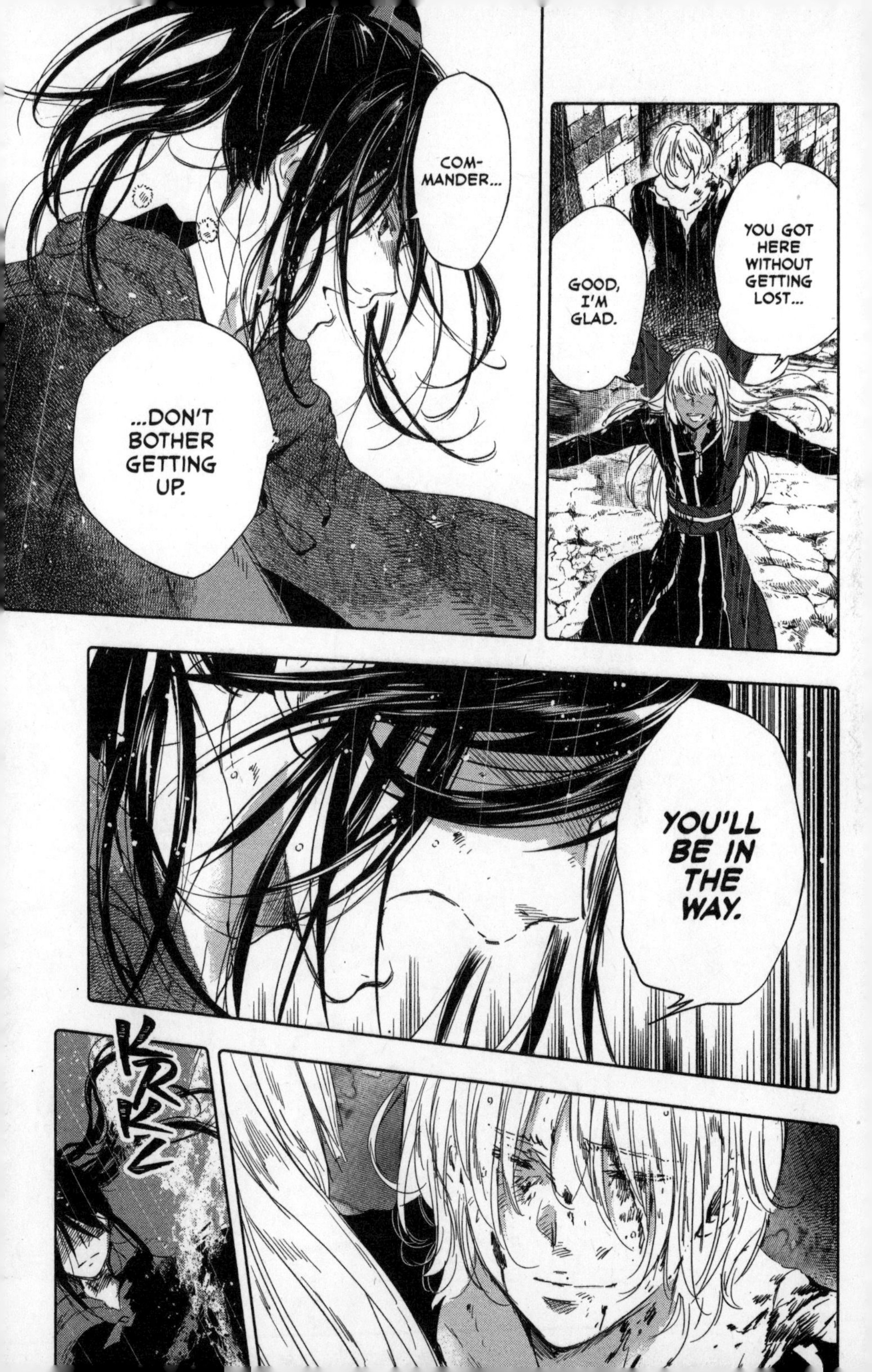
YOU GOT HERE WITHOUT GETTING LOST...
GOOD, I'M GLAD.
COM-MANDER...
...DON'T BOTHER GETTING UP.
YOU'LL BE IN THE WAY.
KRKL

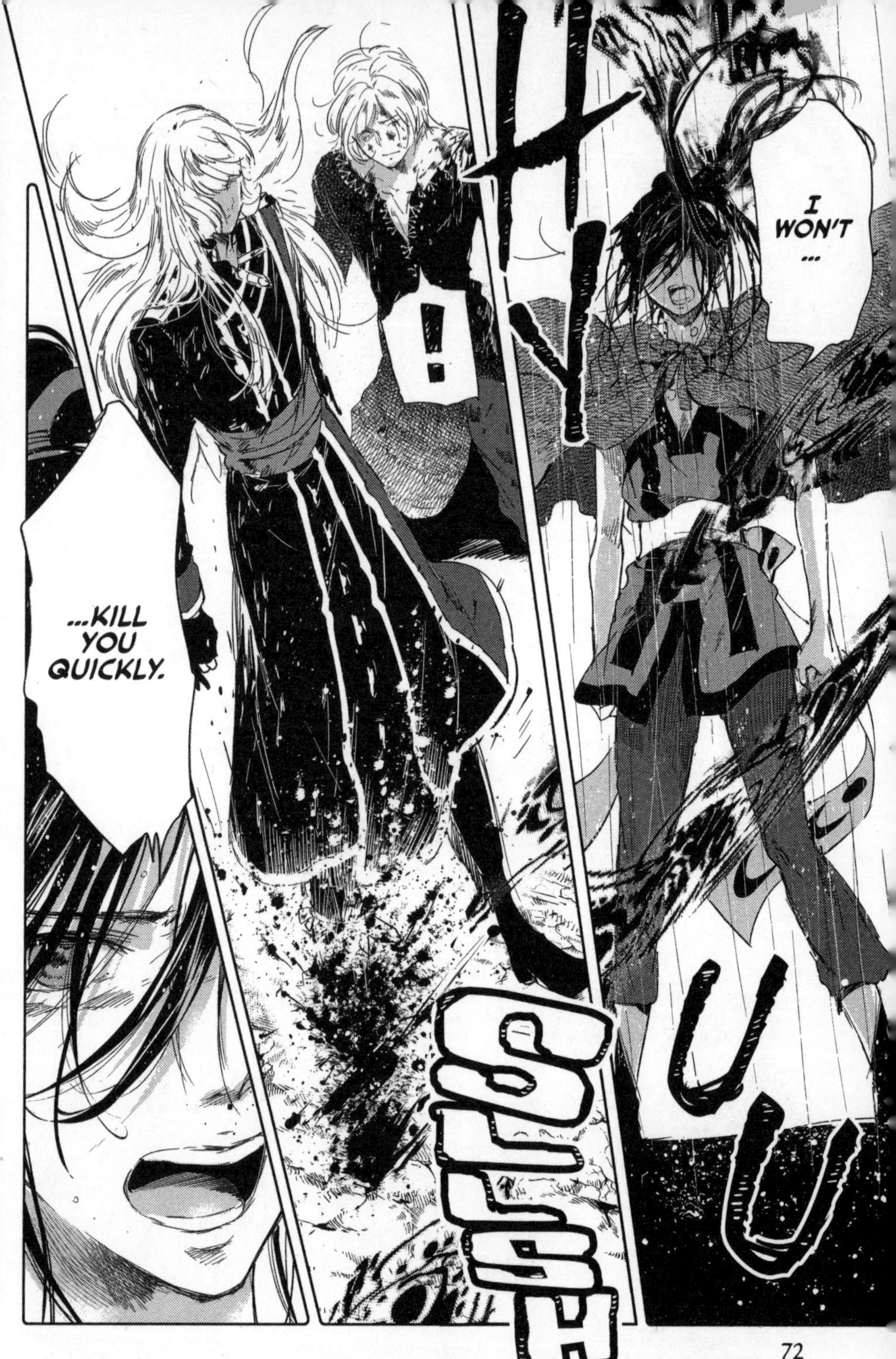
I WON'T ...
...KILL YOU QUICKLY.

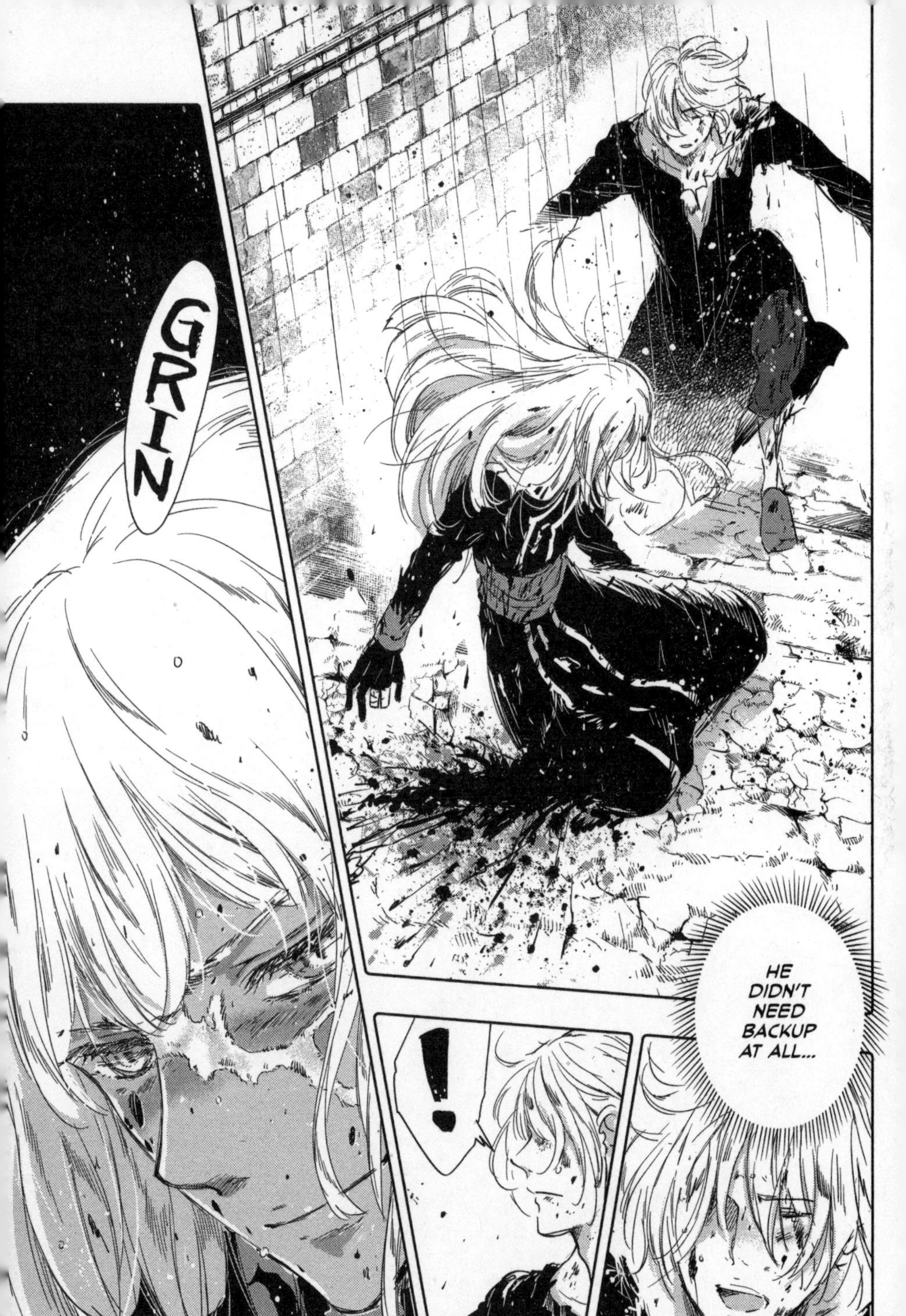
HE DIDN'T NEED BACKUP AT ALL...
GRIN
!

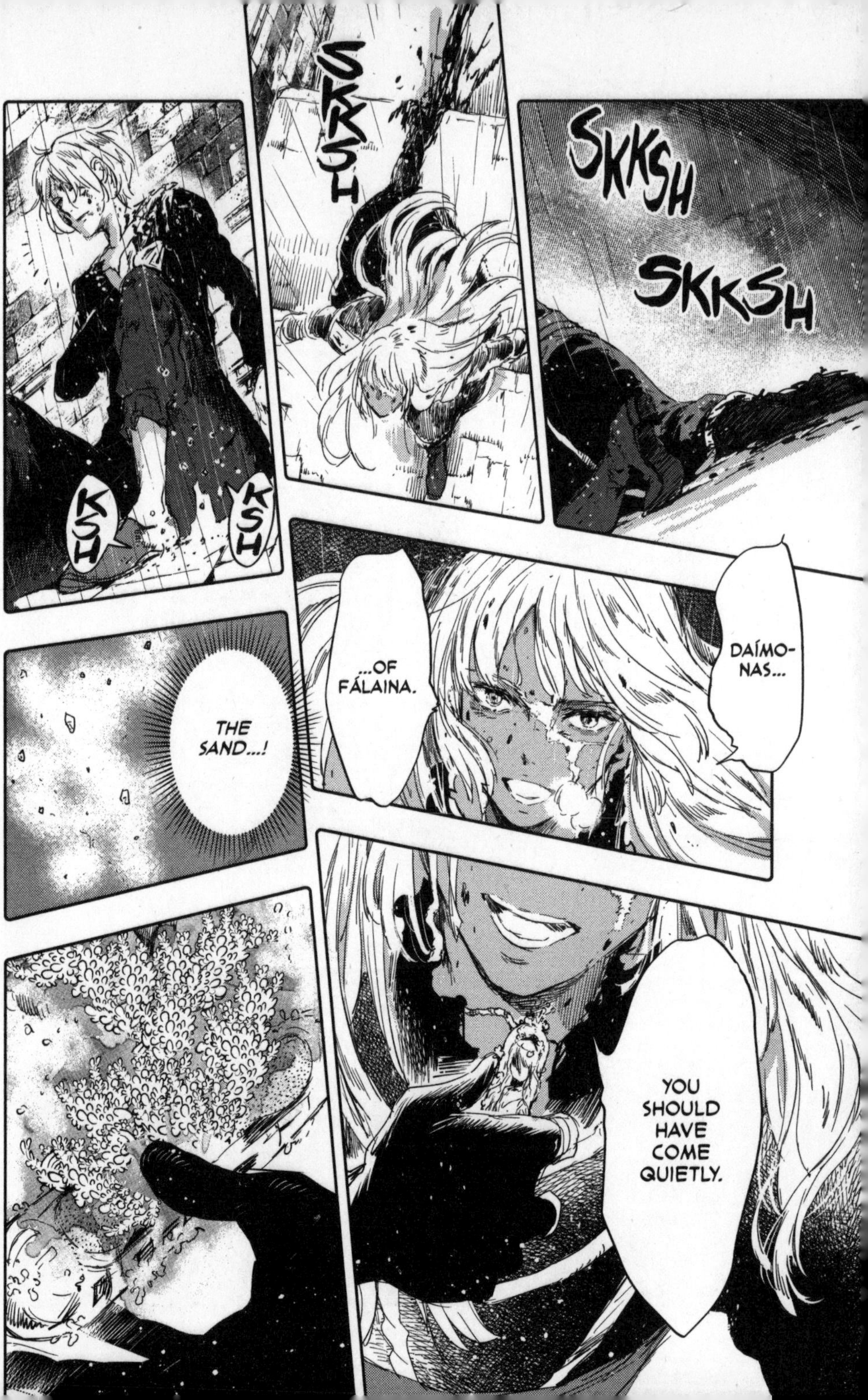
SKKSH
SKKSH
SKKSH
KSH
KSH
DAÍMO-NAS...
...OF FÁLAINA.
THE SAND...!
YOU SHOULD HAVE COME QUIETLY.

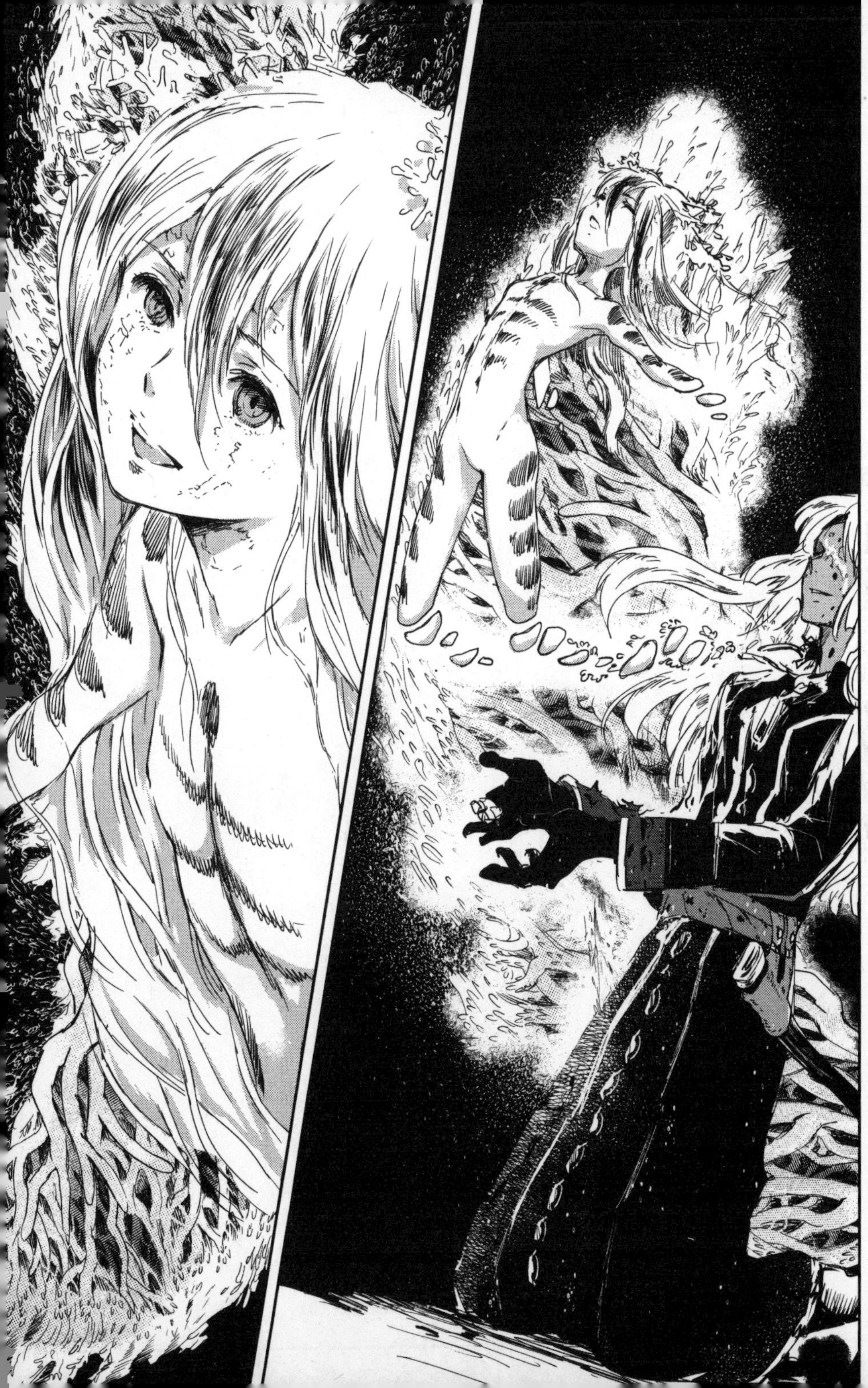

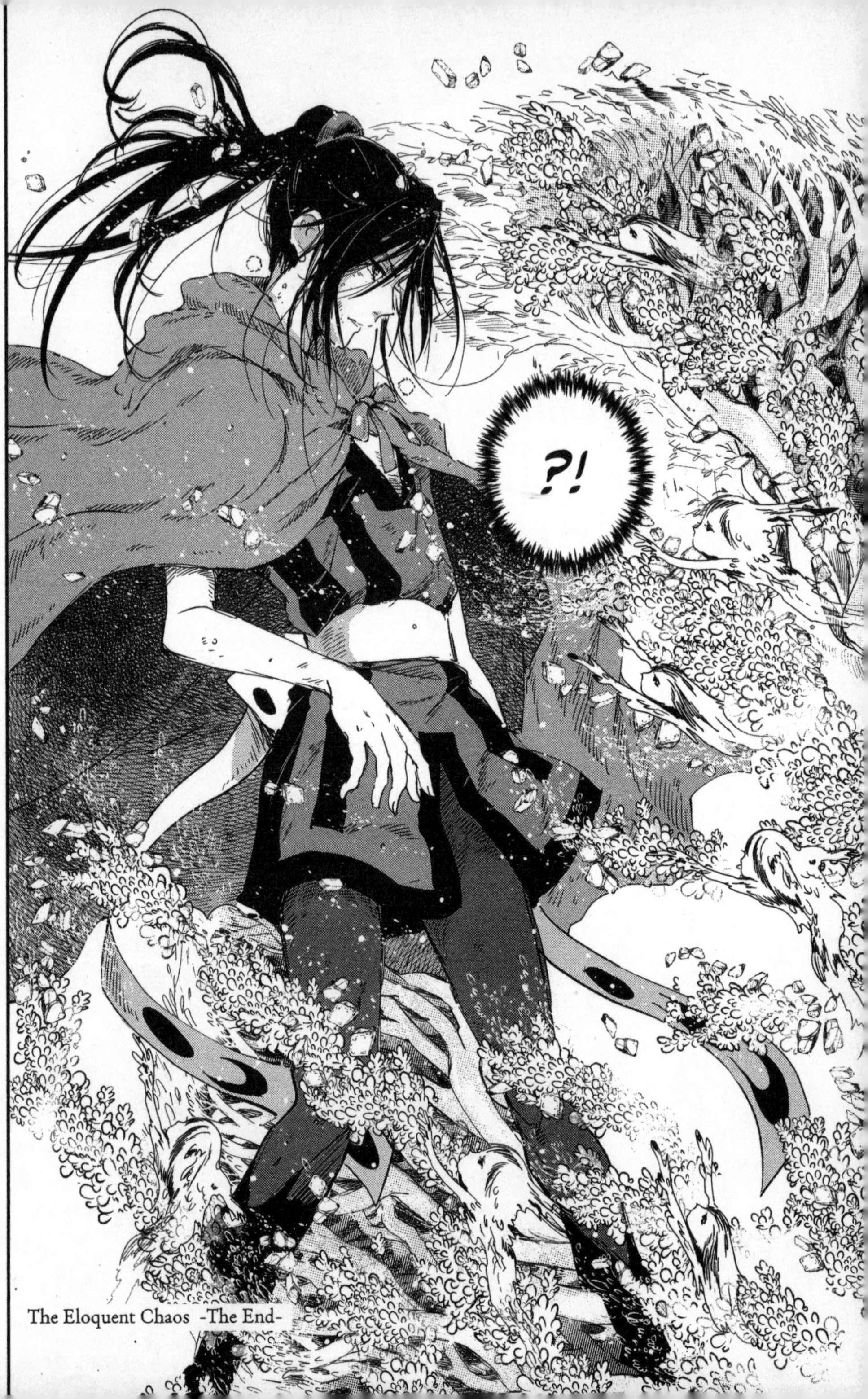
?!
The Eloquent Chaos -The End-

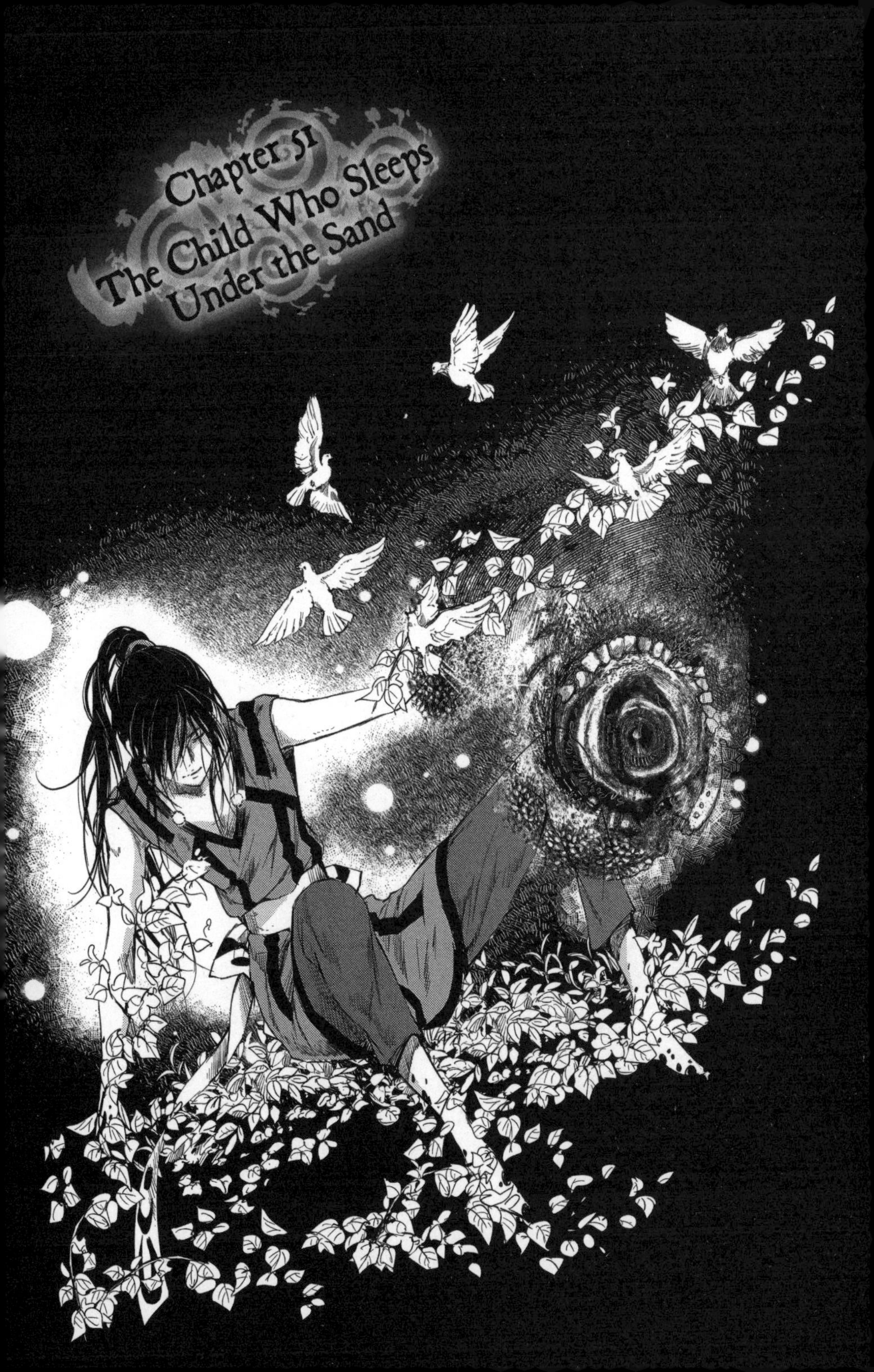
Chapter 51
The Child Who Sleeps Under the Sand

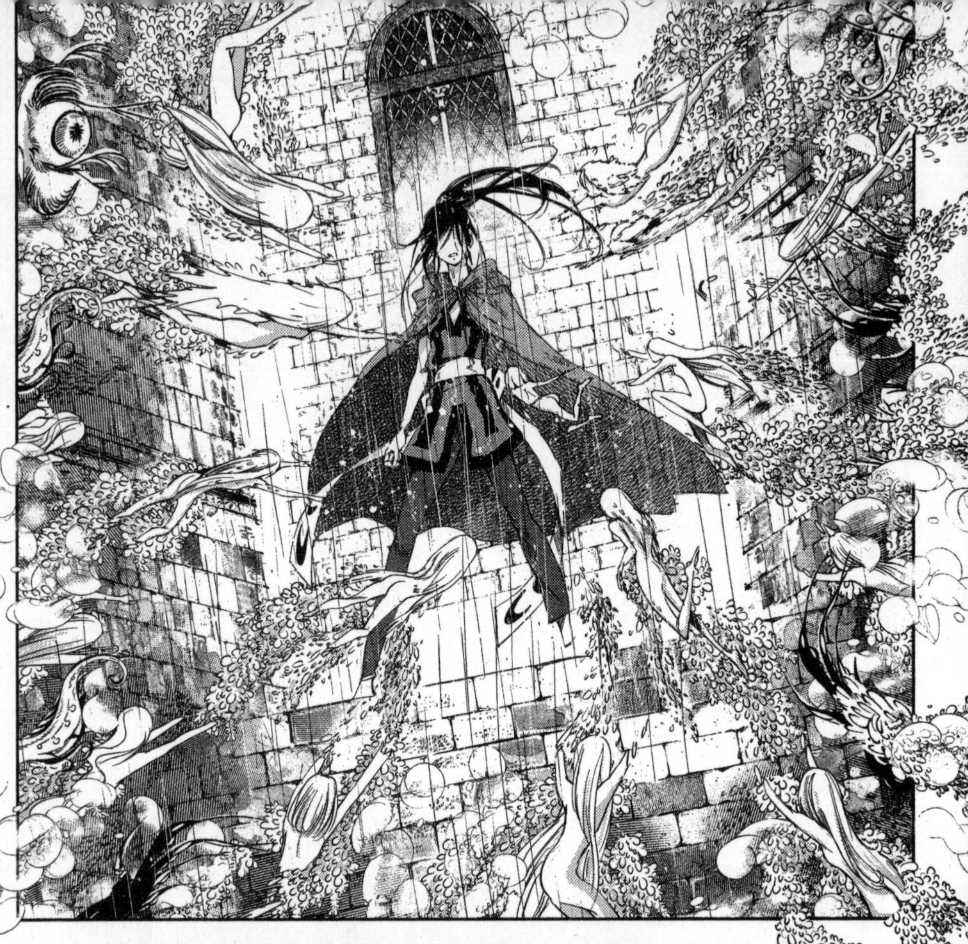
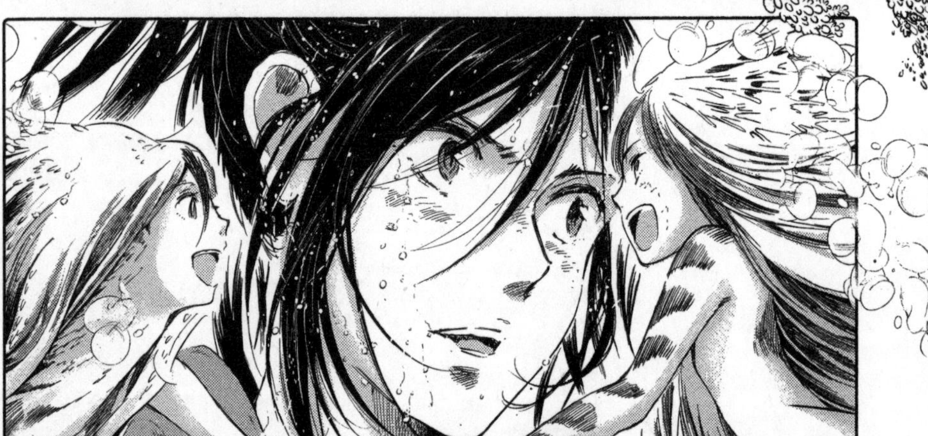

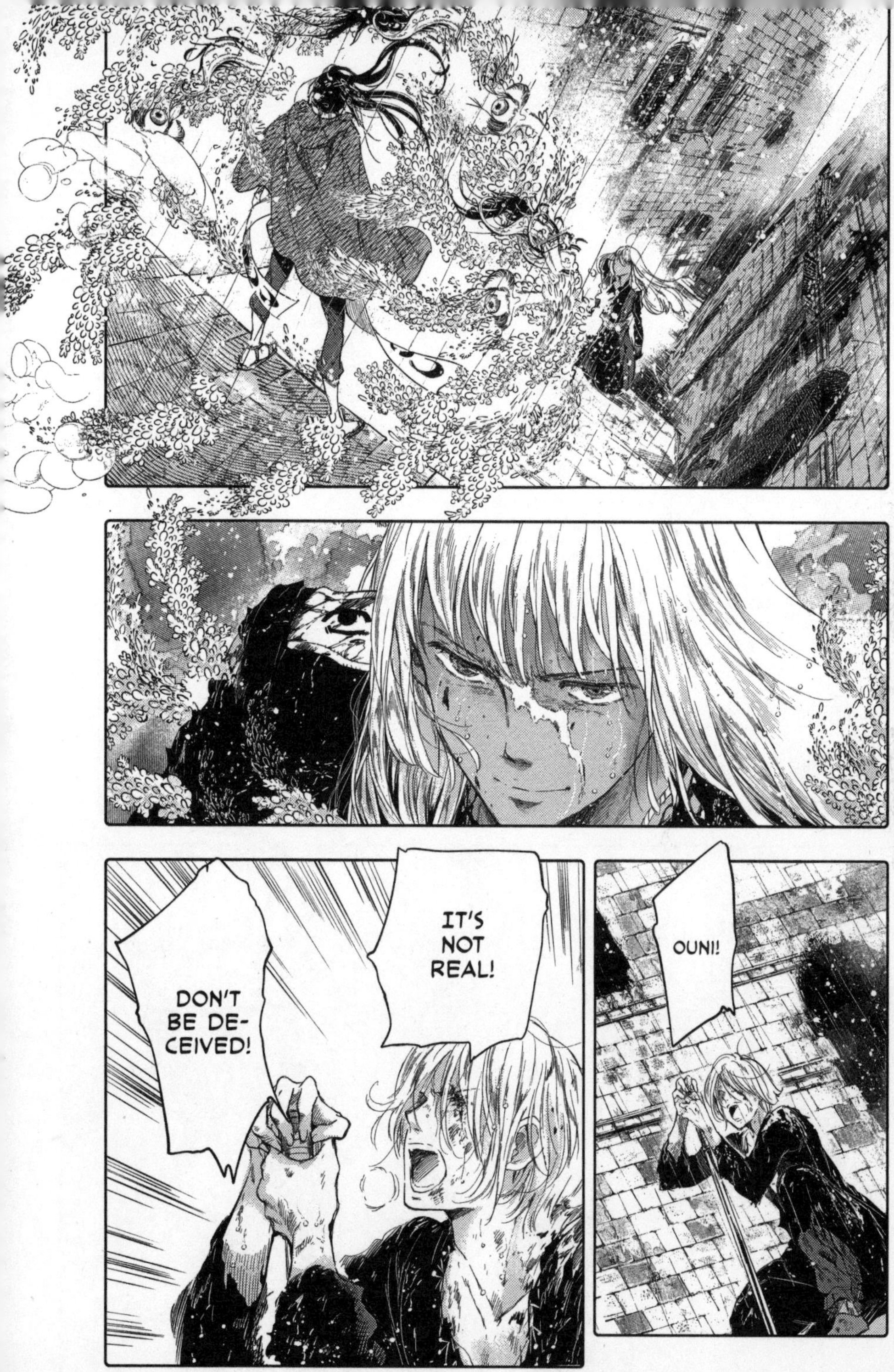
OUNI!
IT'S NOT REAL!
DON'T BE DE-CEIVED!

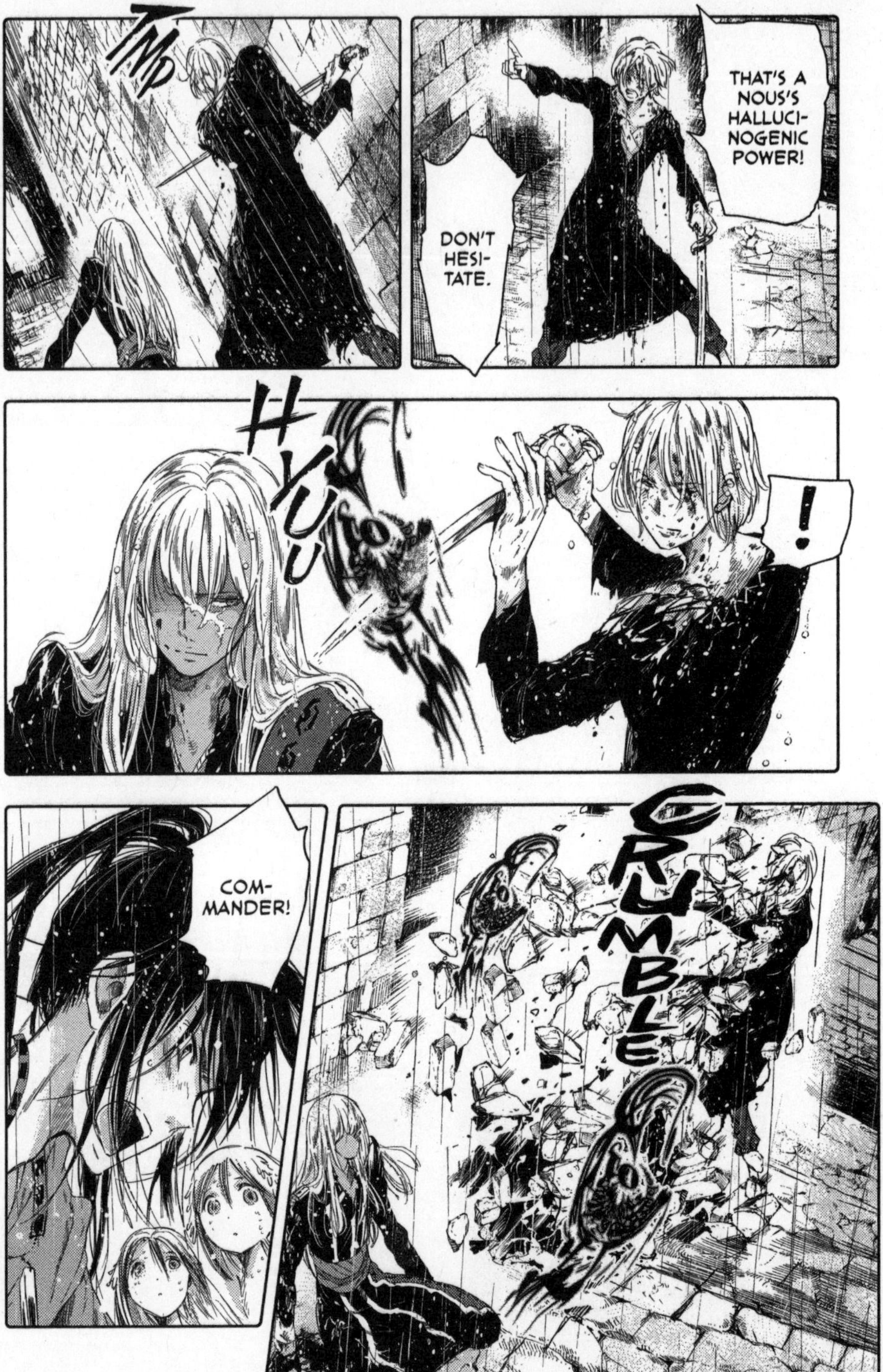
THAT'S A NOUS'S HALLUCI-NOGENIC POWER!
DON'T HESI-TATE.
TMP
HYUU
!
CRUMBLE
COM-MANDER!

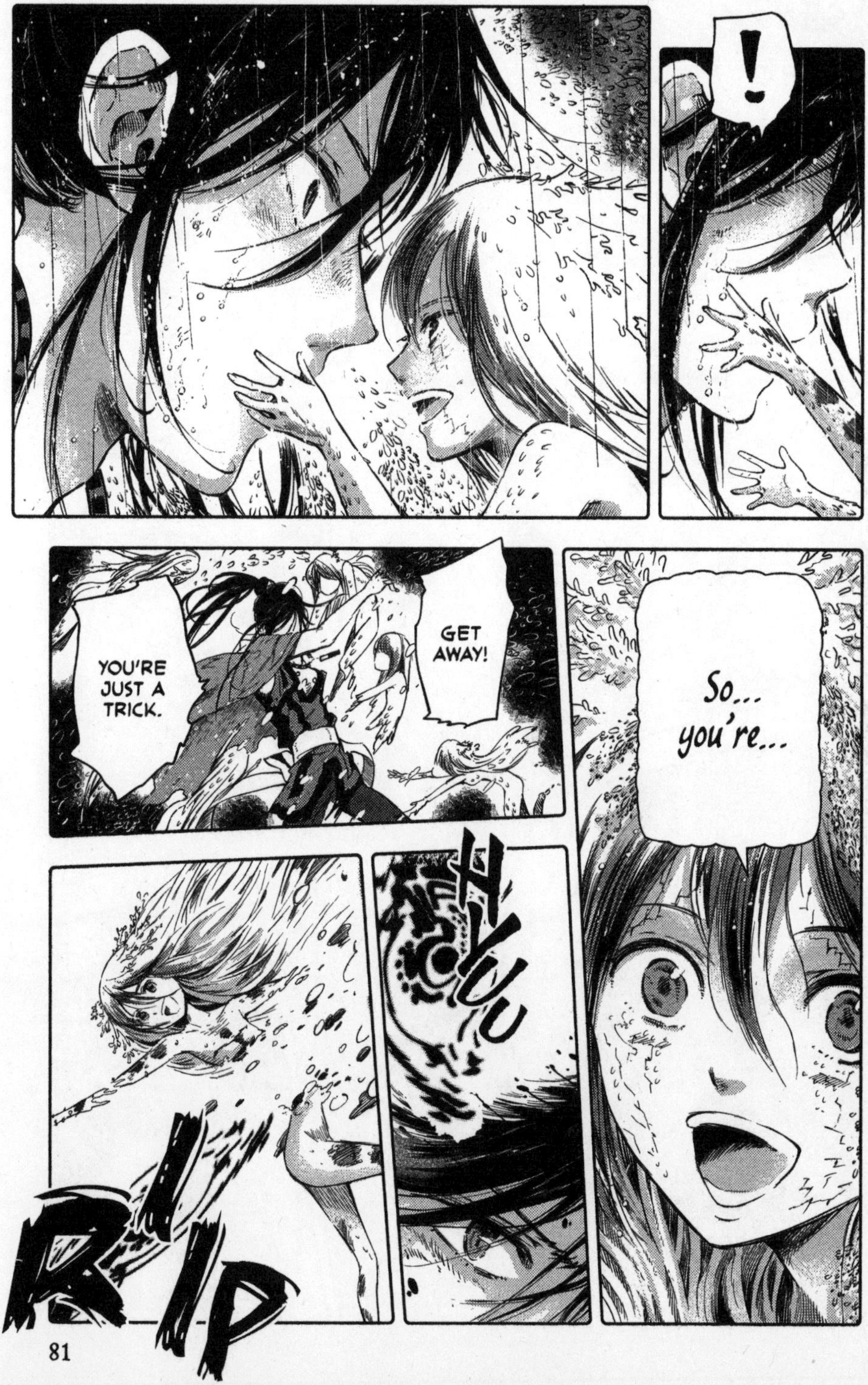
!
So... you're...
GET AWAY!
YOU'RE JUST A TRICK.
HYUU
RIP

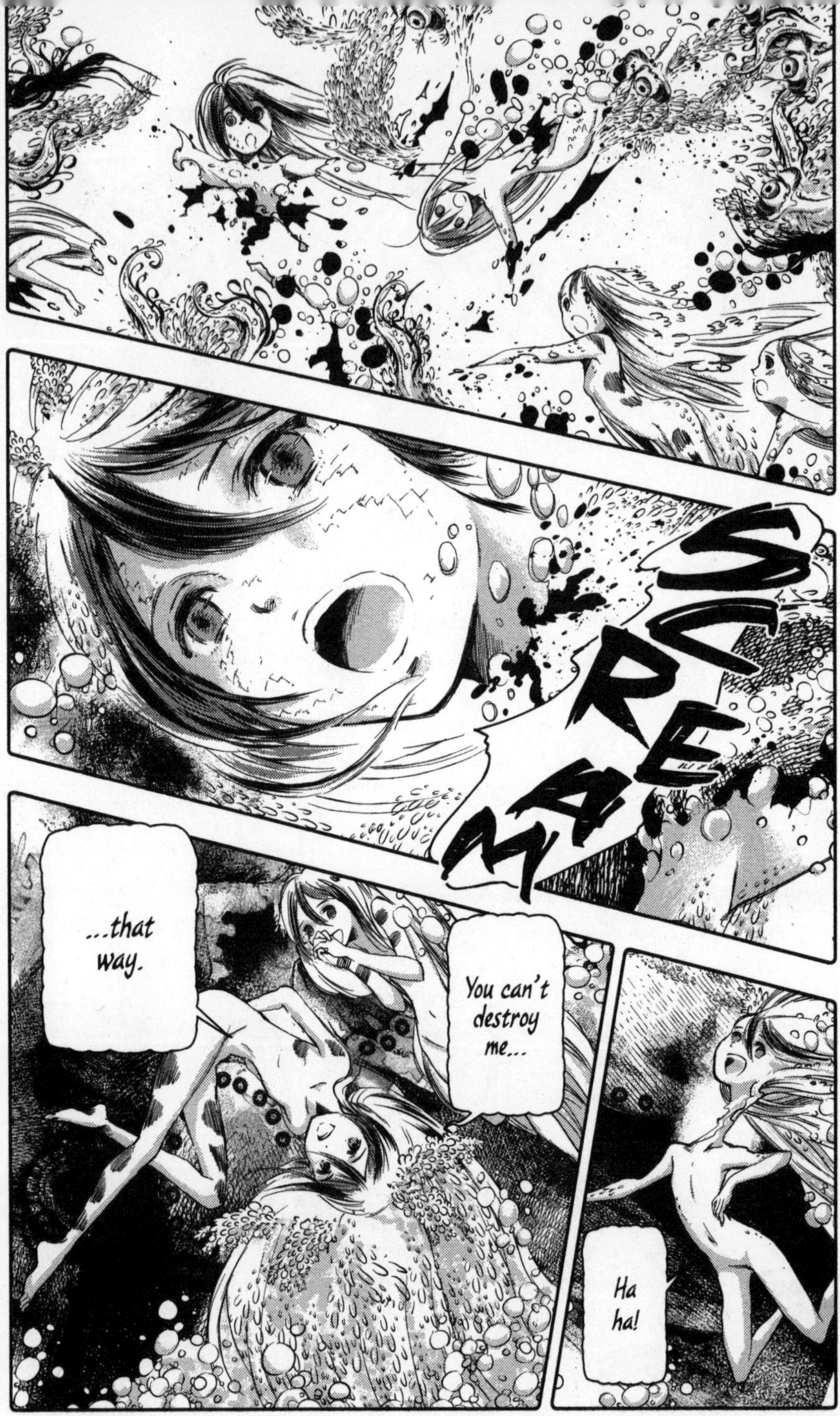
SCREAM
Ha ha!
You can't destroy me...
...that way.

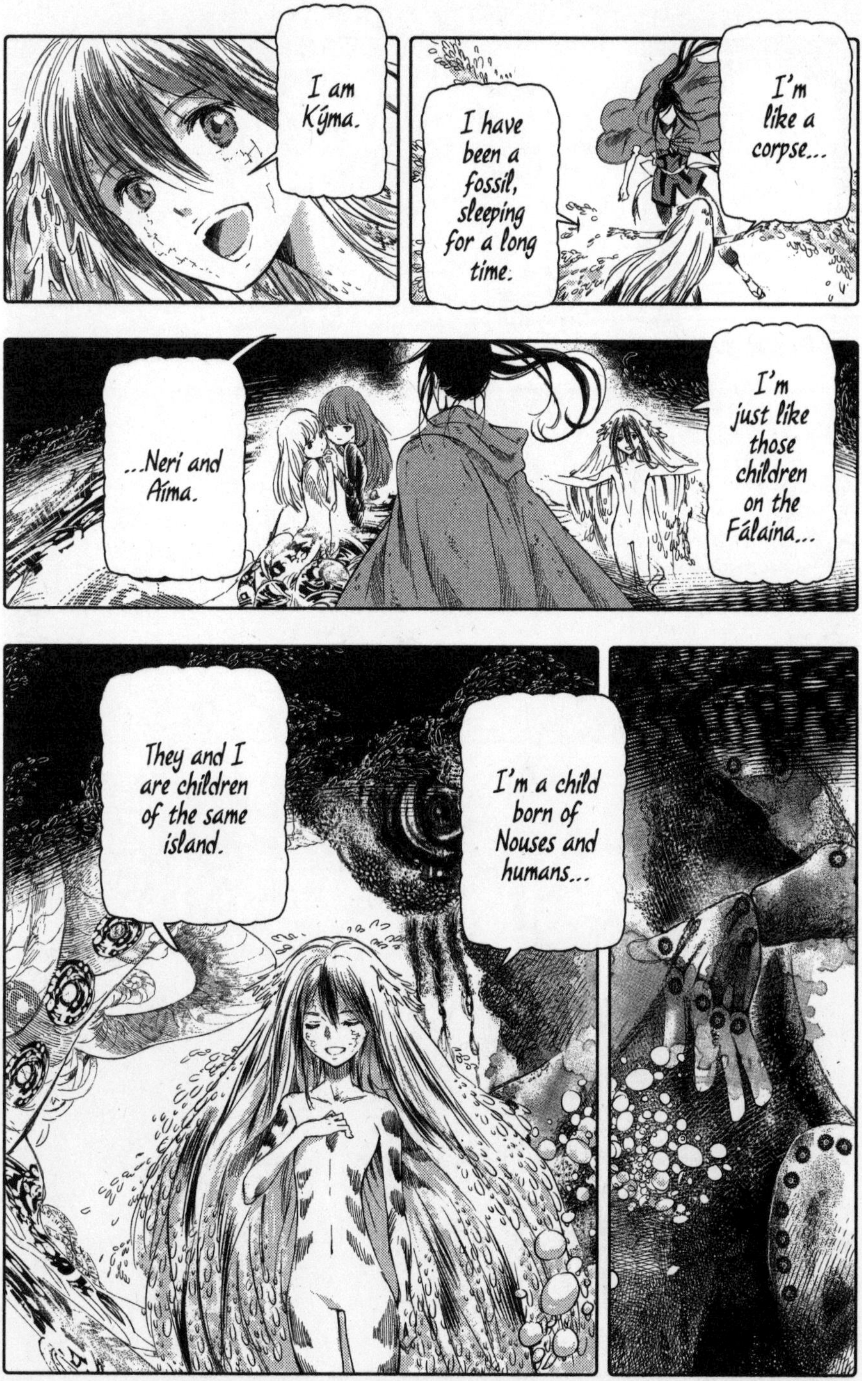
I'm like a corpse...
I have been a fossil, sleeping for a long time.
I am Kýma.
I'm just like those children on the Fálaina...
...Neri and Aíma.
I'm a child born of Nouses and humans...
They and I are children of the same island.

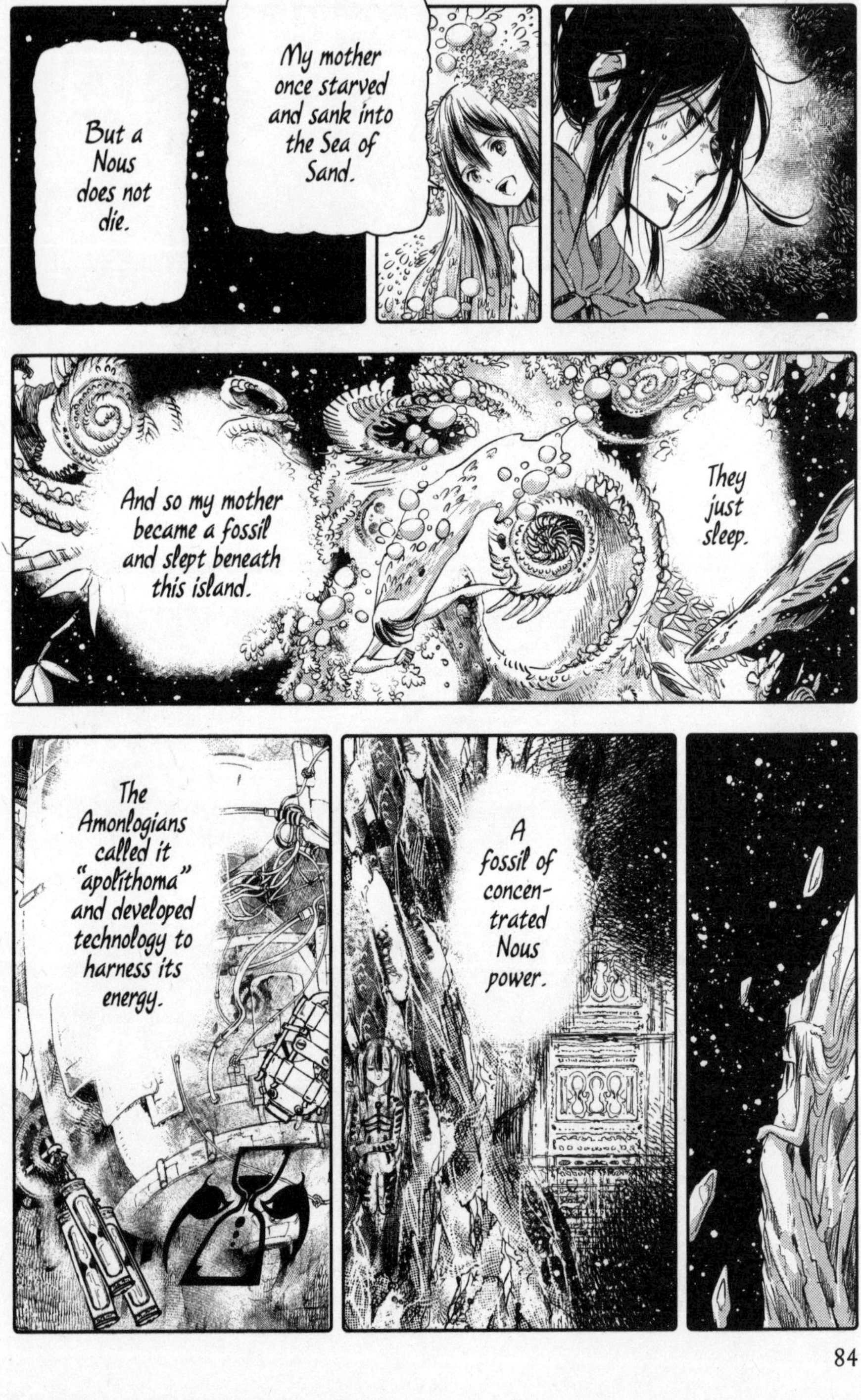
My mother once starved and sank into the Sea of Sand.
But a Nous does not die.
They just sleep.
And so my mother became a fossil and slept beneath this island.
A fossil of concen-trated Nous power.
The Amonlogians called it "apolithoma" and developed technology to harness its energy.

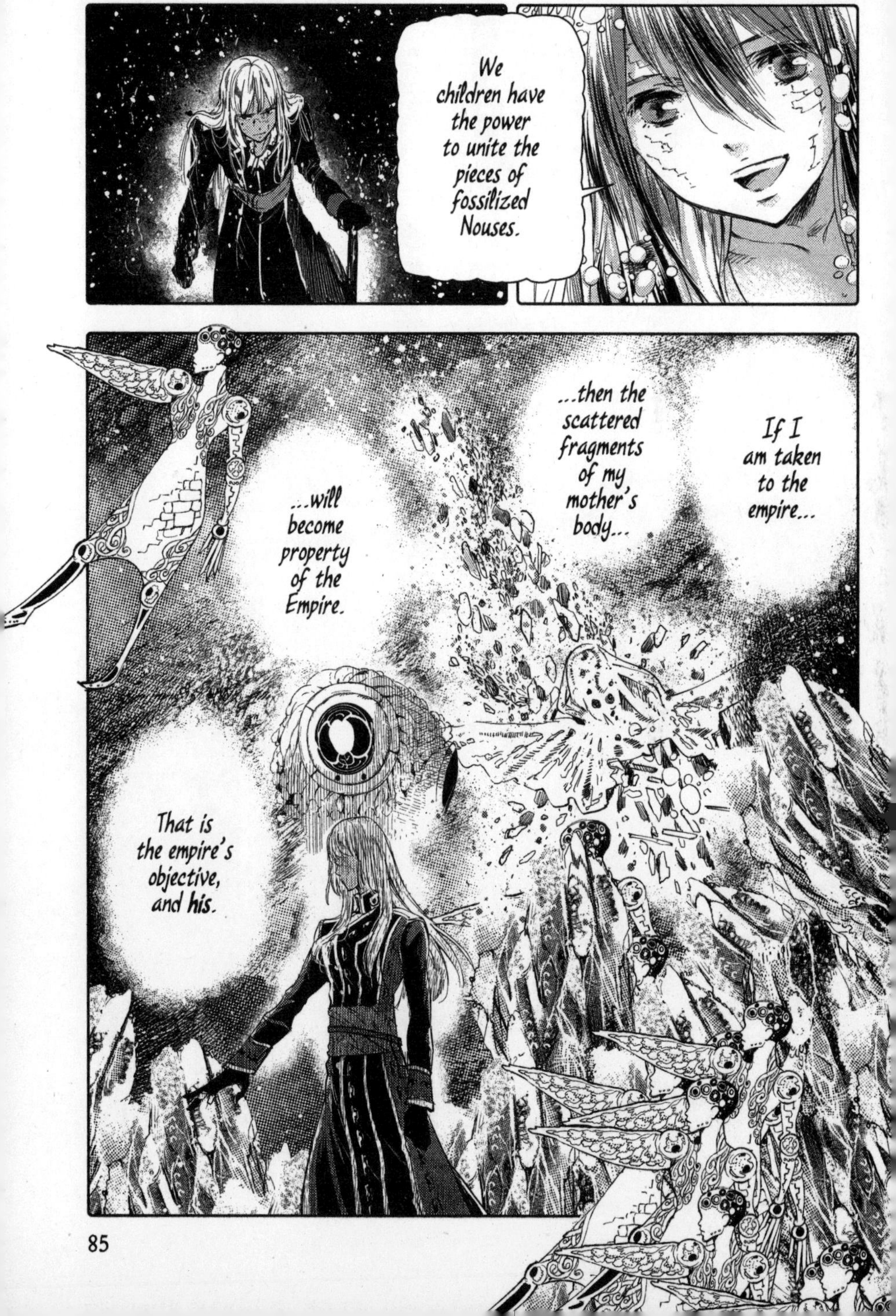
We children have the power to unite the pieces of fossilized Nouses.
If I am taken to the empire...
...then the scattered fragments of my mother's body...
...will become property of the Empire.
That is the empire's objective, and his.

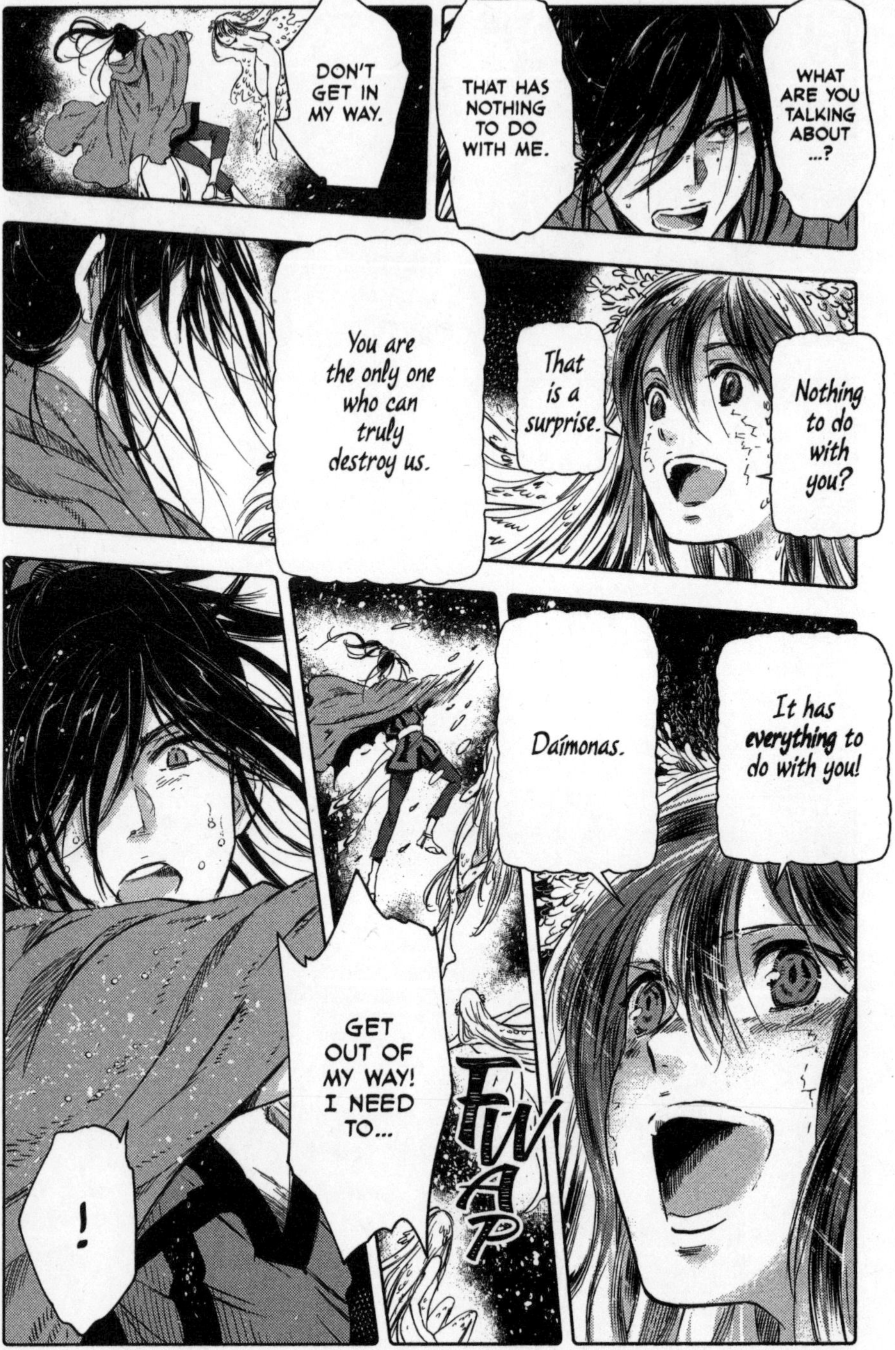
WHAT ARE YOU TALKING ABOUT ...?
THAT HAS NOTHING TO DO WITH ME.
DON'T GET IN MY WAY.
Nothing to do with you?
That is a surprise.
You are the only one who can truly destroy us.
It has everything to do with you!
Daímonas.
FWAP
GET OUT OF MY WAY! I NEED TO...
!

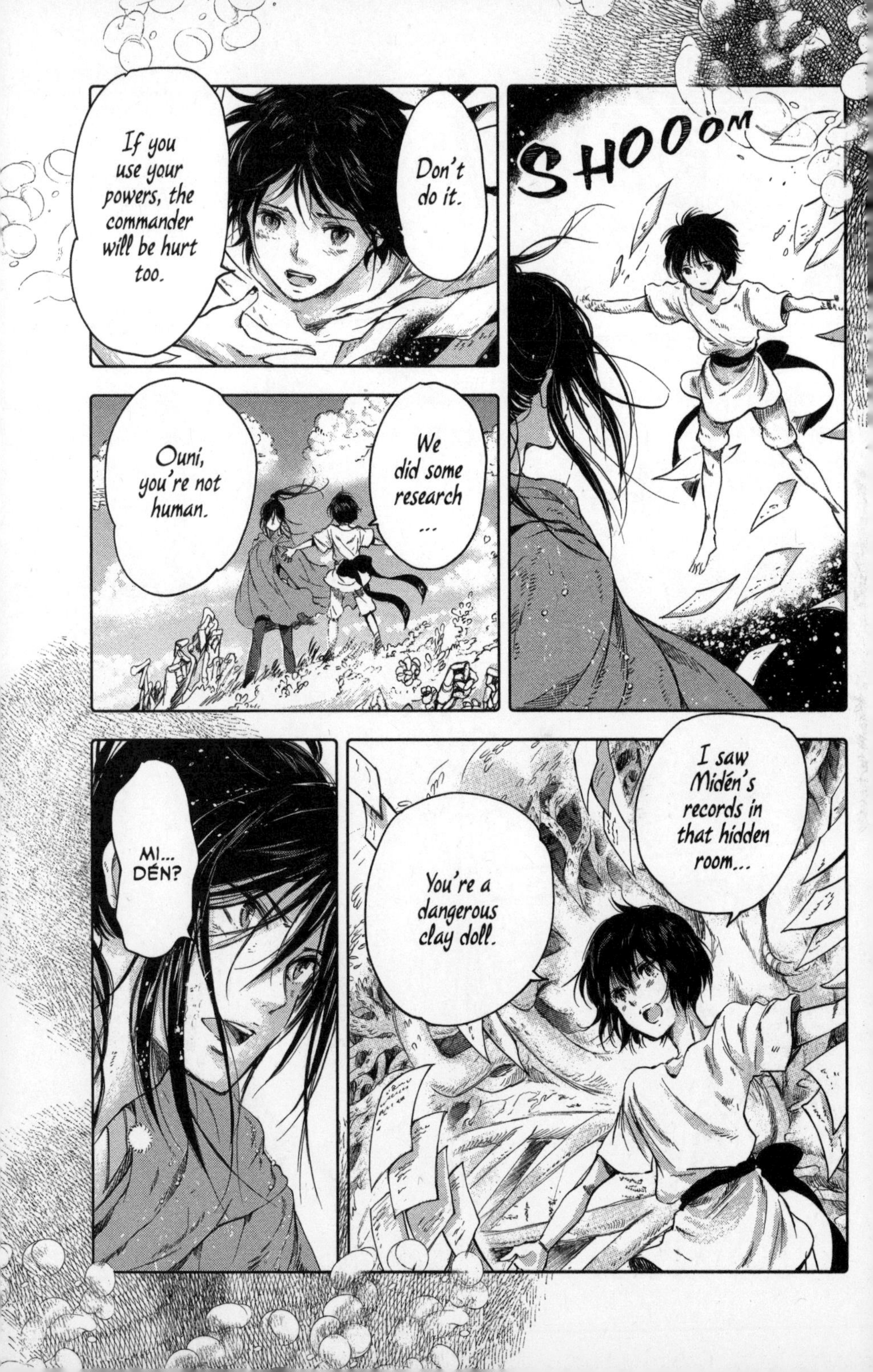
SHOOOOM
Don't do it.
If you use your powers, the commander will be hurt too.
We did some research ...
Ouni, you're not human.
I saw Midén's records in that hidden room...
You're a dangerous clay doll.
MI... DÉN?

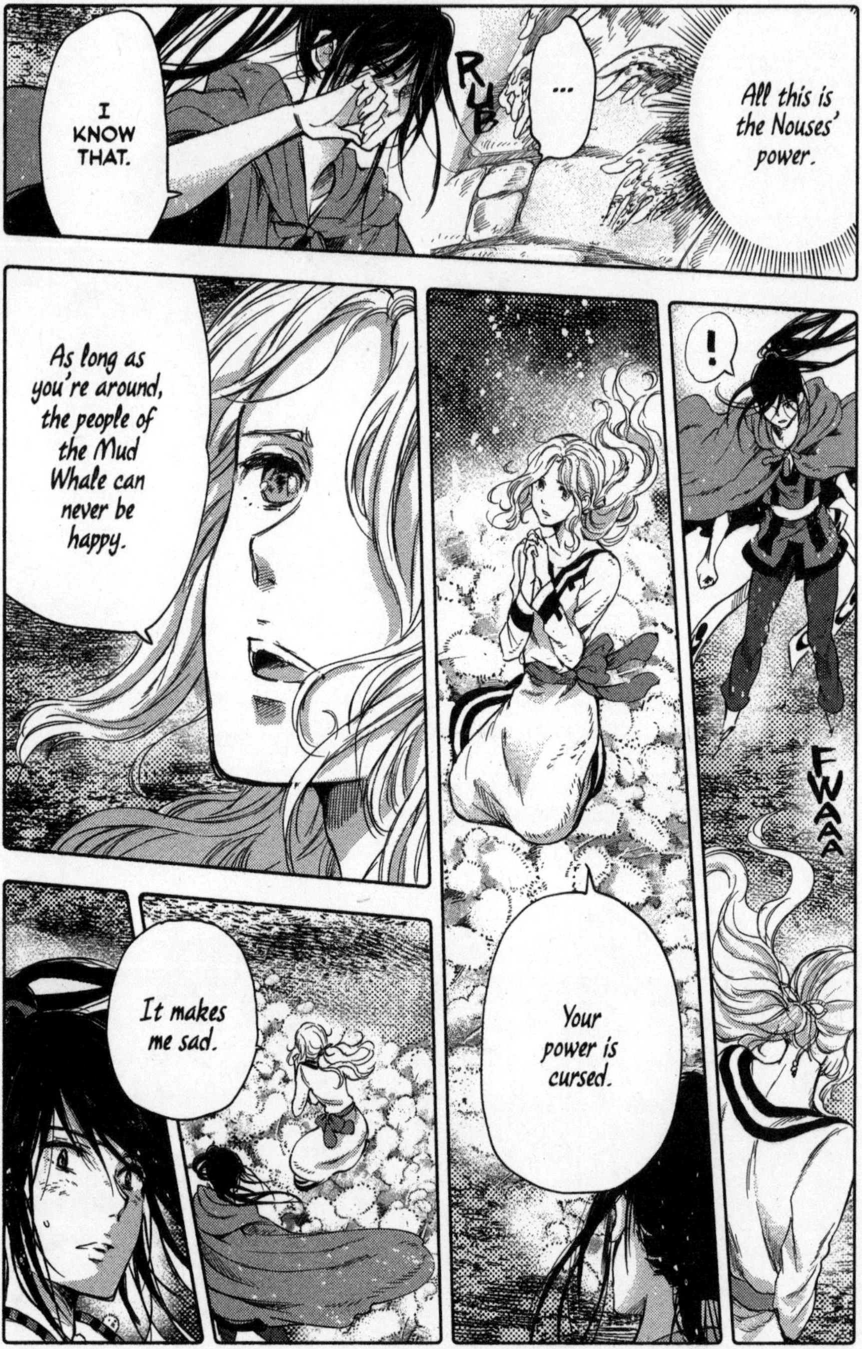
All this is the Nouses' power.
...
RUB
I KNOW THAT.
!
FWAAA
Your power is cursed.
As long as you're around, the people of the Mud Whale can never be happy.
It makes me sad.

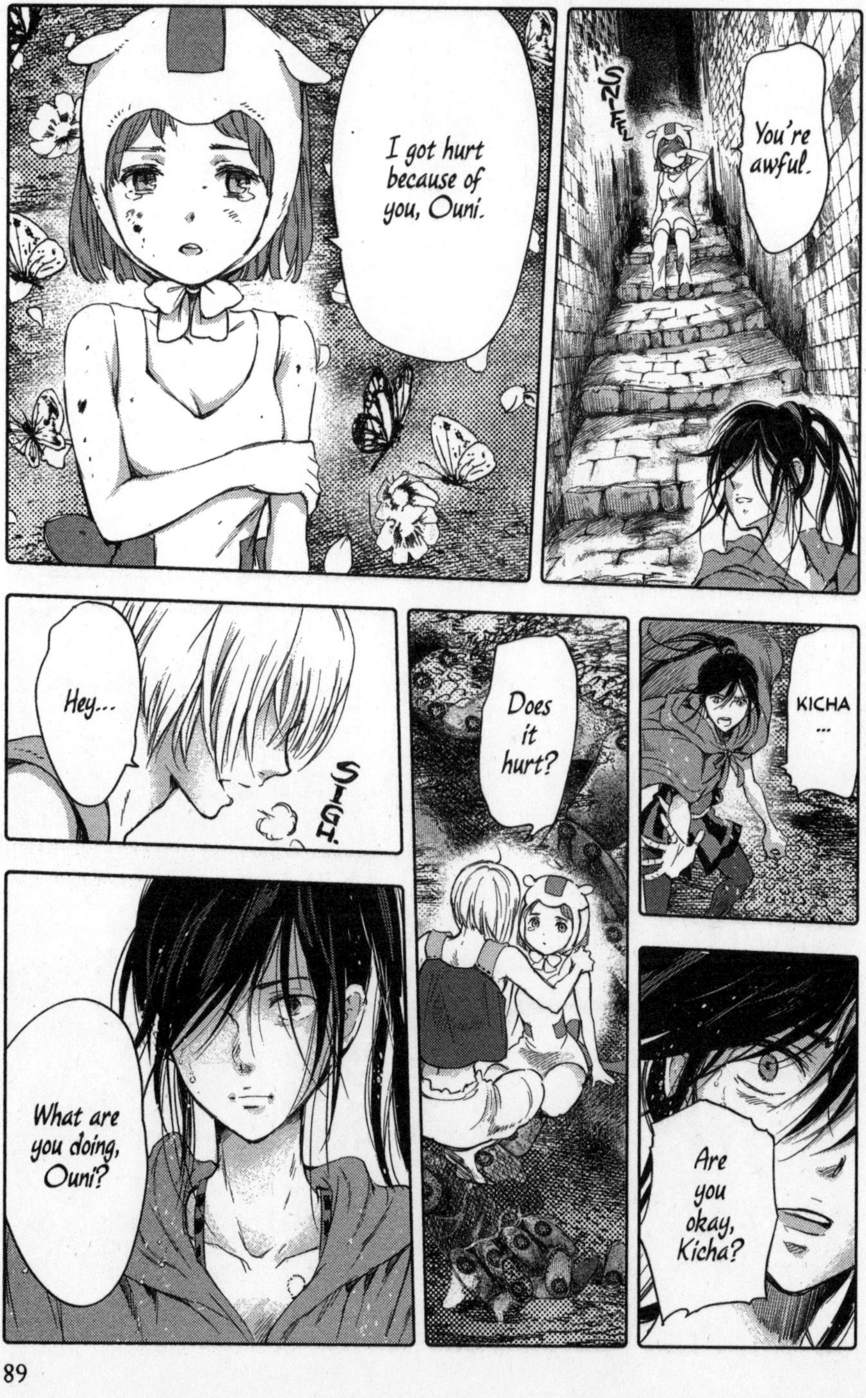
SNIFFLE
You're awful.
I got hurt because of you, Ouni.
KICHA ...
Are you okay, Kicha?
Does it hurt?
Hey...
SIGH.
What are you doing, Ouni?

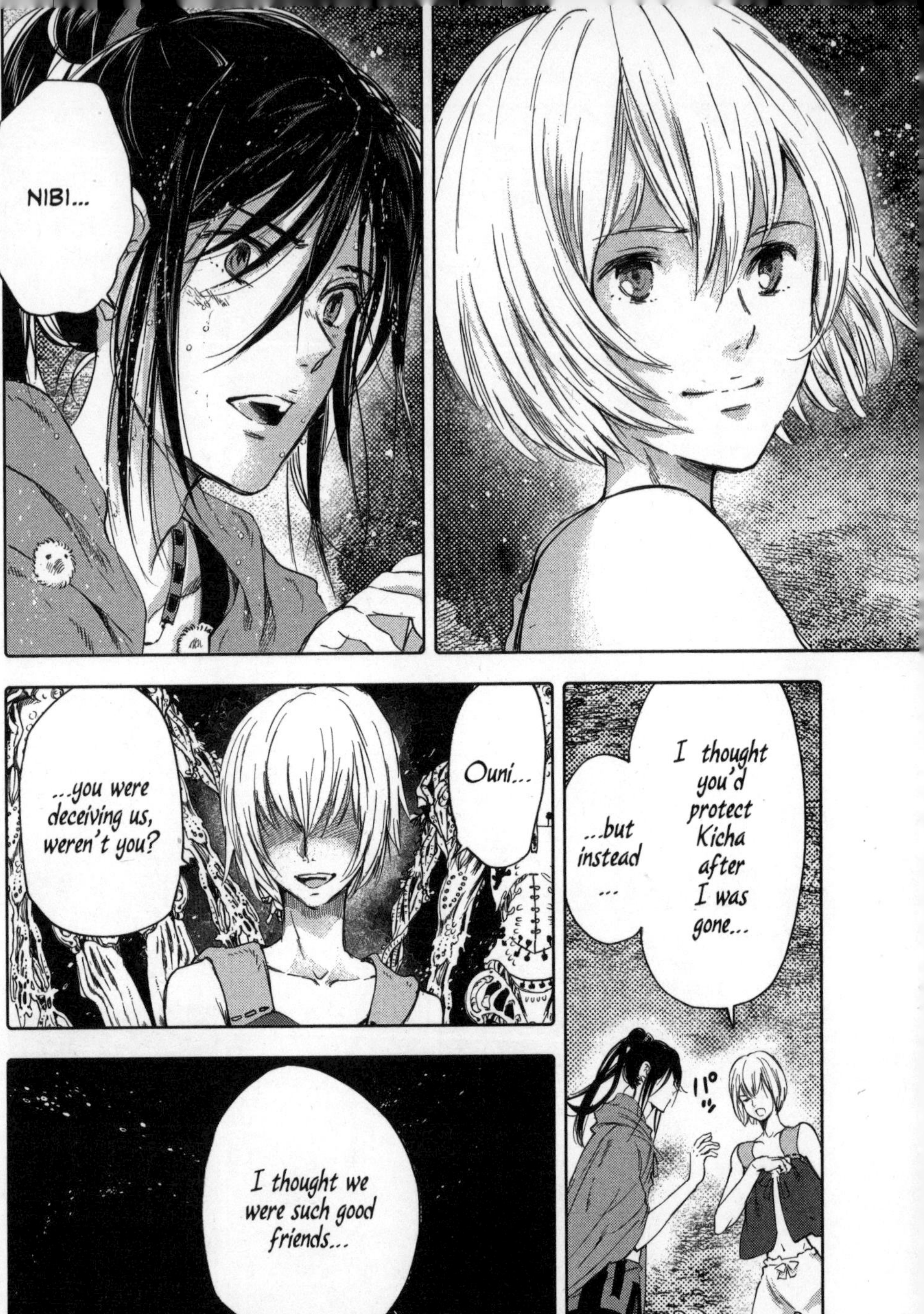
NIBI...
I thought you'd protect Kicha after I was gone...
...but instead...
Ouni...
...you were deceiving us, weren't you?
I thought we were such good friends...

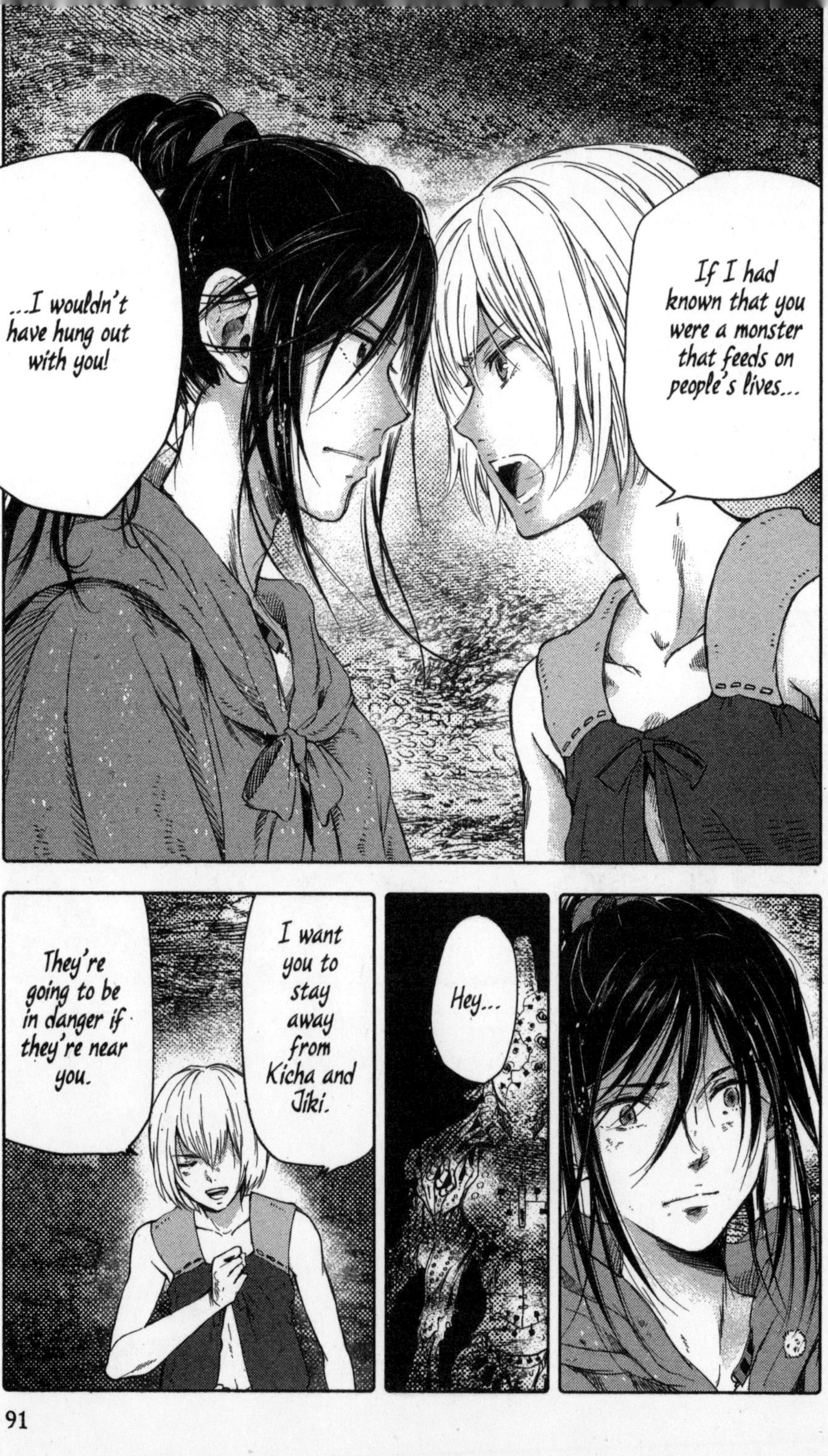
If I had known that you were a monster that feeds on people's lives...
...I wouldn't have hung out with you!
Hey...
I want you to stay away from Kicha and Jiki.
They're going to be in danger if they're near you.

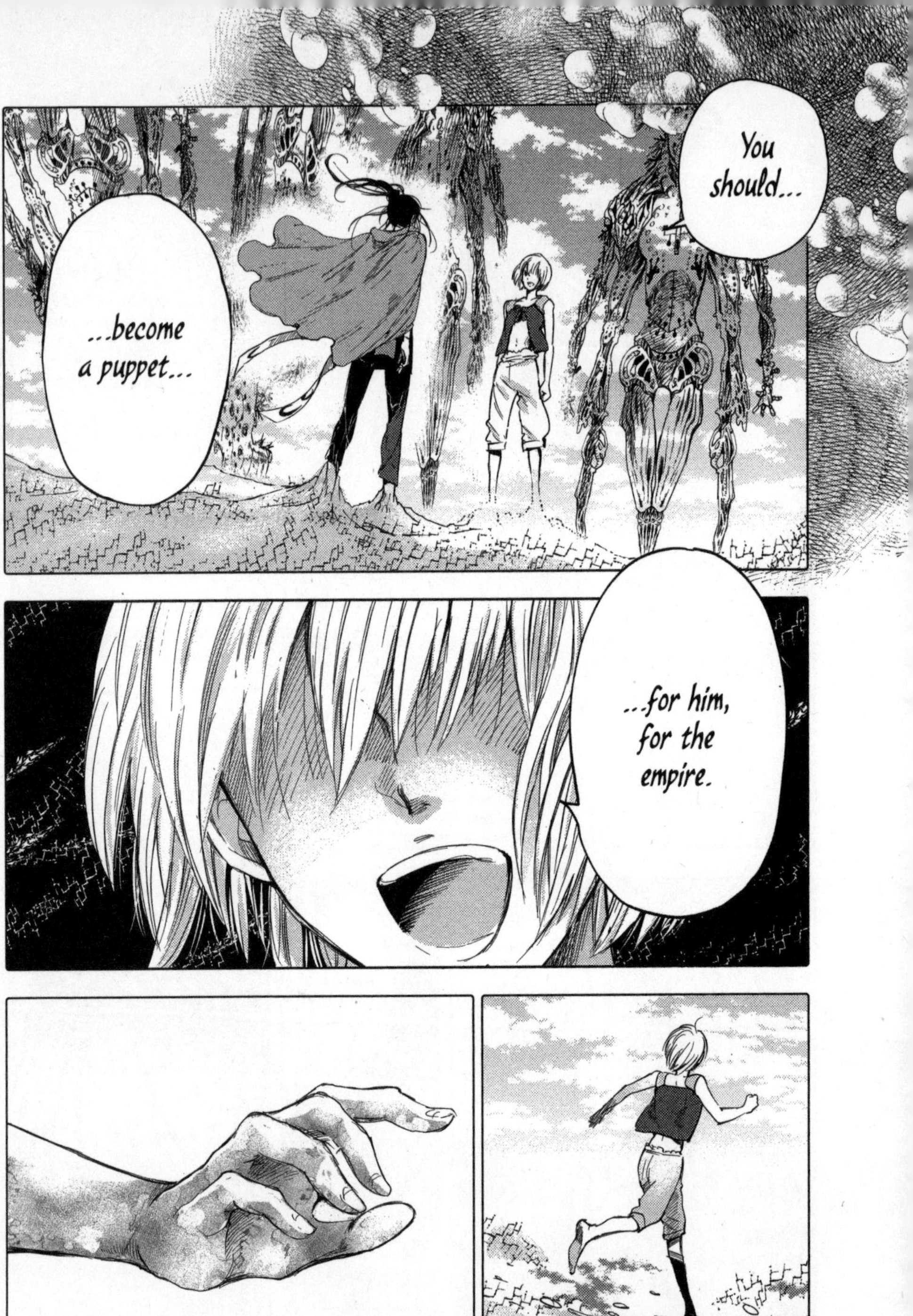
You should...
...become a puppet...
...for him, for the empire.

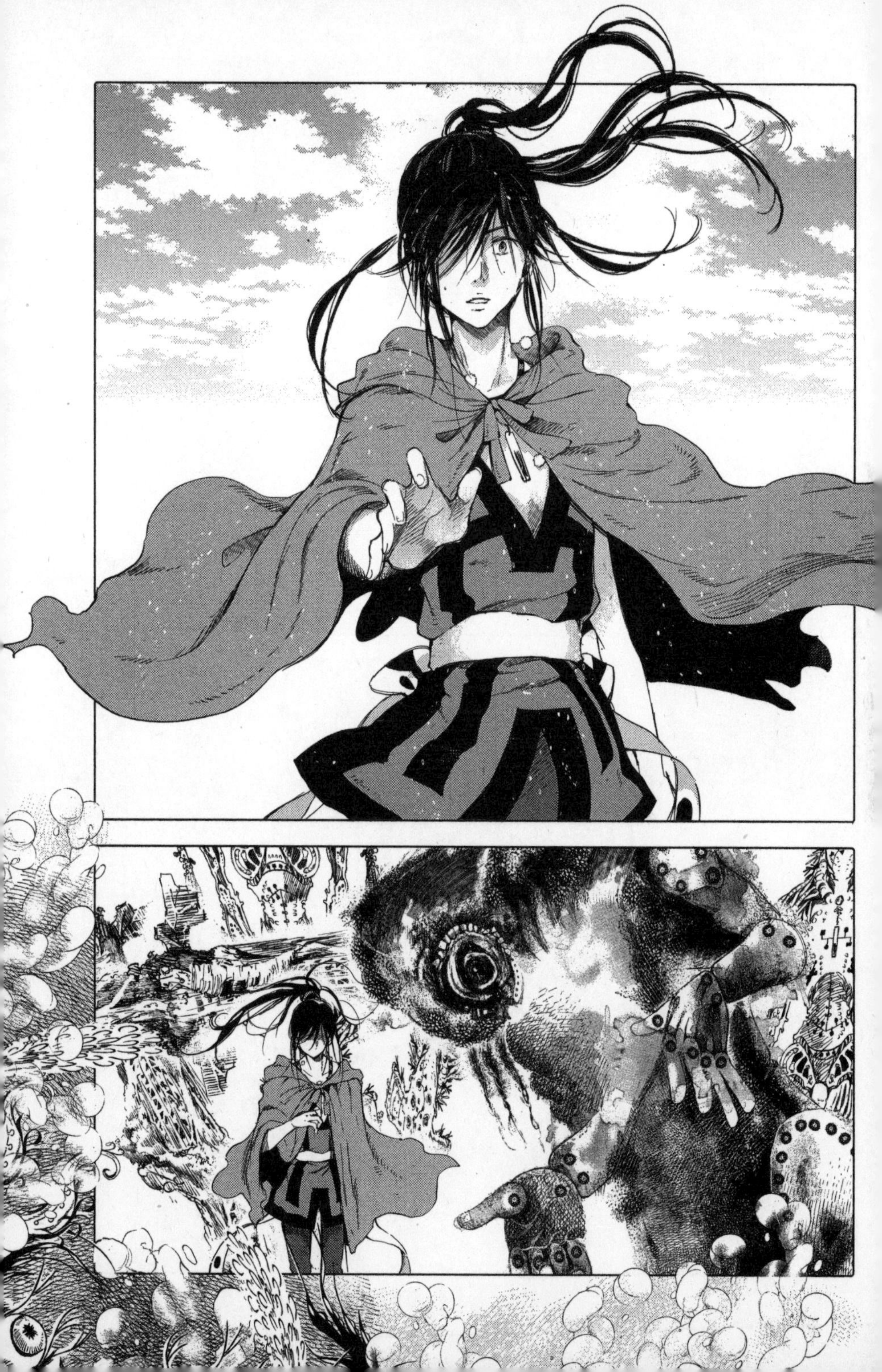

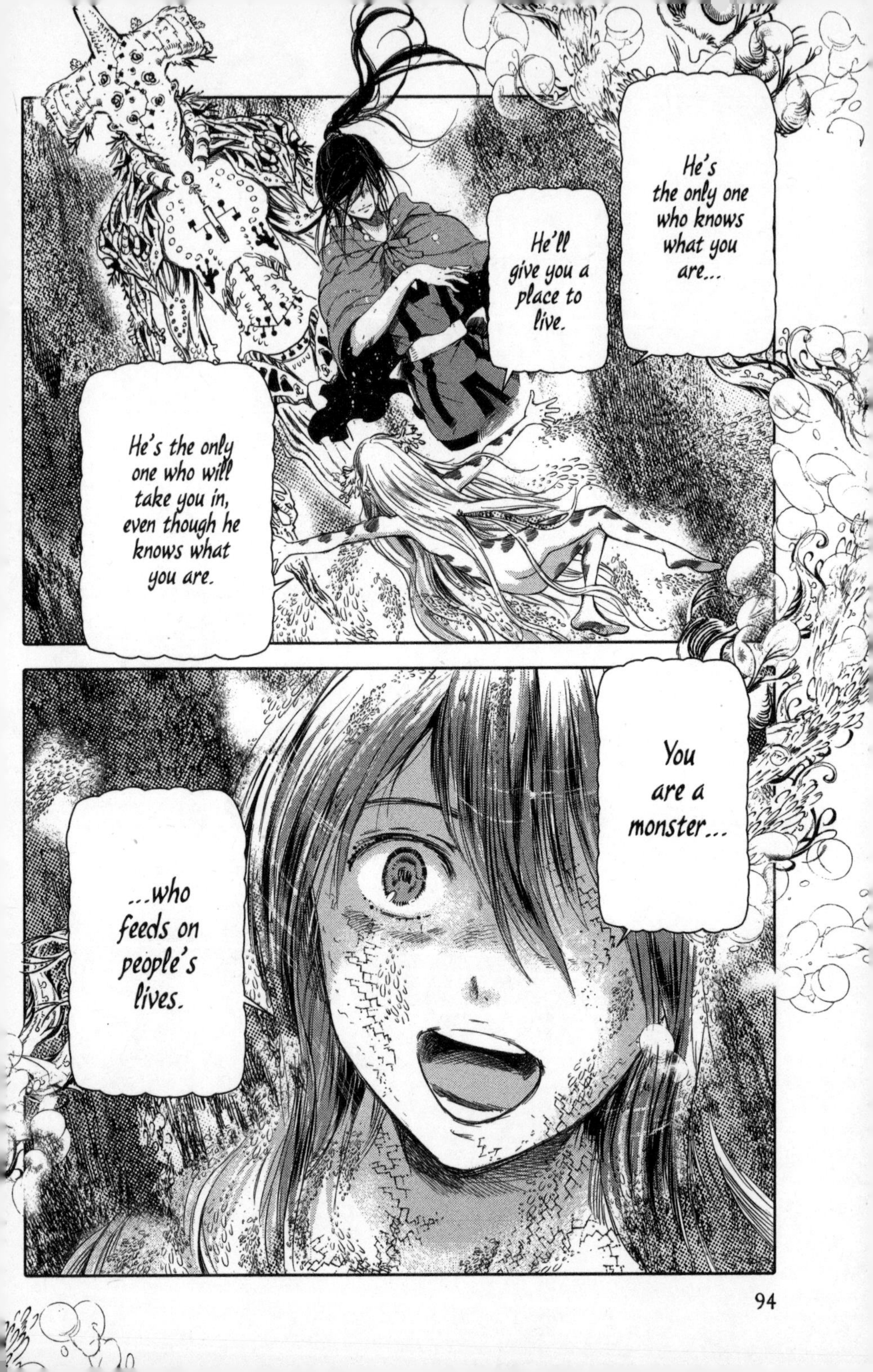
He's the only one who knows what you are...
He'll give you a place to live.
He's the only one who will take you in, even though he knows what you are.
You are a monster...
...who feeds on people's lives.

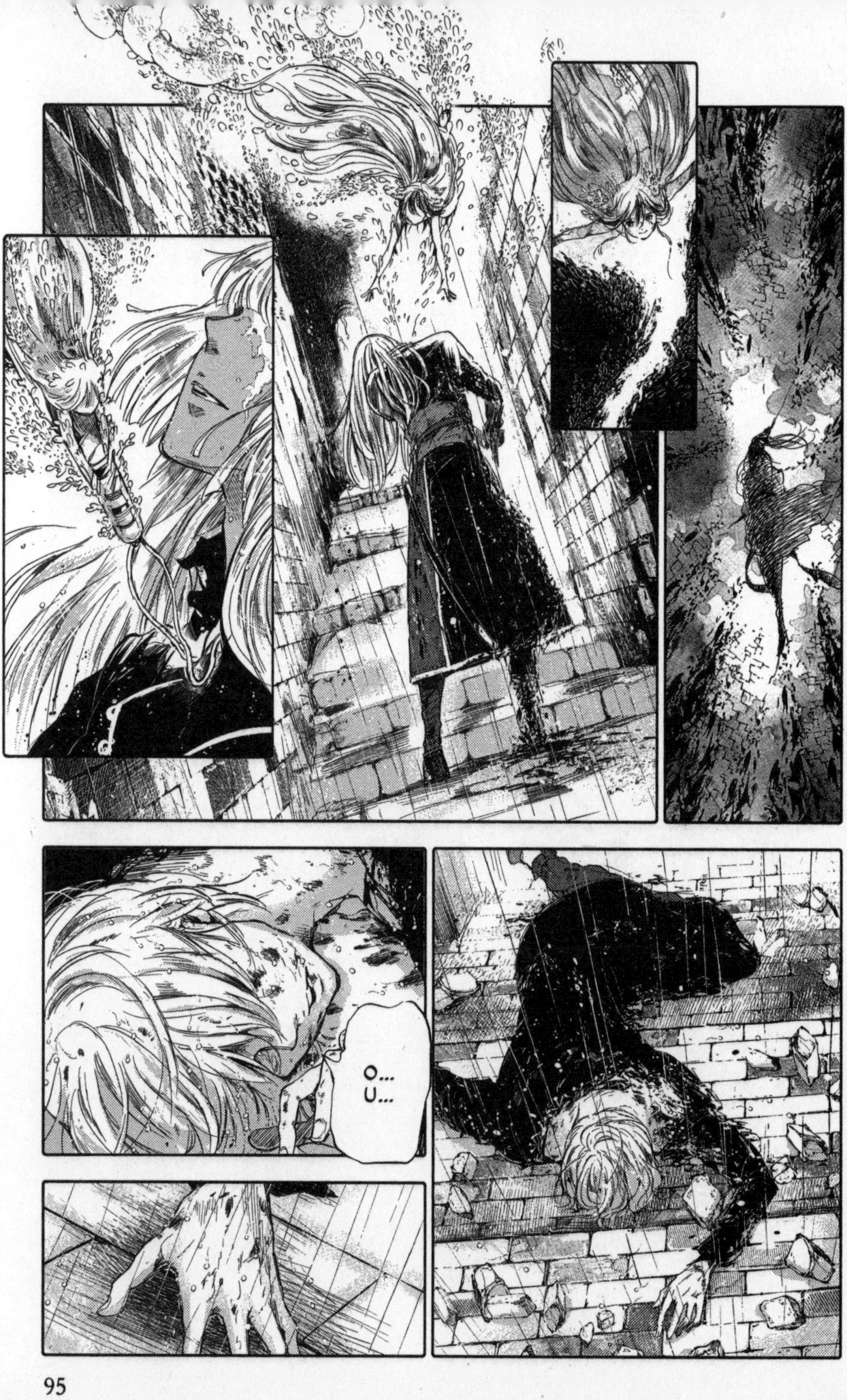
O... U...

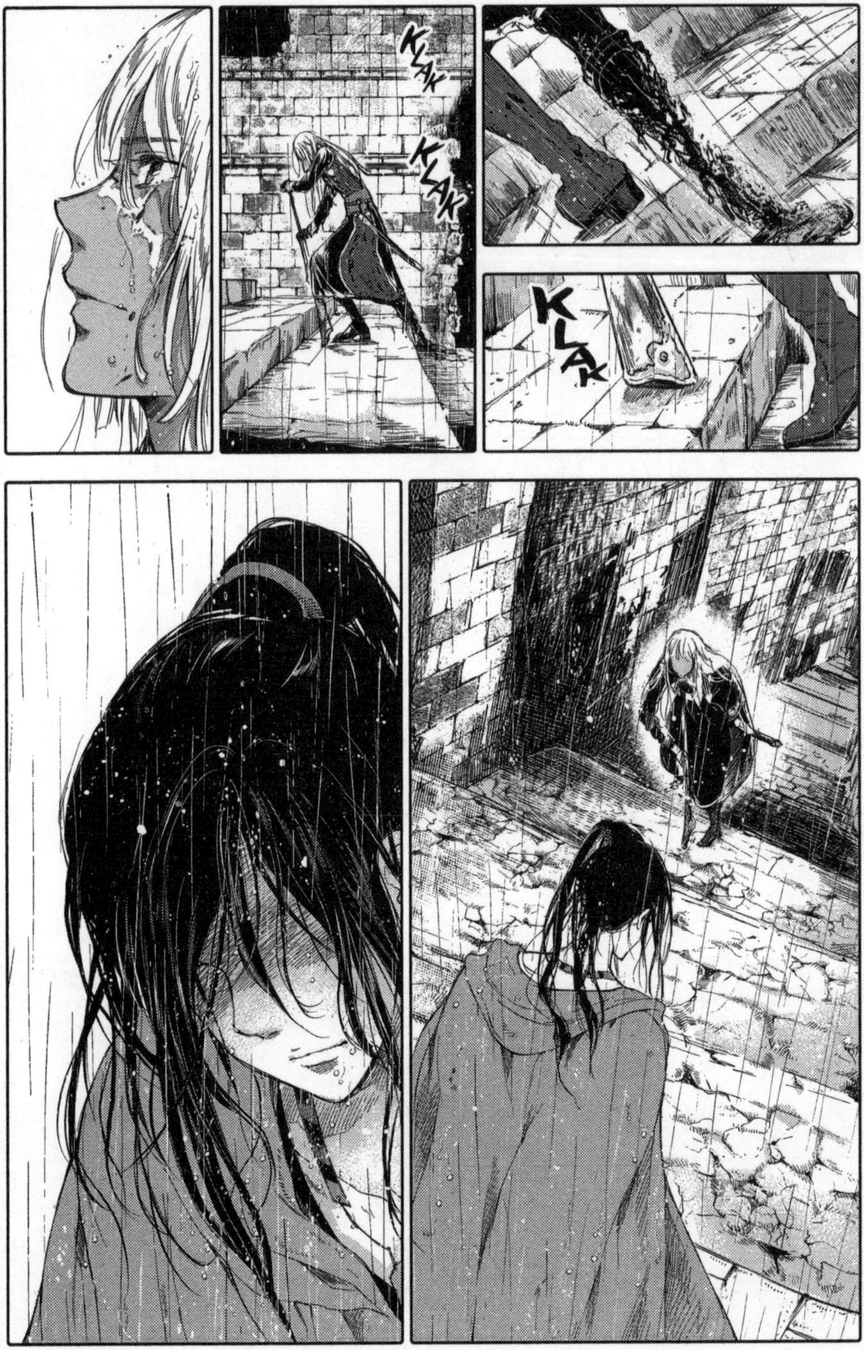
KLAK
KLAK
KLAK

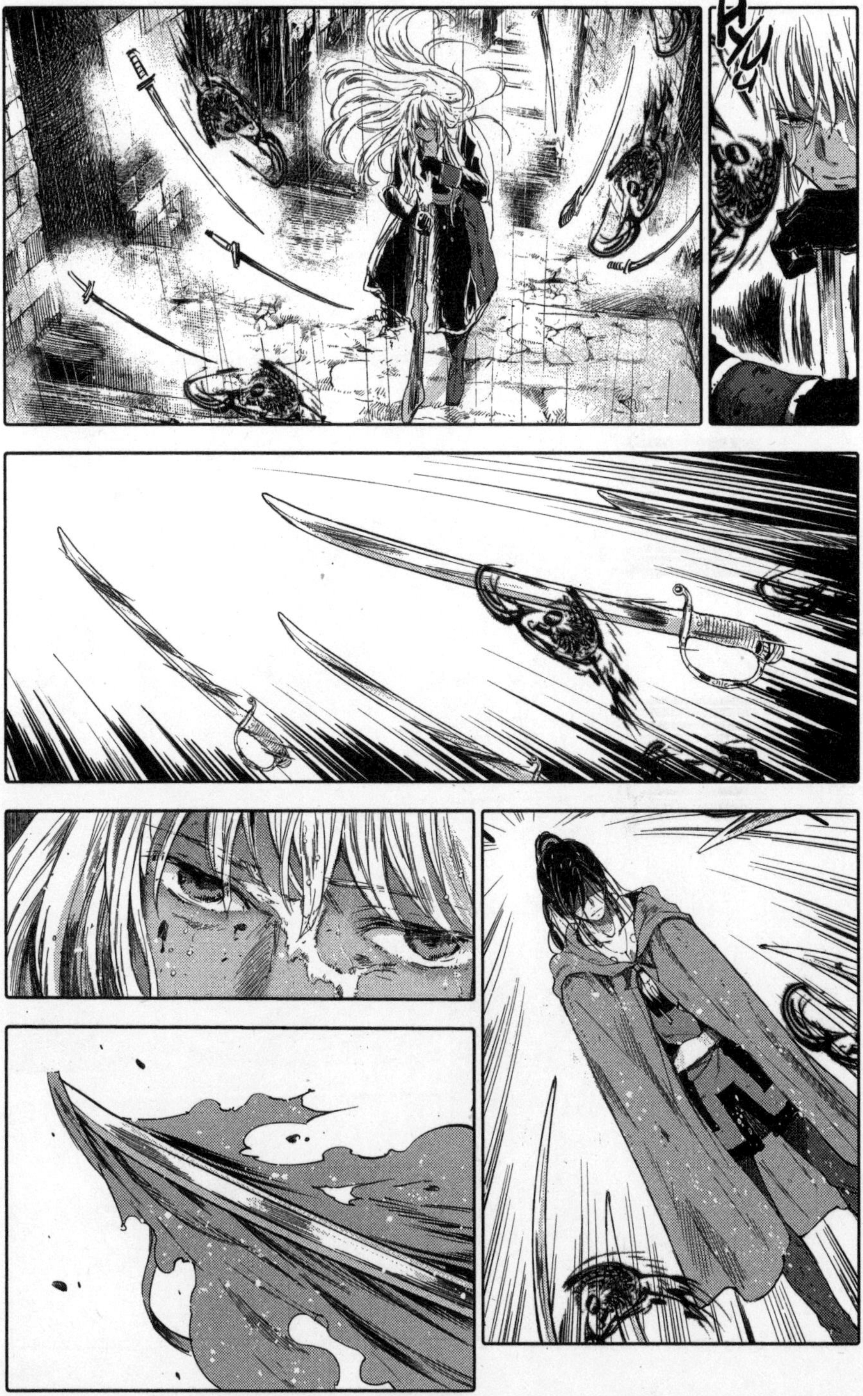
HYUU

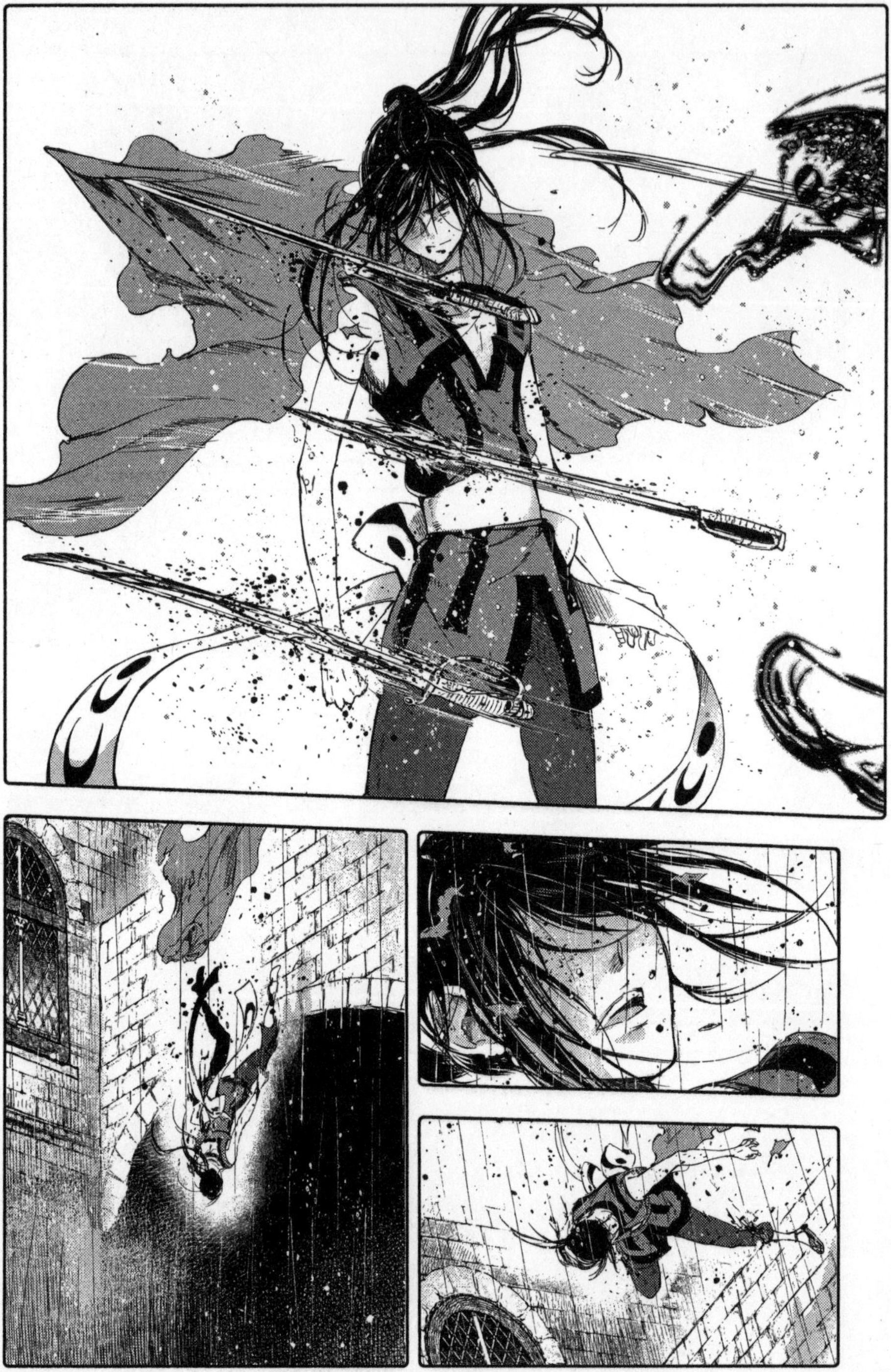

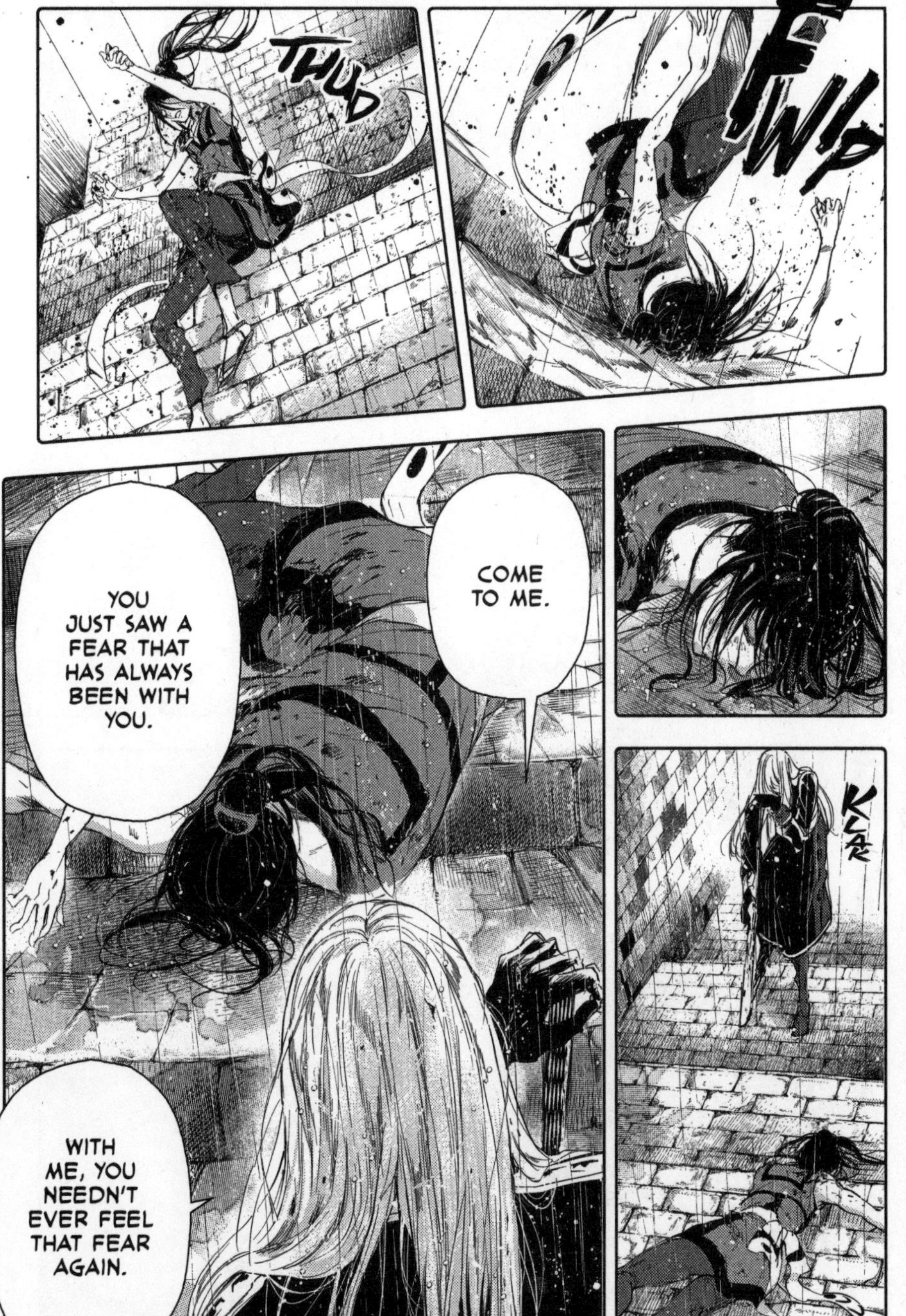
FWIP
THUD
KLAK
COME TO ME.
YOU JUST SAW A FEAR THAT HAS ALWAYS BEEN WITH YOU.
WITH ME, YOU NEEDN'T EVER FEEL THAT FEAR AGAIN.

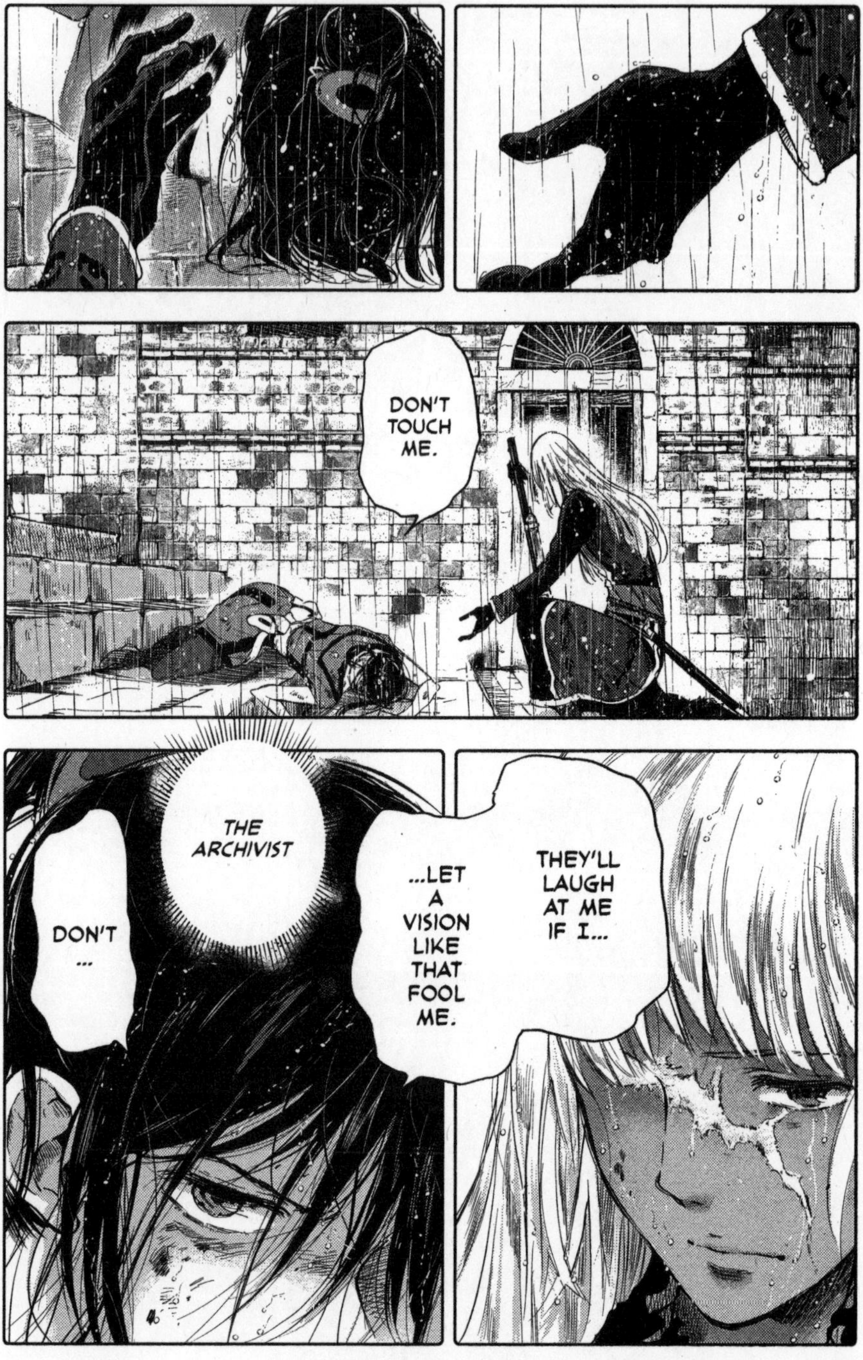
DON'T TOUCH ME.
THEY'LL LAUGH AT ME IF I...
...LET A VISION LIKE THAT FOOL ME.
THE ARCHIVIST
DON'T ...

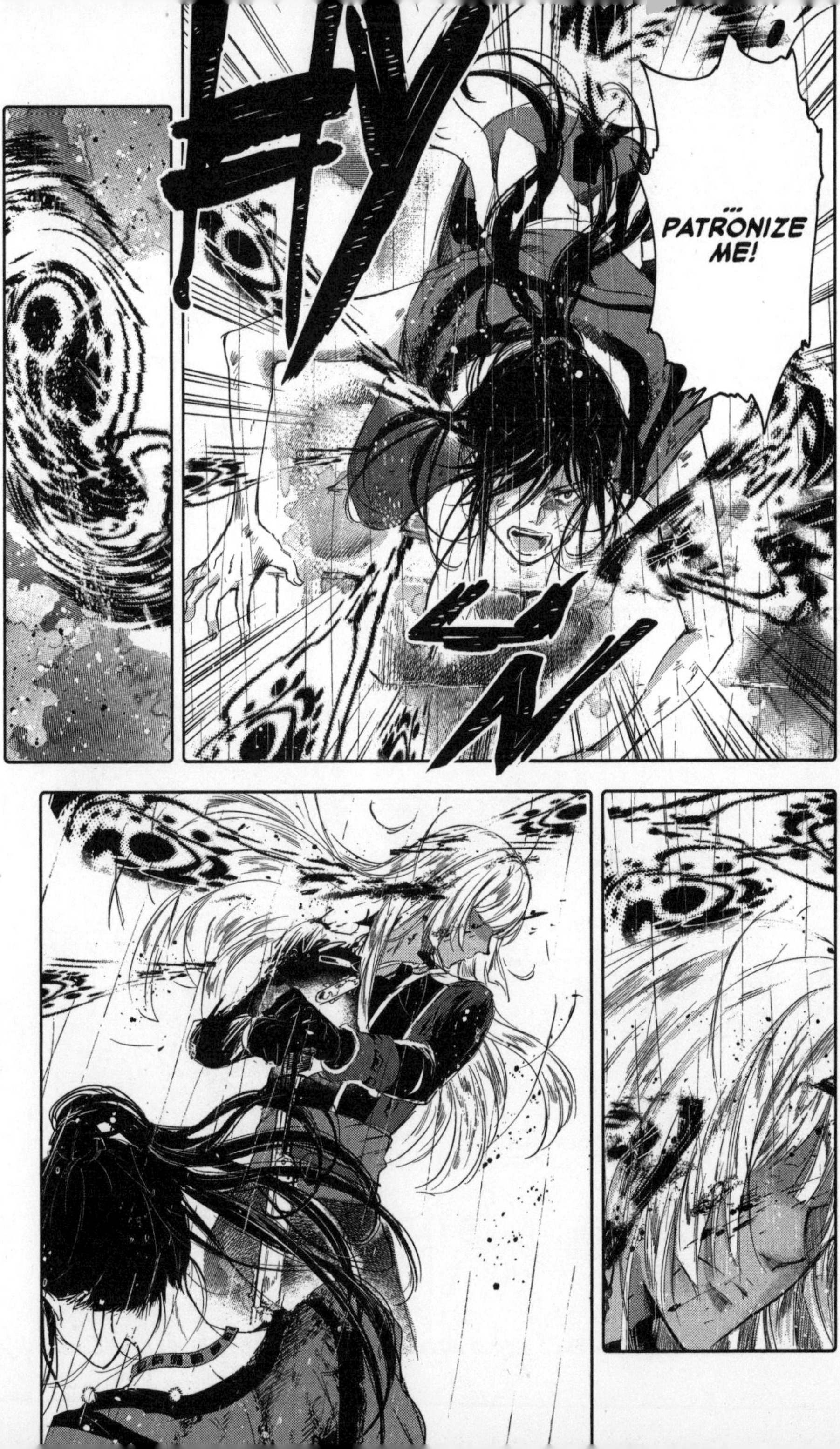
...PATRONIZE ME!

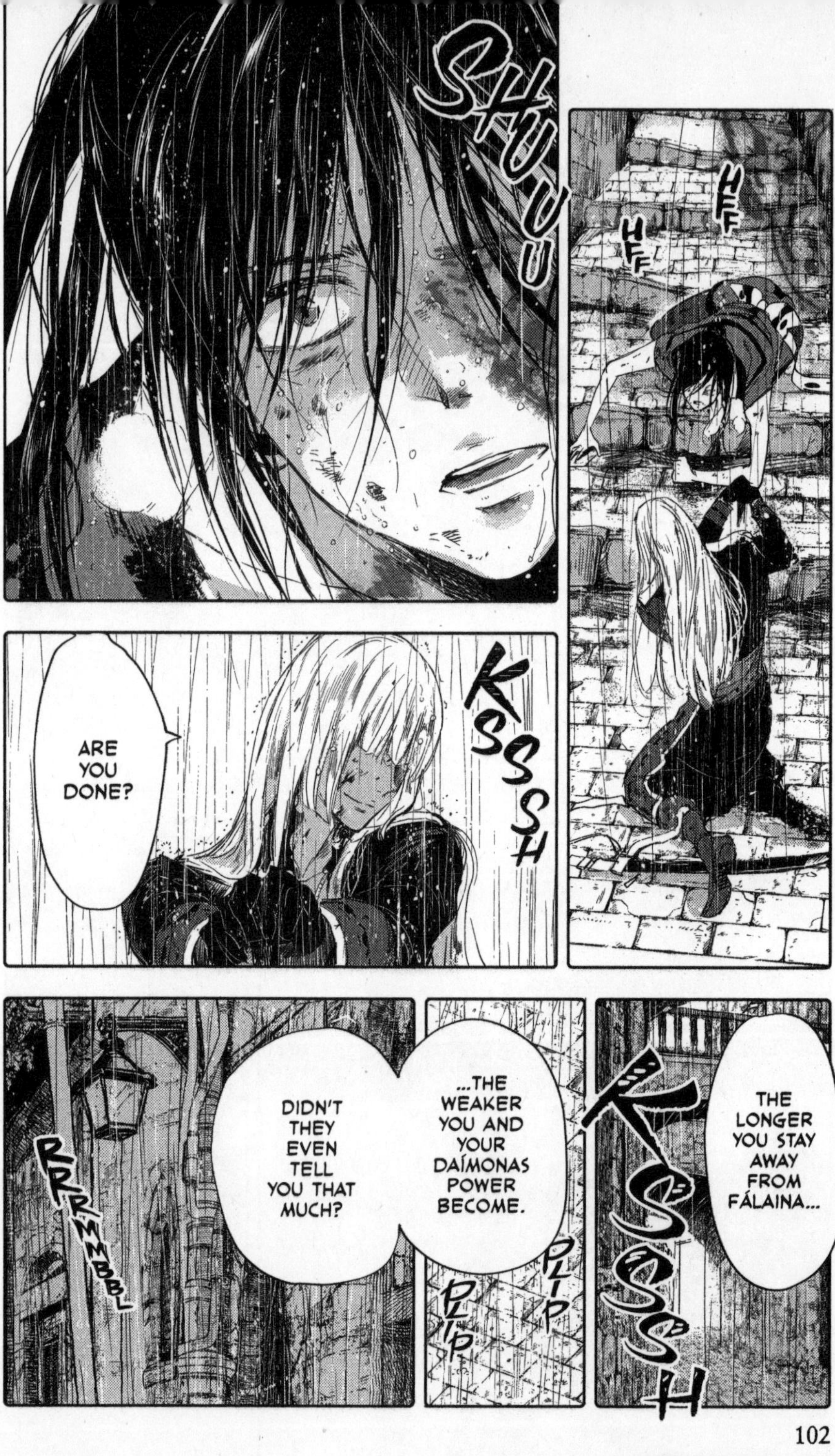
HFF
HFF
SHUUU
KSSSH
ARE YOU DONE?
KSSSH
THE LONGER YOU STAY AWAY FROM FÁLAINA...
...THE WEAKER YOU AND YOUR DAÍMONAS POWER BECOME.
PLIP
PLIP
DIDN'T THEY EVEN TELL YOU THAT MUCH?
RRRMMBBL

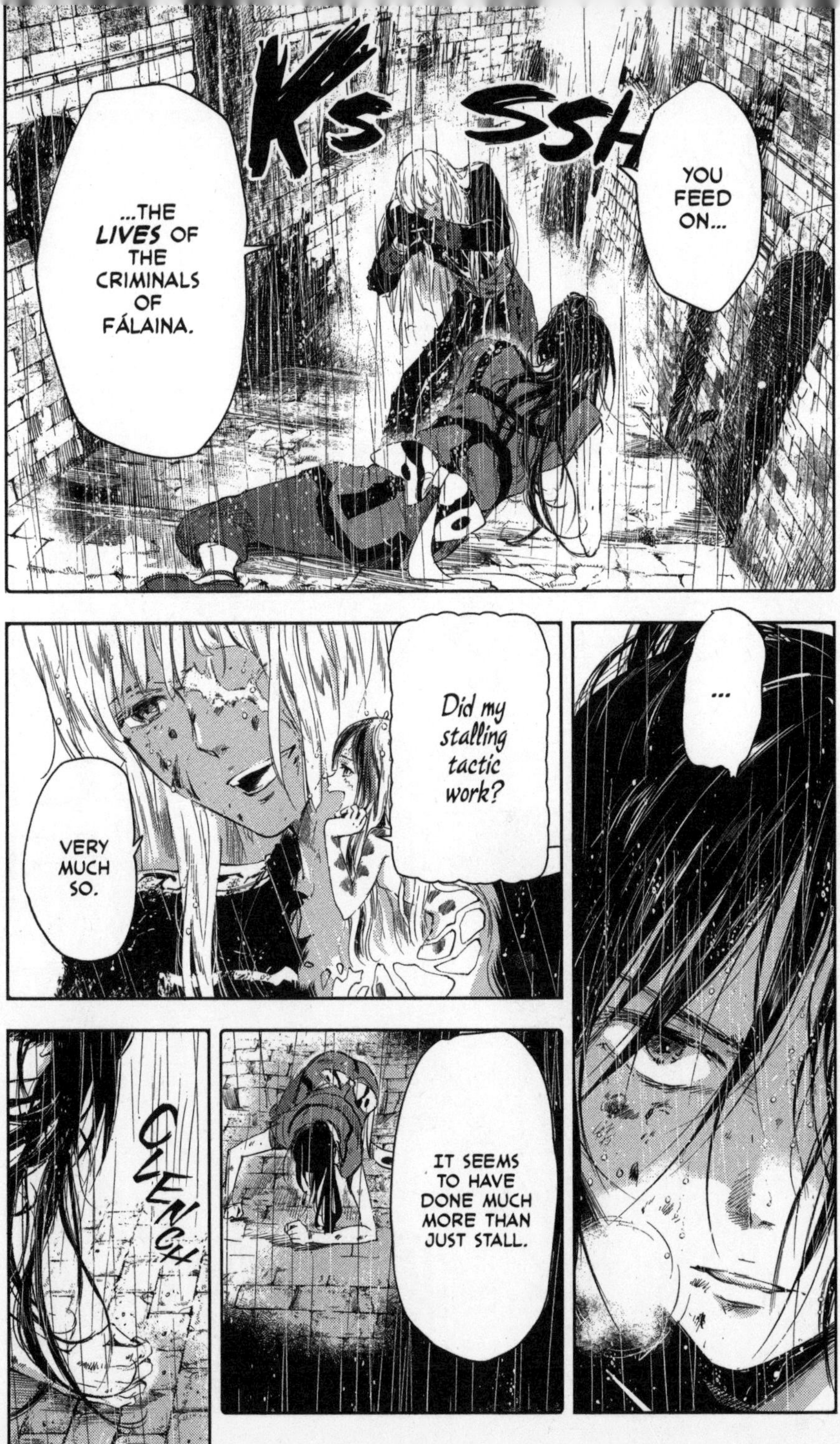
KS SSH
YOU FEED ON...
...THE *LIVES* OF THE CRIMINALS OF FÁLAINA.
...
Did my stalling tactic work?
VERY MUCH SO.
IT SEEMS TO HAVE DONE MUCH MORE THAN JUST STALL.
CLENCH

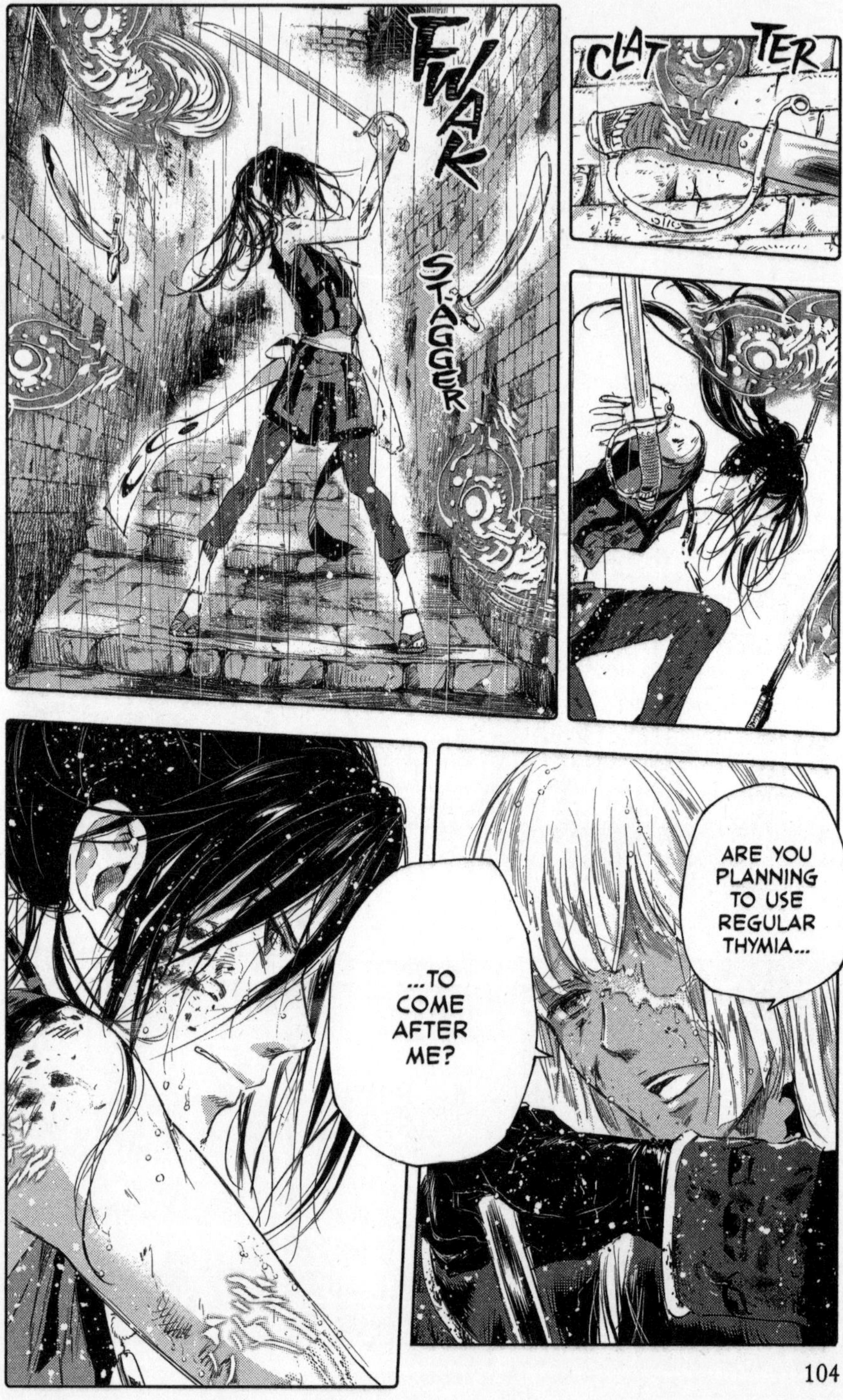
CLATTER
FWAK
STAGGER
ARE YOU PLANNING TO USE REGULAR THYMIA...
...TO COME AFTER ME?

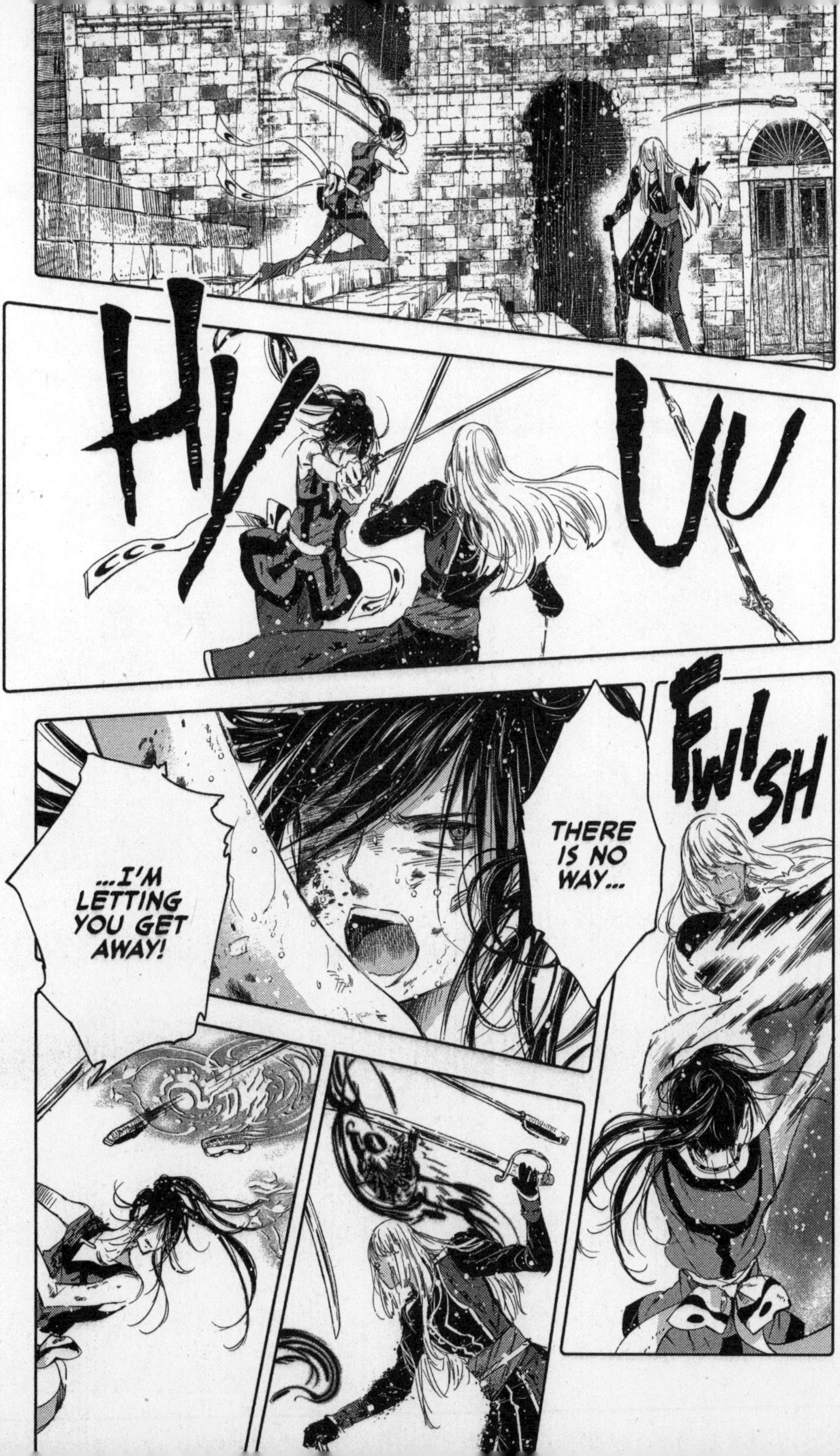
HYUU
FWISH
THERE IS NO WAY...
...I'M LETTING YOU GET AWAY!

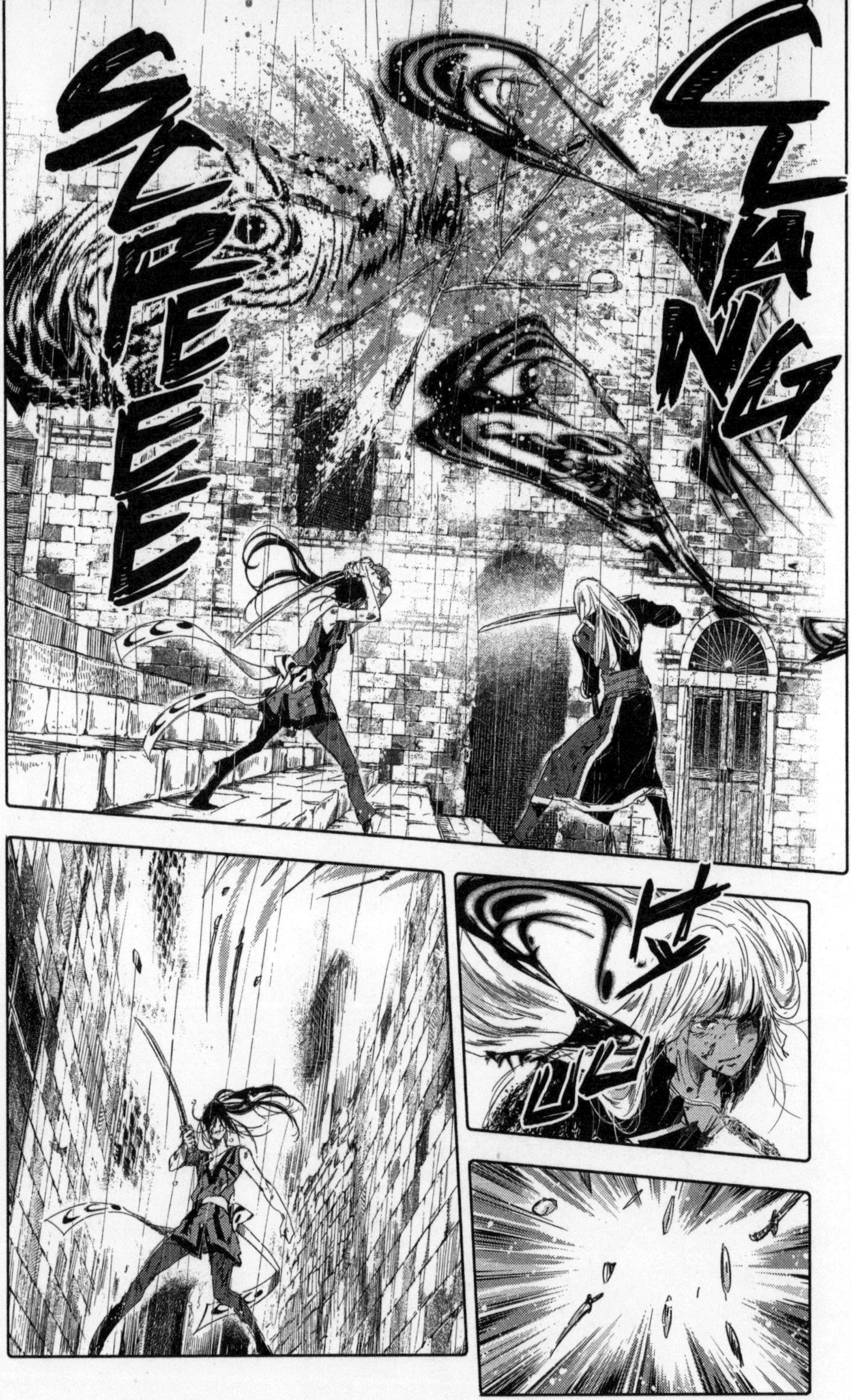
CLANG
SCREEE

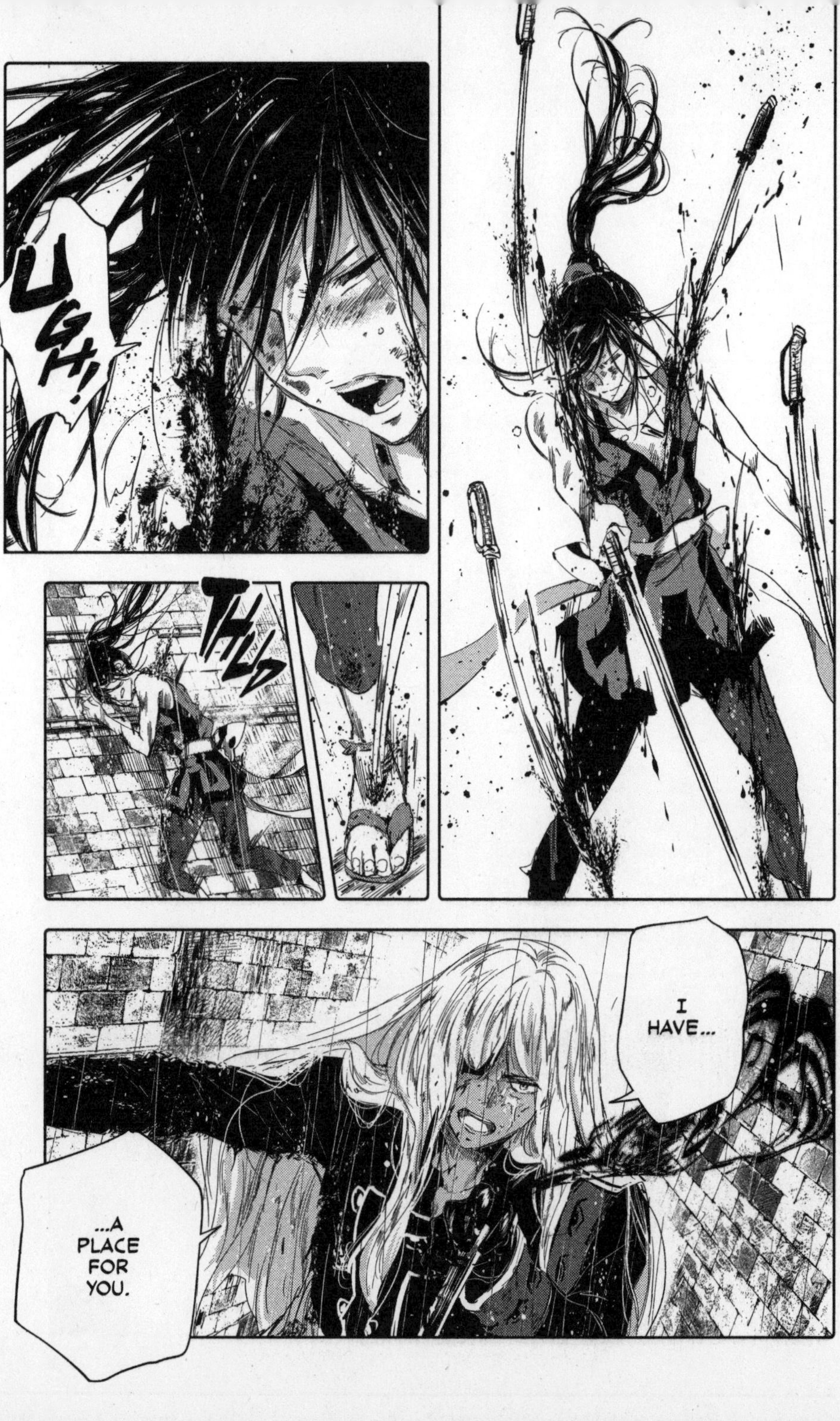
UGH!
THUD
I HAVE...
...A PLACE FOR YOU.

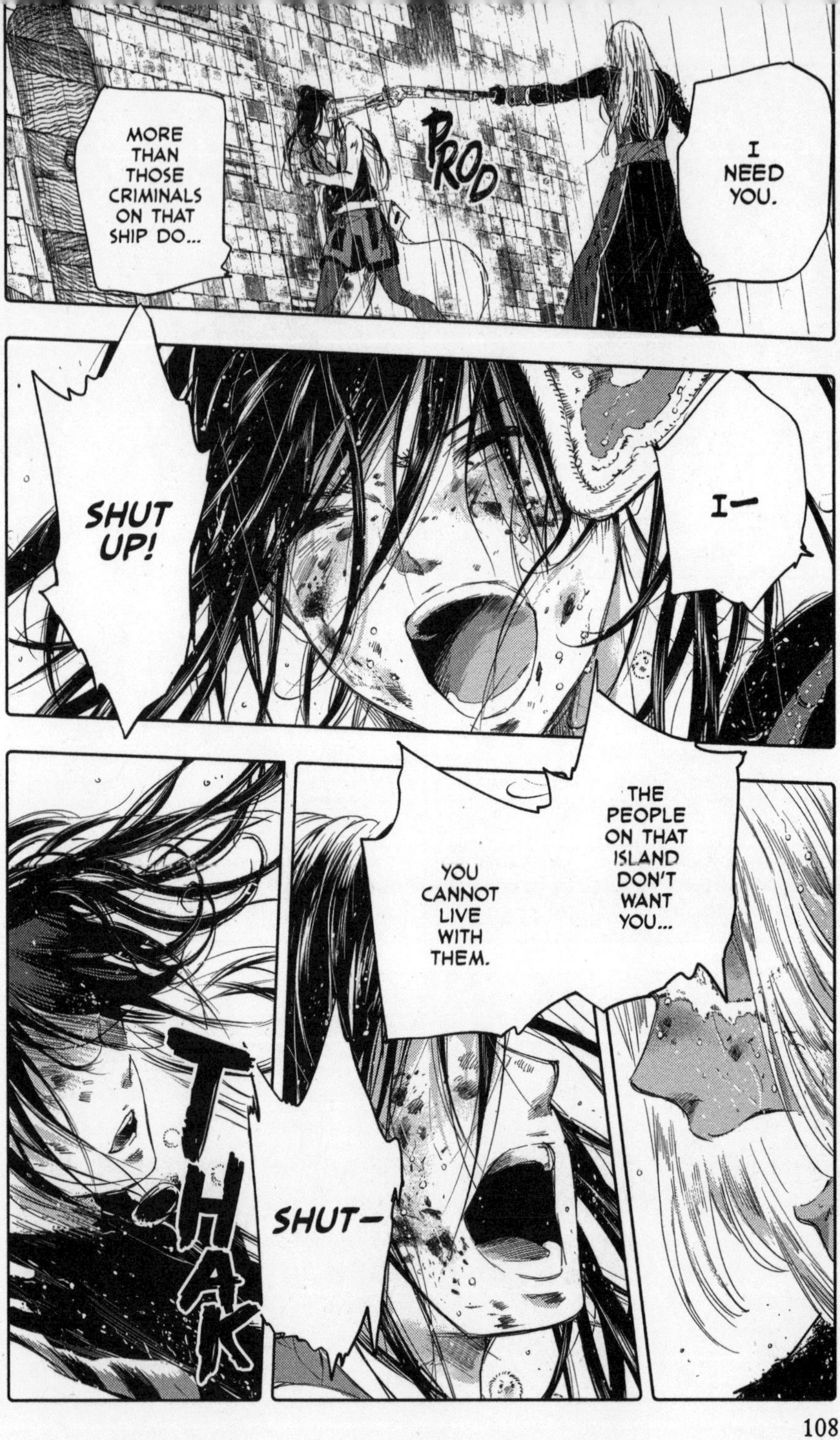
I NEED YOU.
MORE THAN THOSE CRIMINALS ON THAT SHIP DO...
PROD
I—
SHUT UP!
THE PEOPLE ON THAT ISLAND DON'T WANT YOU...
YOU CANNOT LIVE WITH THEM.
SHUT—
THAK

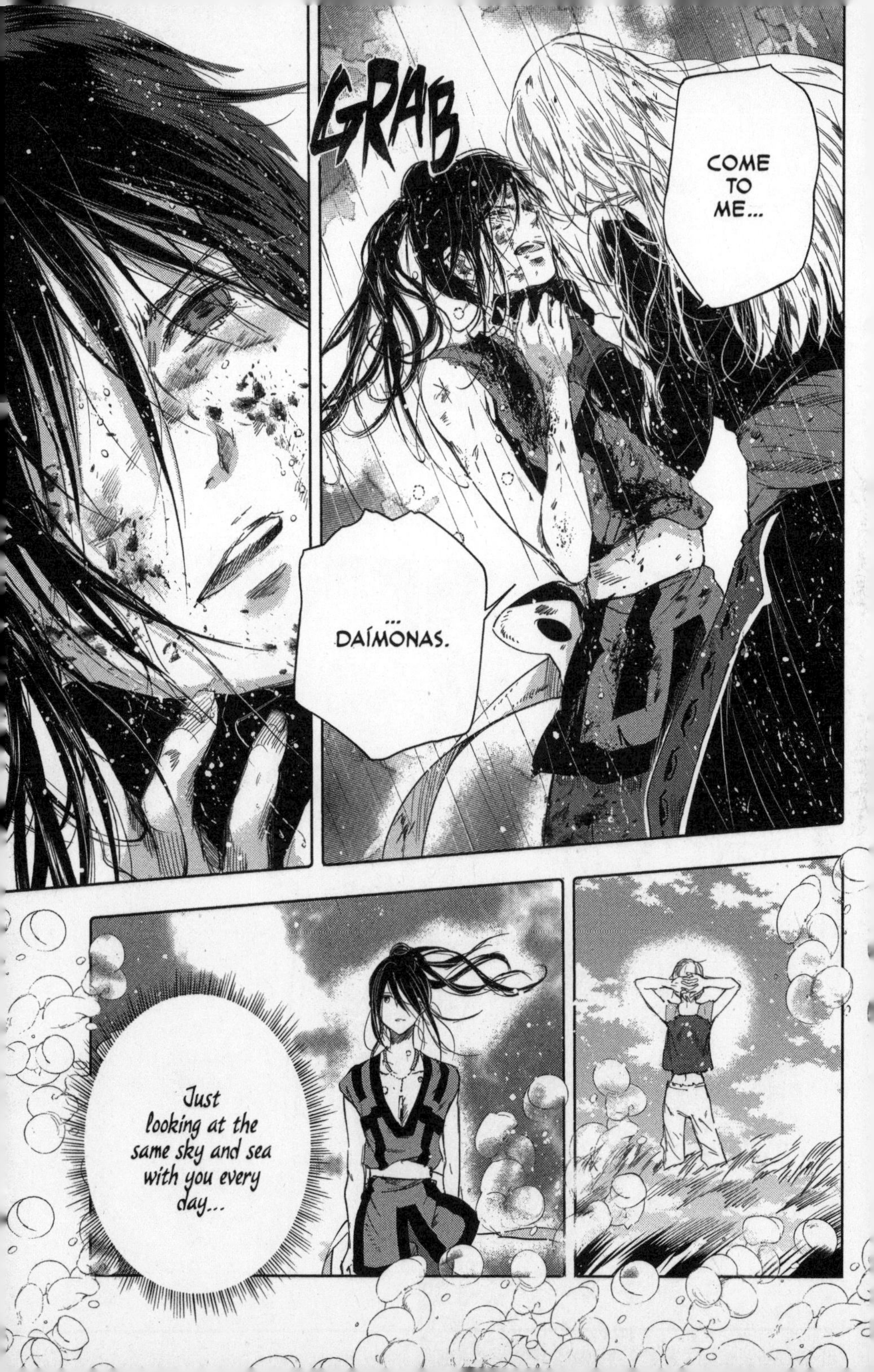
COME TO ME...
GRAB
...DAÍMONAS.
Just looking at the same sky and sea with you every day...

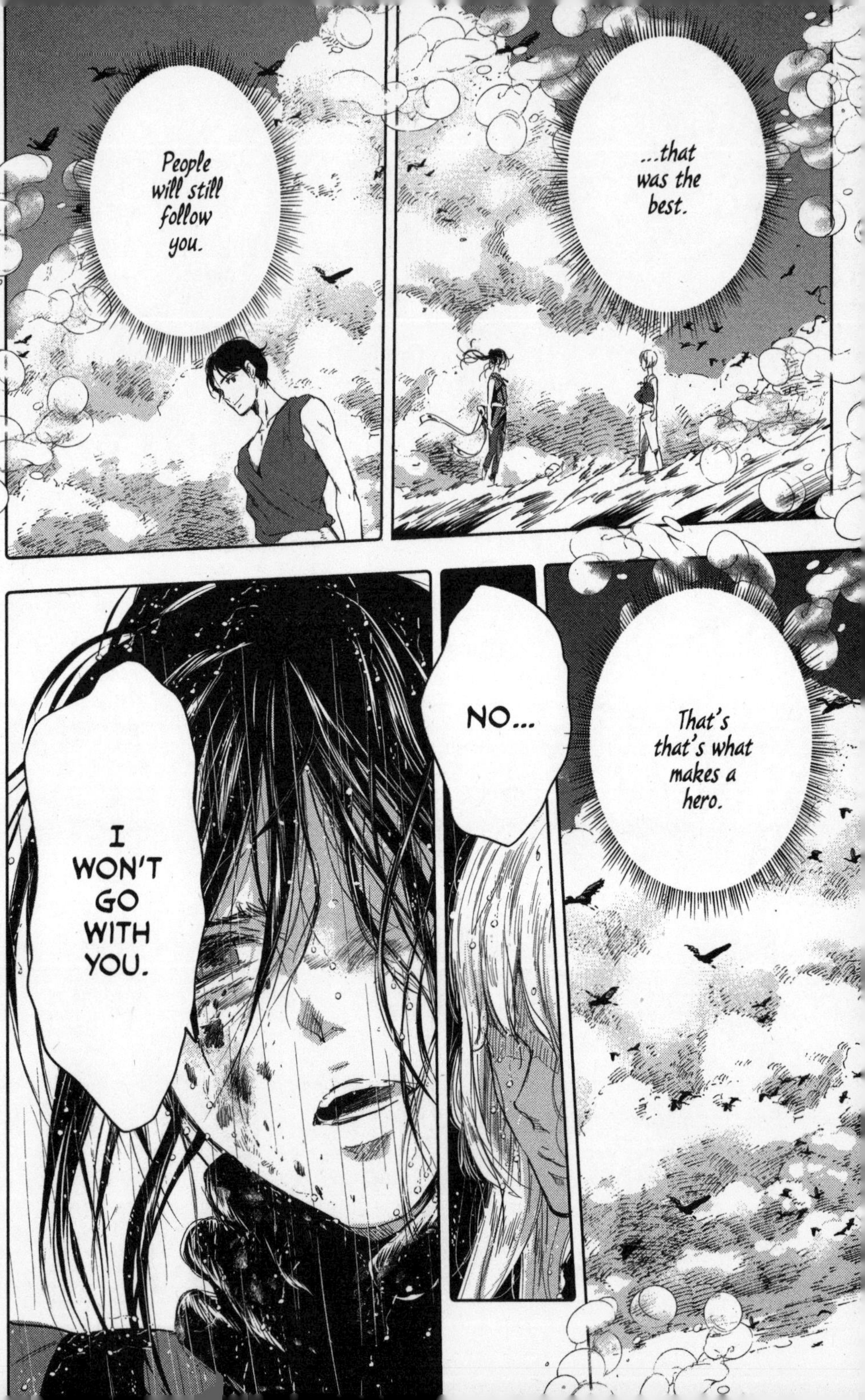
...that was the best.
People will still follow you.
That's that's what makes a hero.
NO...
I WON'T GO WITH YOU.

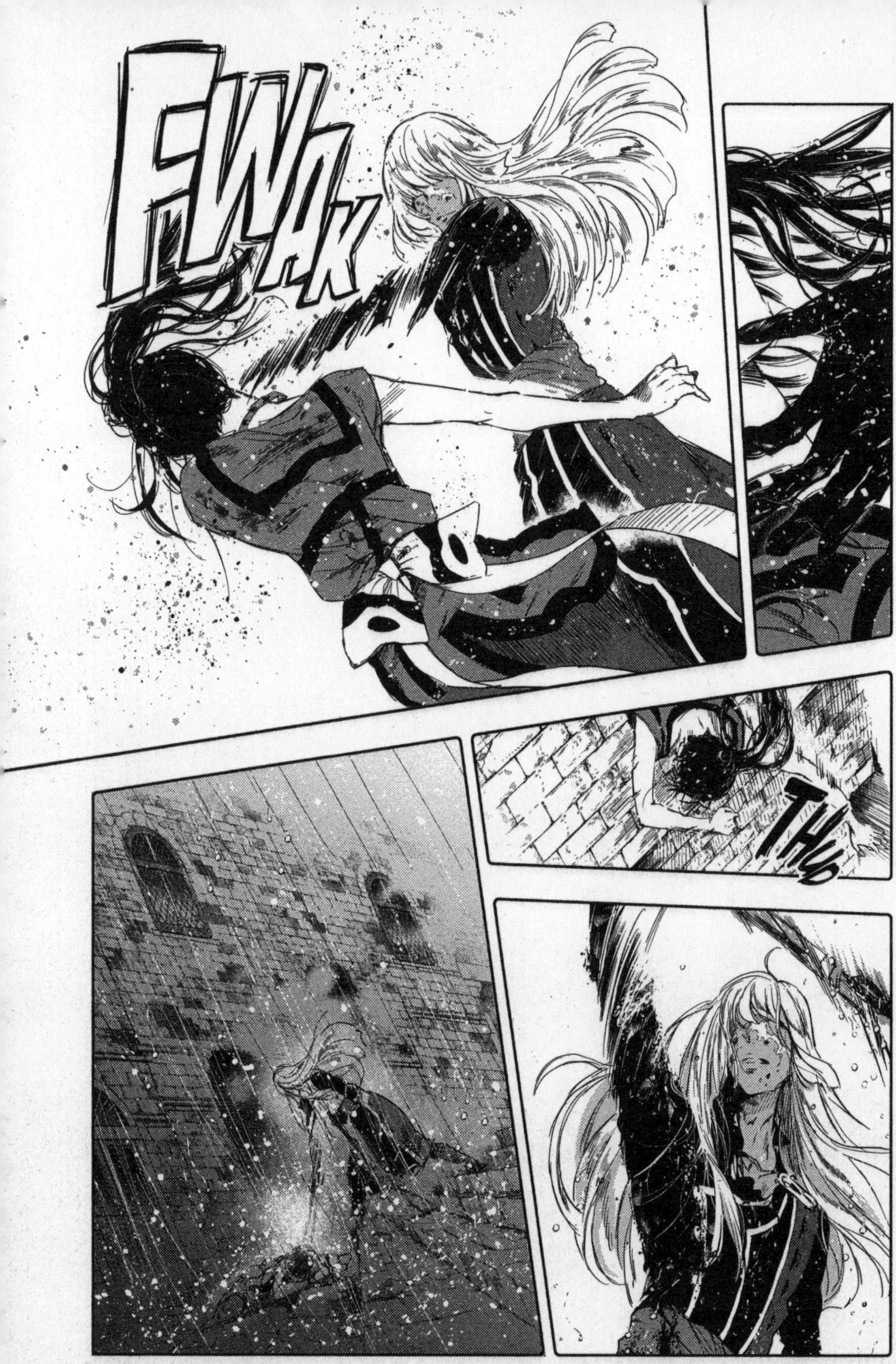
FWAK
THUD

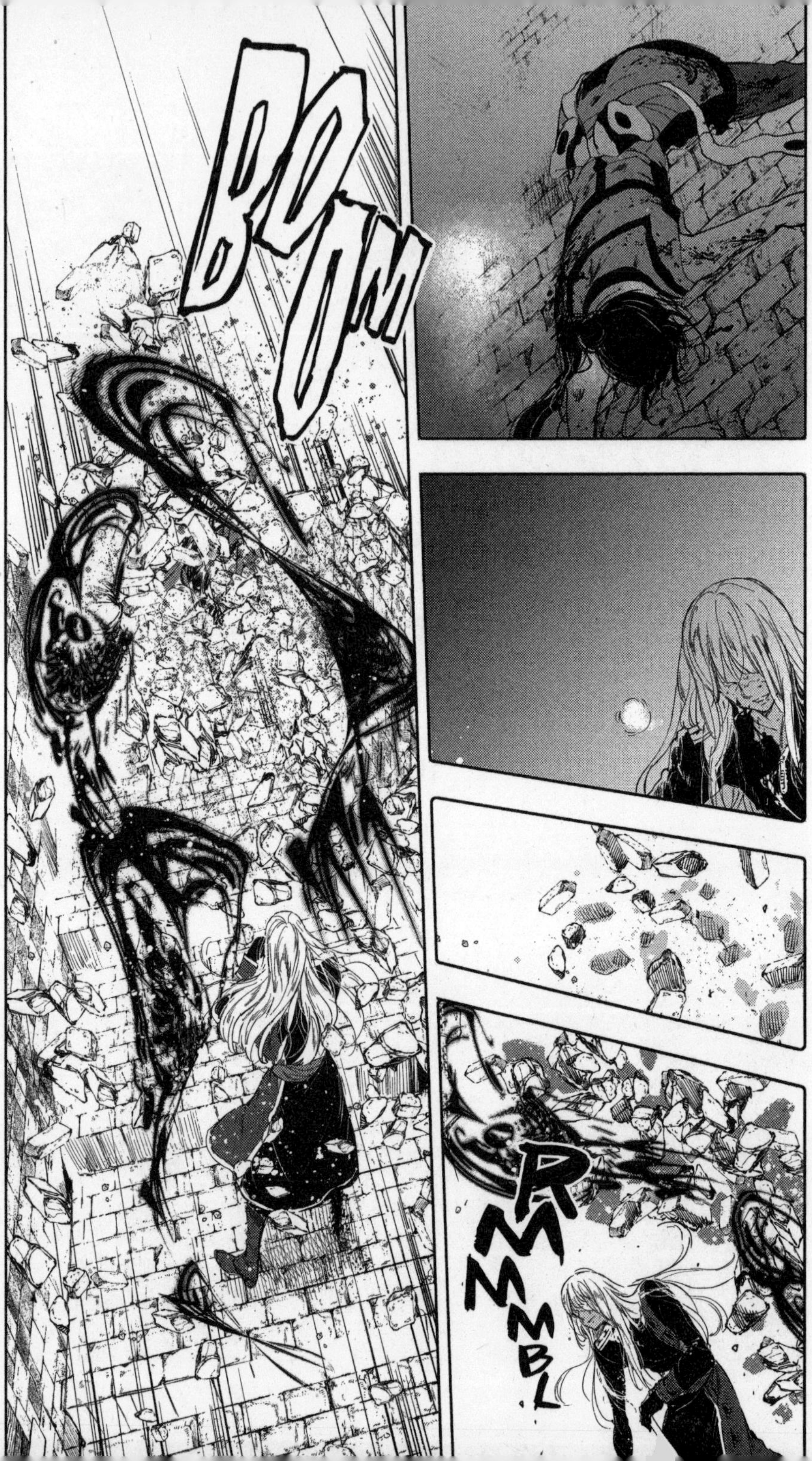
RMMMBL
BOOM

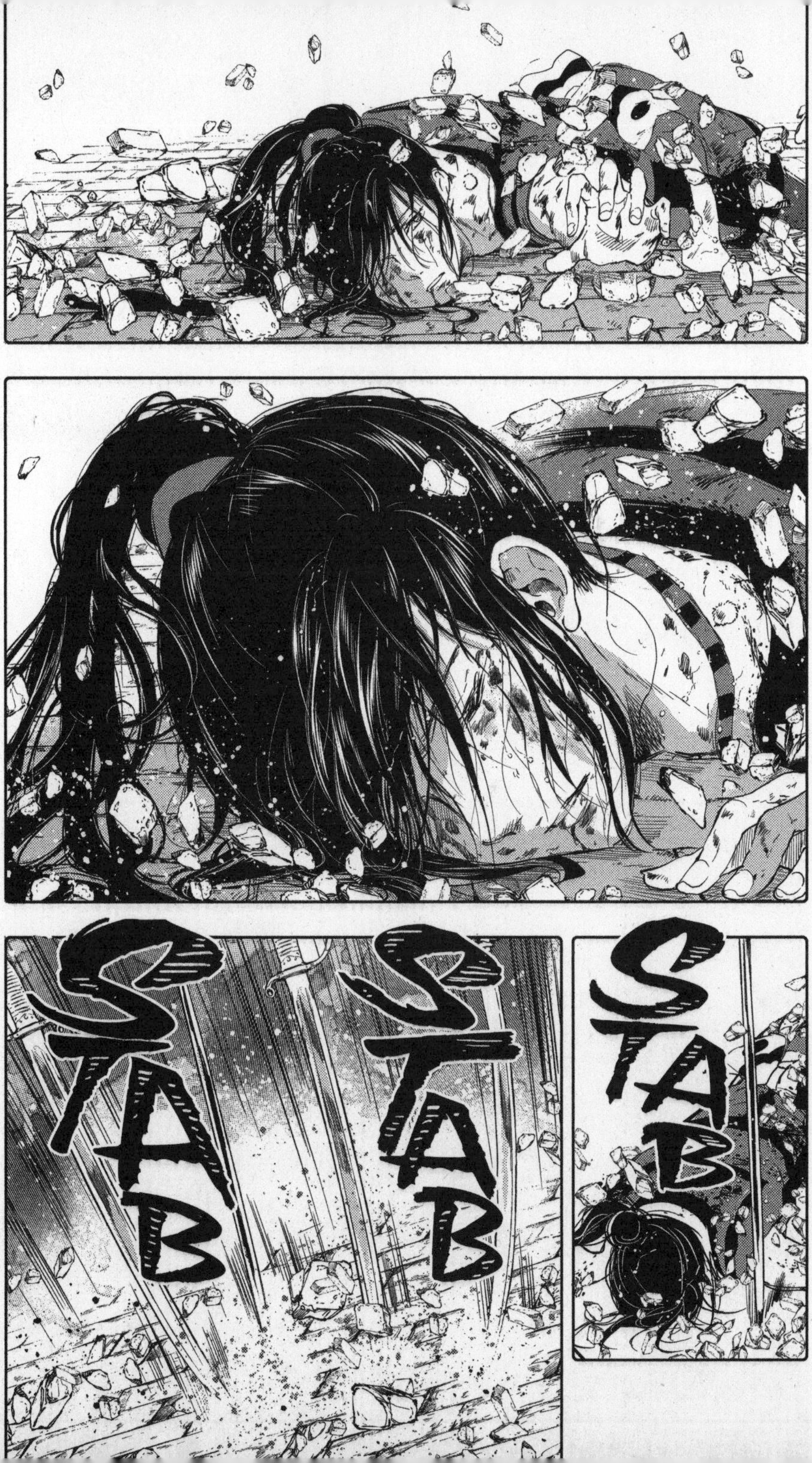
STAB
STAB
STAB

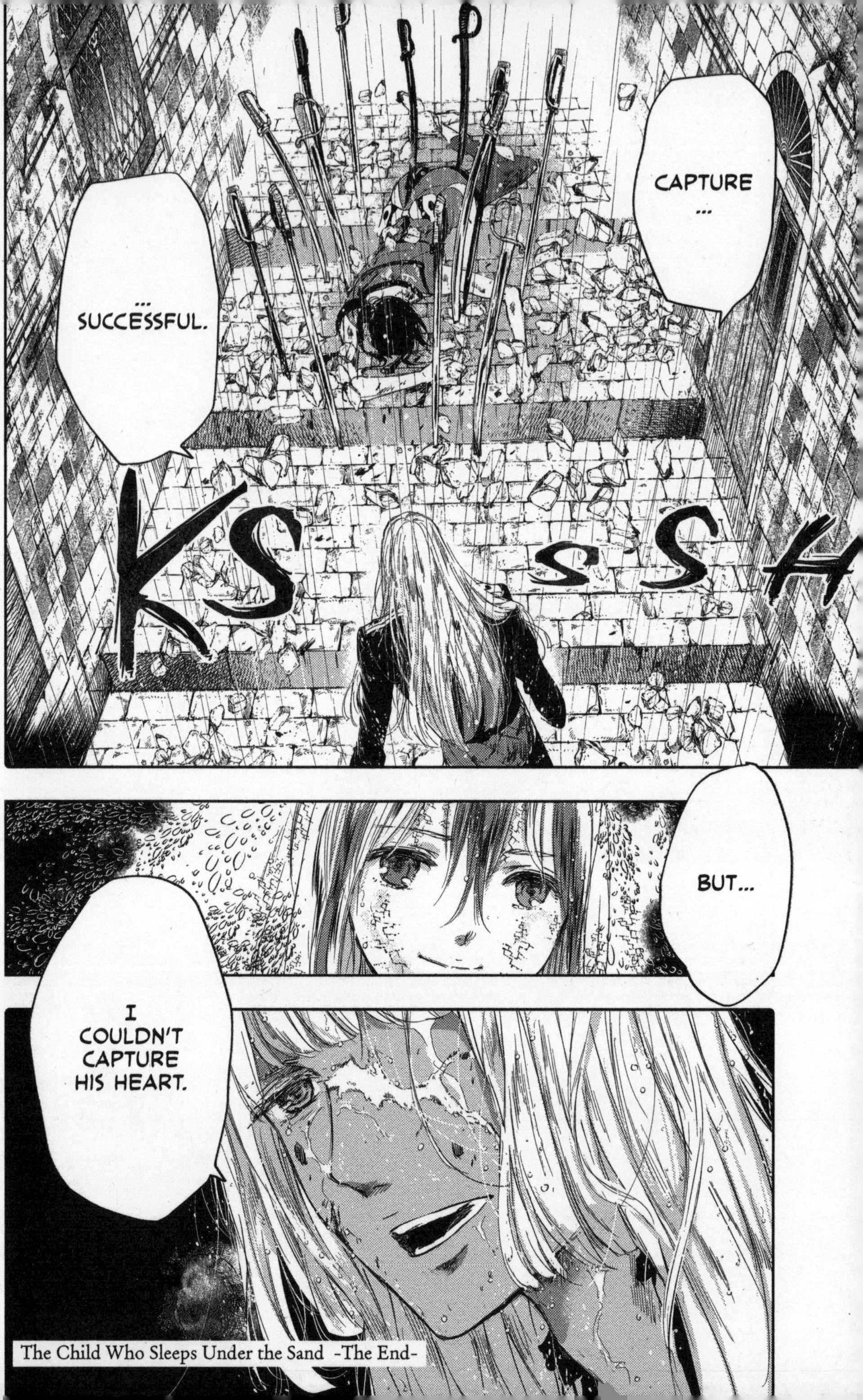
CAPTURE ...
... SUCCESSFUL.
KSSSH
BUT...
I COULDN'T CAPTURE HIS HEART.
The Child Who Sleeps Under the Sand -The End-

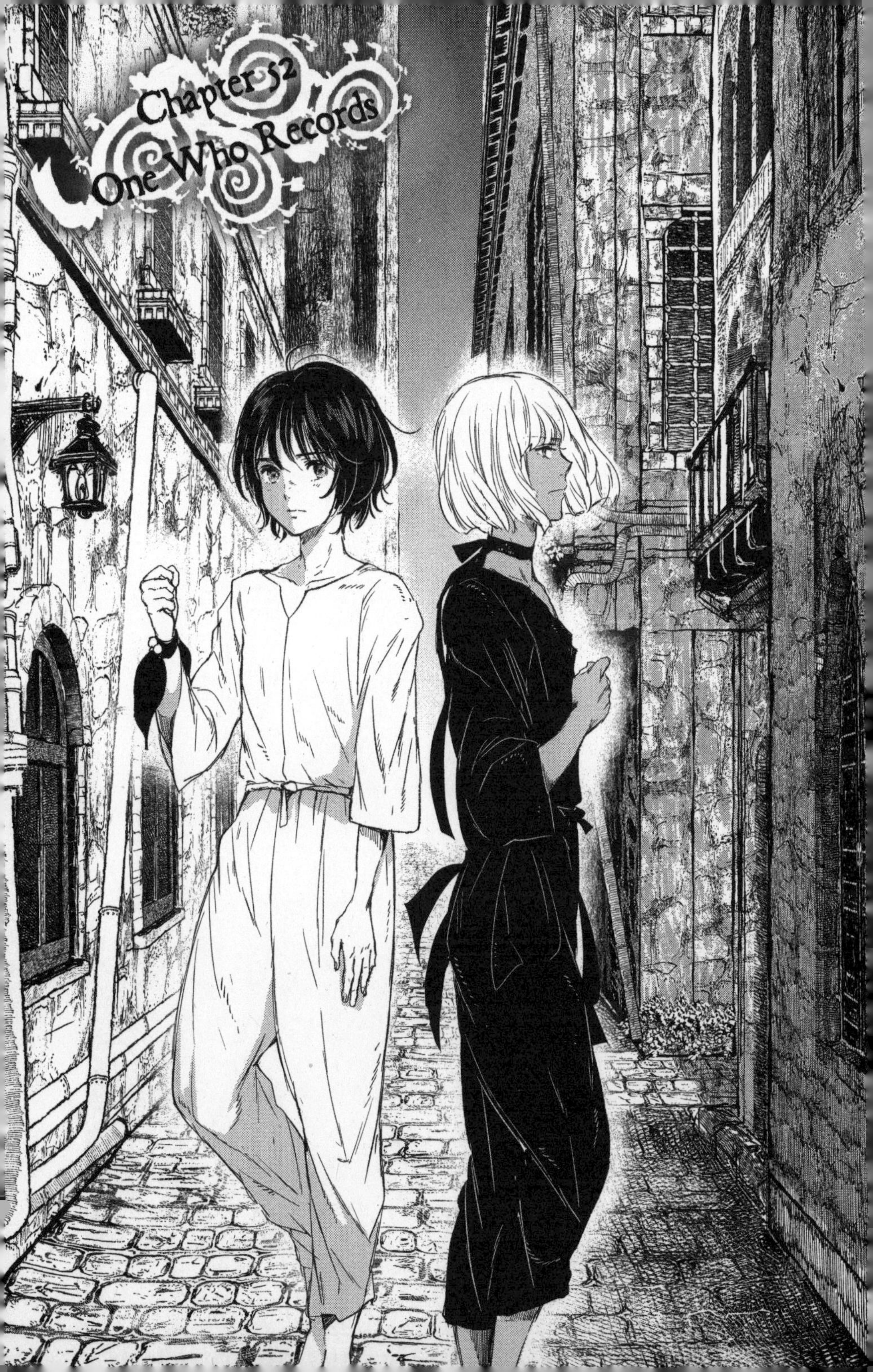
Chapter 52
One Who Records

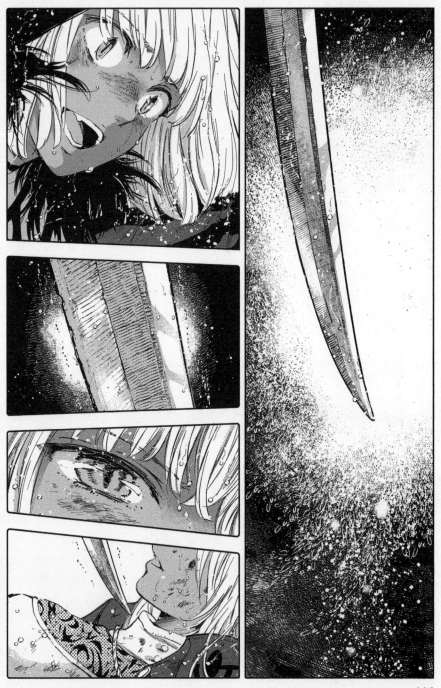

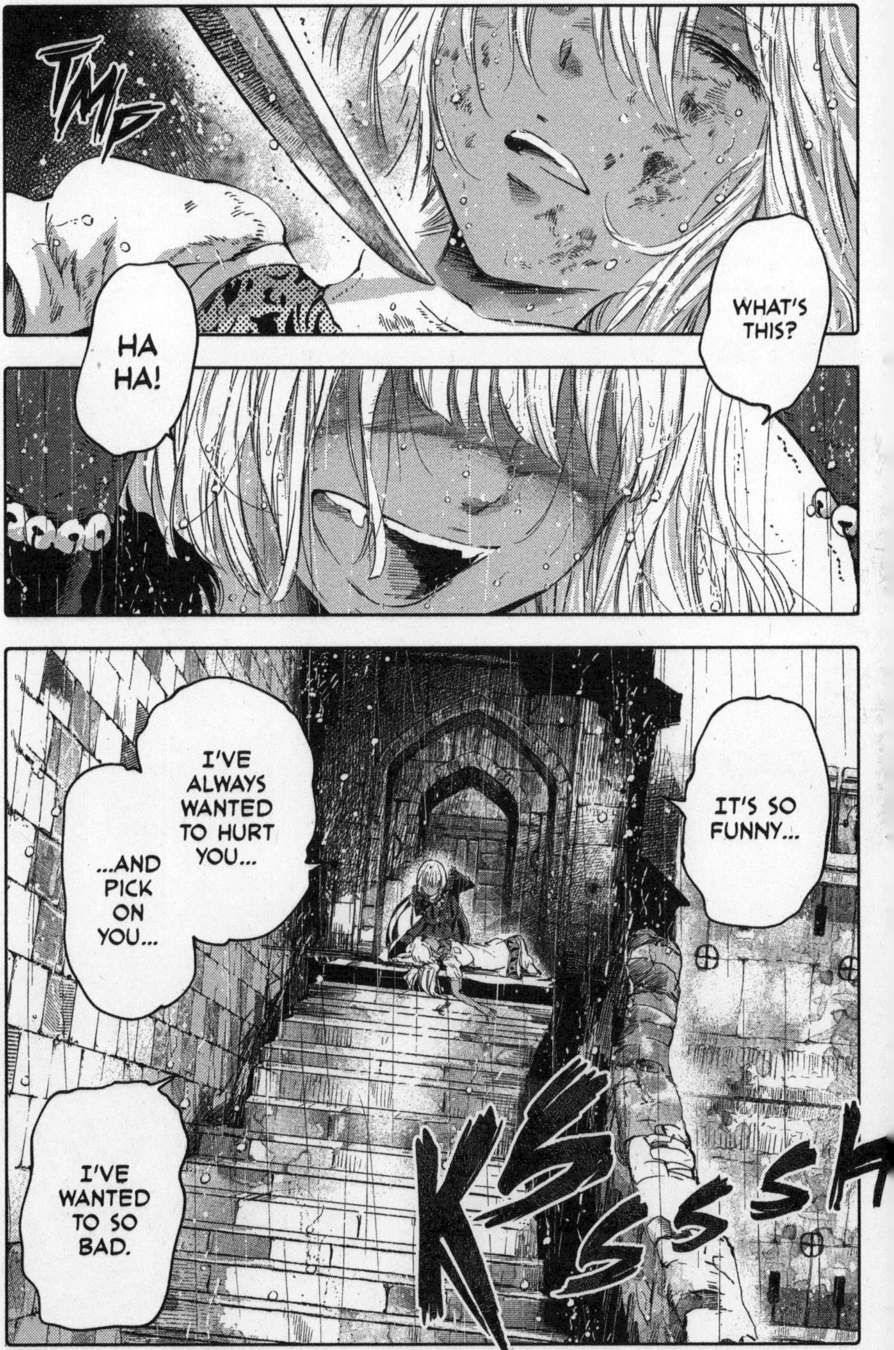
WHAT'S THIS?
TMP
HA HA!
IT'S SO FUNNY...
I'VE ALWAYS WANTED TO HURT YOU...
...AND PICK ON YOU...
I'VE WANTED TO SO BAD.
KSSSSH

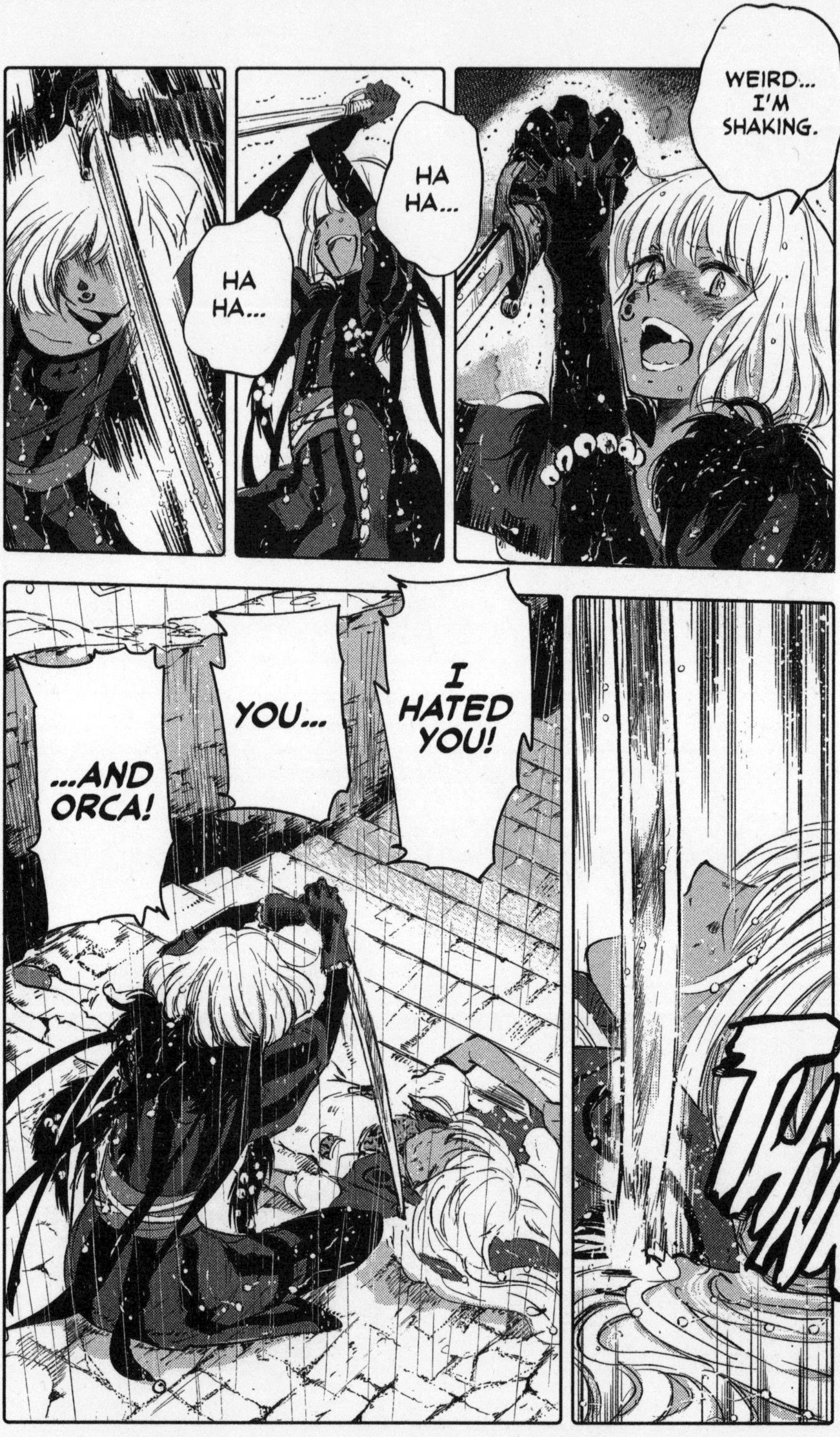
WEIRD... I'M SHAKING.
HA HA...
HA HA...
THUNK
I HATED YOU!
YOU...
...AND ORCA!

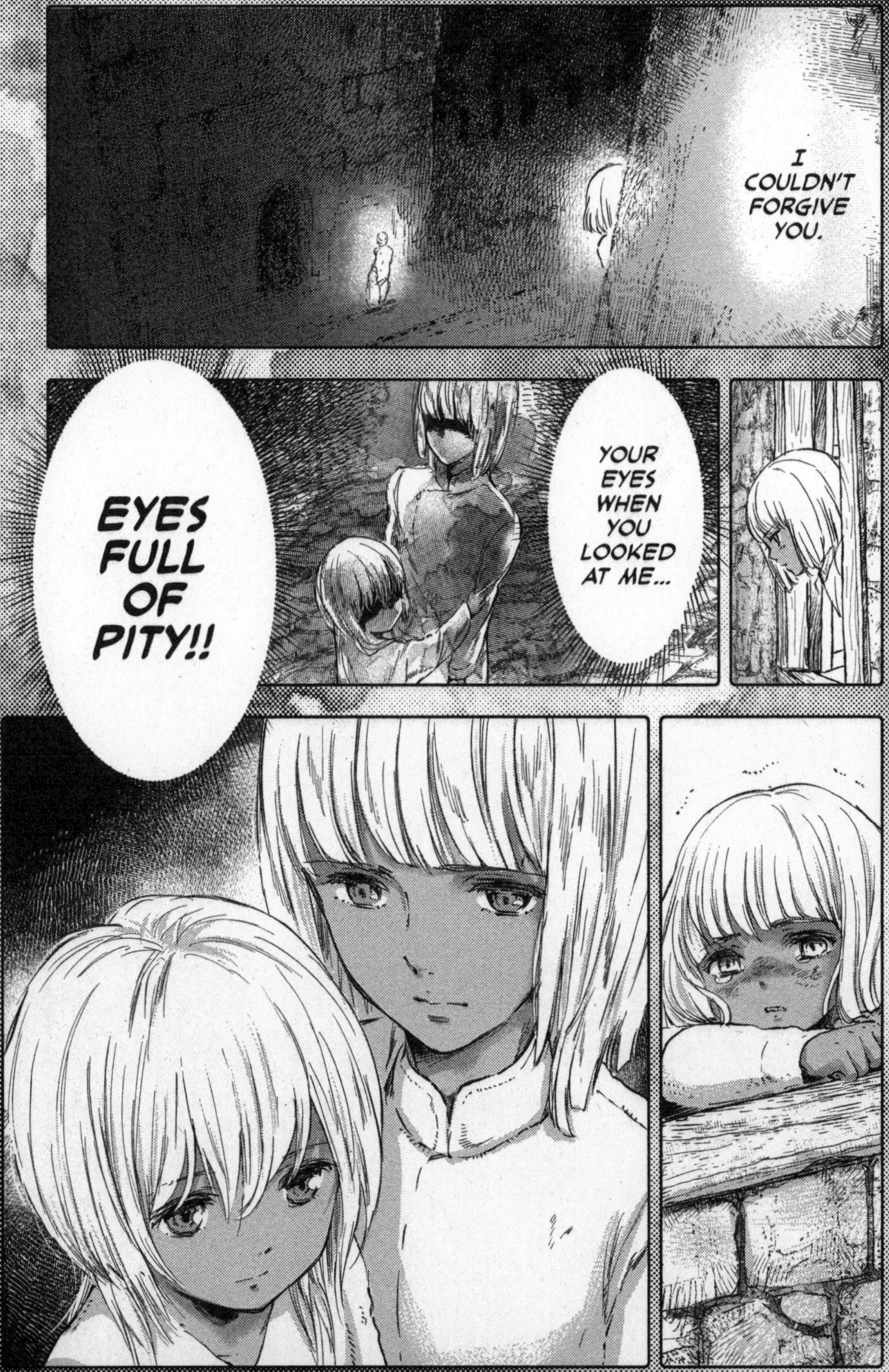

I COULDN'T FORGIVE YOU.
YOUR EYES WHEN YOU LOOKED AT ME...
EYES FULL OF PITY!!
......

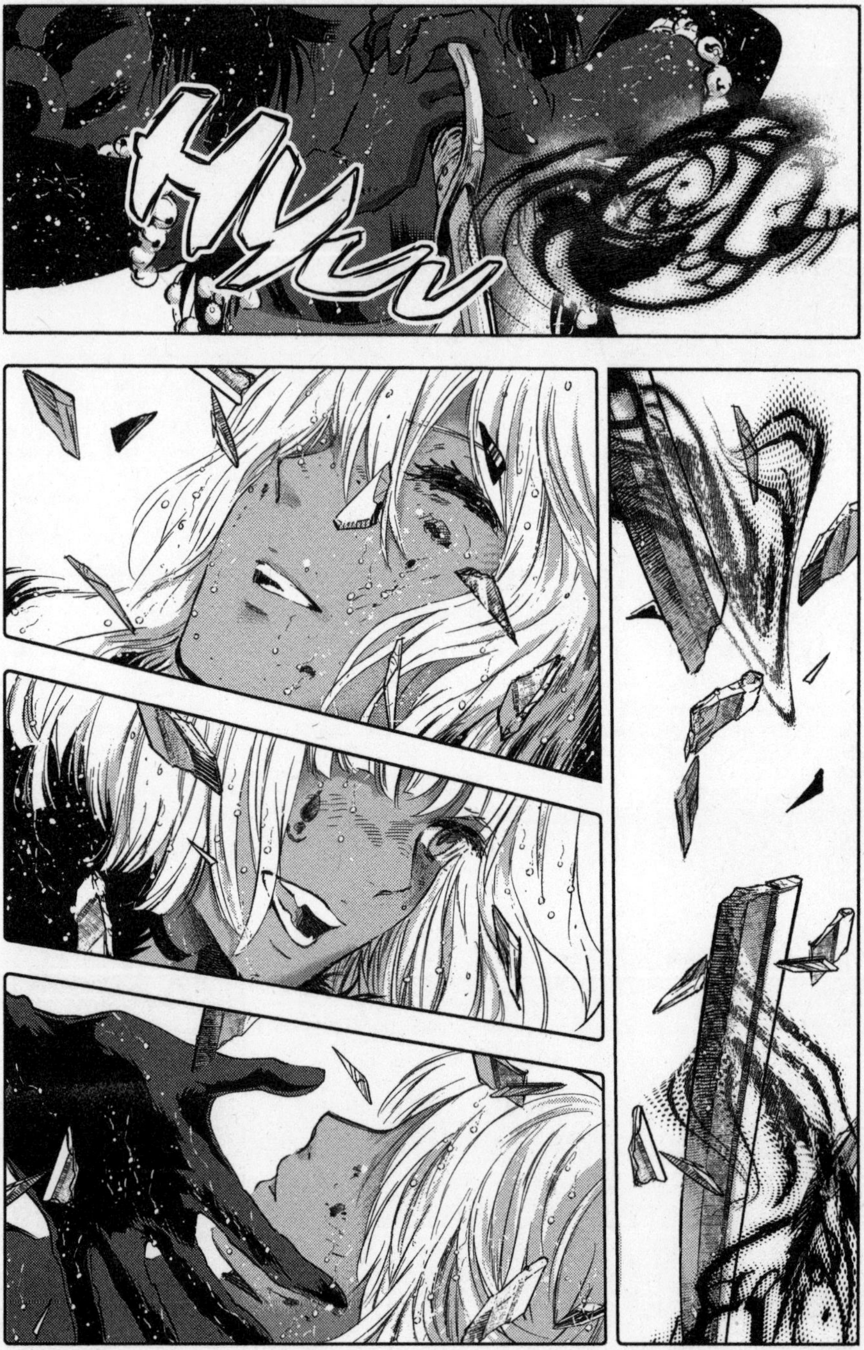
HYUU

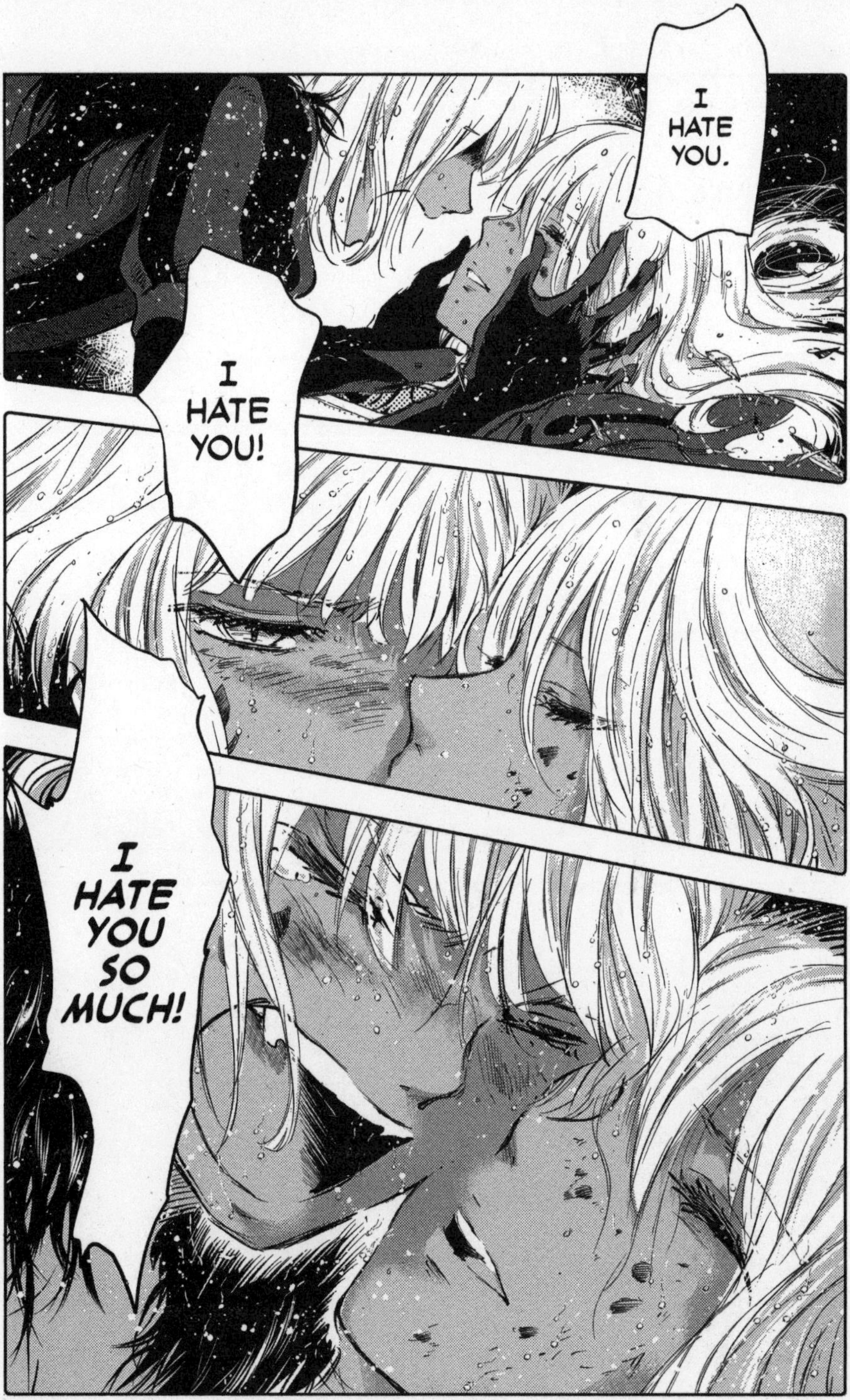
I HATE YOU.
I HATE YOU!
I HATE YOU SO MUCH!

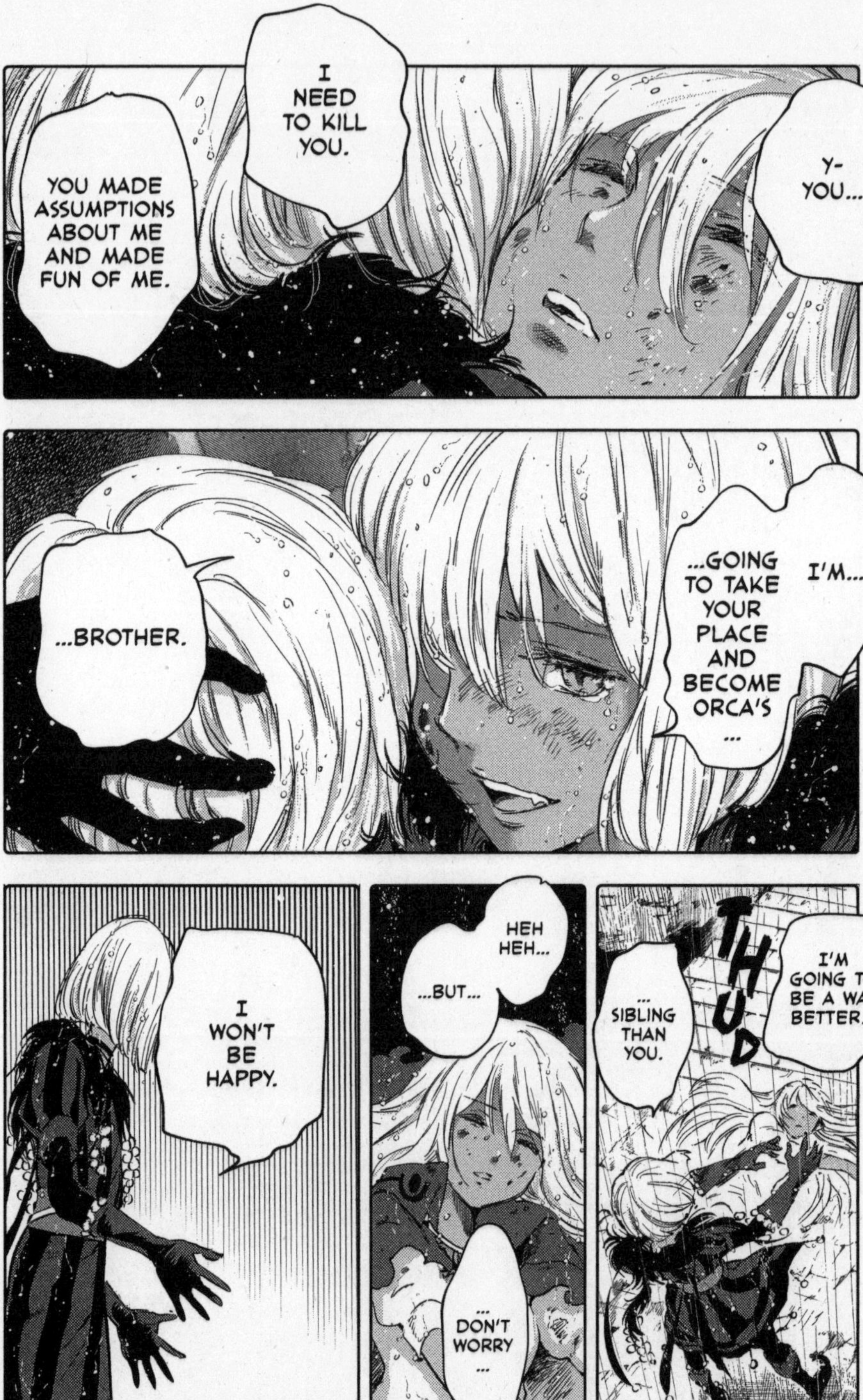
Y- YOU...
I NEED TO KILL YOU.
YOU MADE ASSUMPTIONS ABOUT ME AND MADE FUN OF ME.
I'M...
...GOING TO TAKE YOUR PLACE AND BECOME ORCA'S ...
...BROTHER.
I'M GOING TO BE A WAY BETTER...
THUD
... SIBLING THAN YOU.
HEH HEH...
...BUT...
... DON'T WORRY ...
I WON'T BE HAPPY.

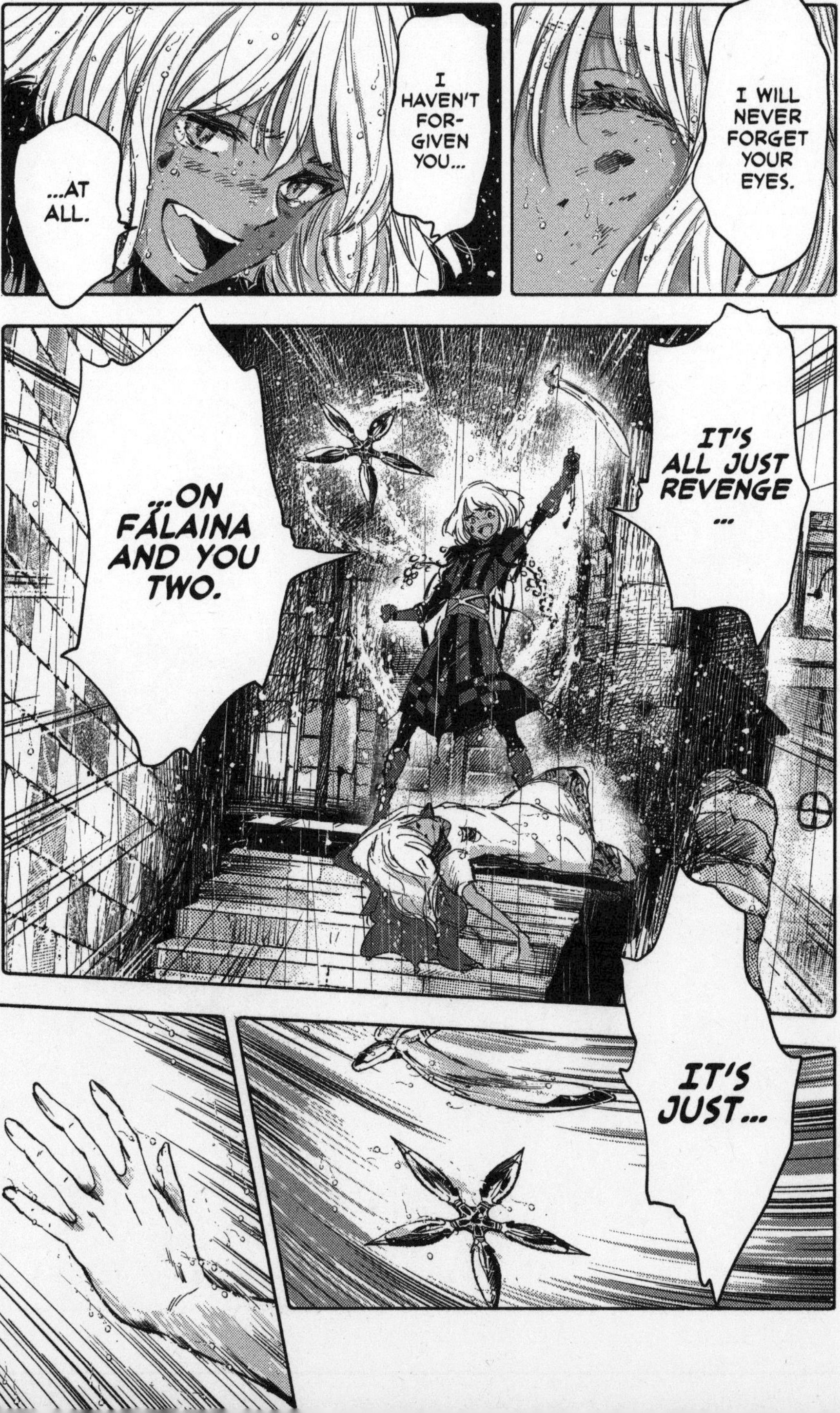
I WILL NEVER FORGET YOUR EYES.
I HAVEN'T FOR-GIVEN YOU...
...AT ALL.
IT'S ALL JUST REVENGE ...
...ON FĀLAINA AND YOU TWO.
IT'S JUST...

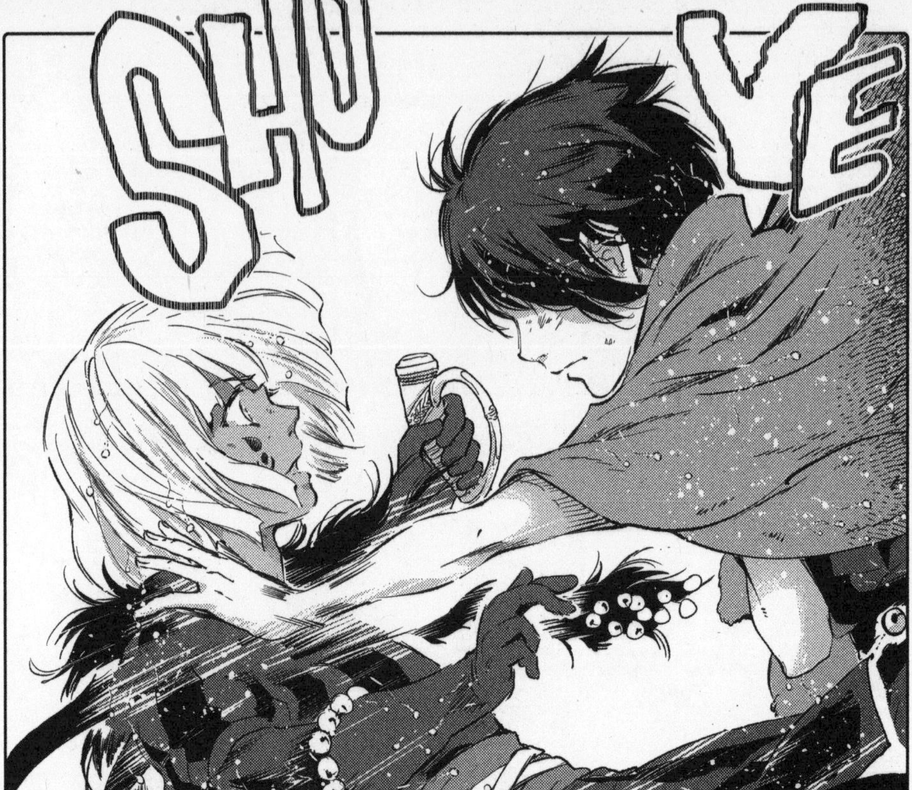
SHOVE
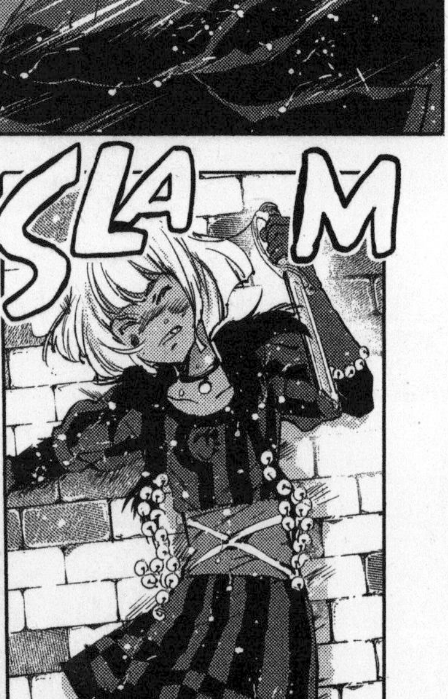
SLAM
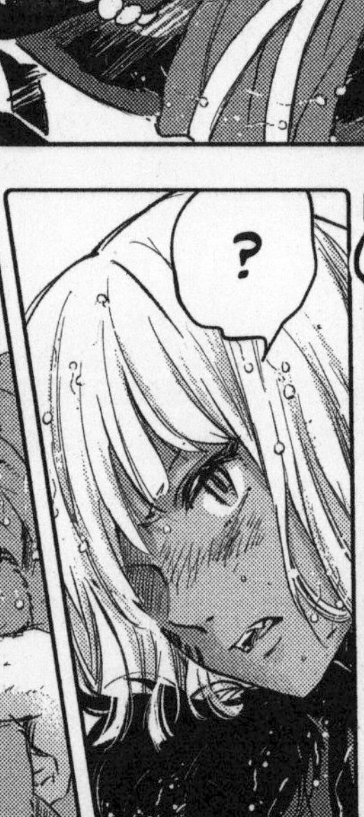
?
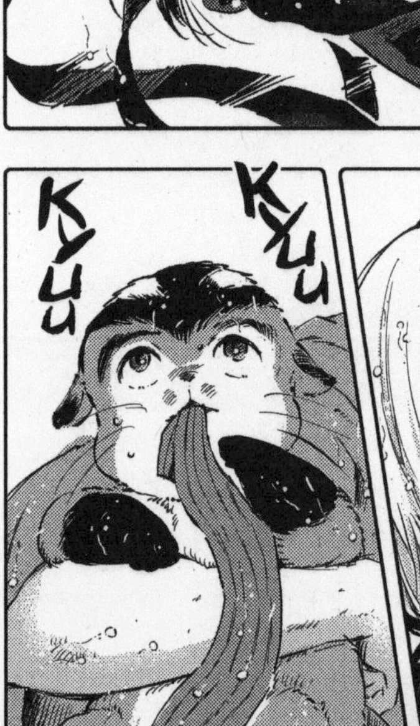
KYUU
KYUU

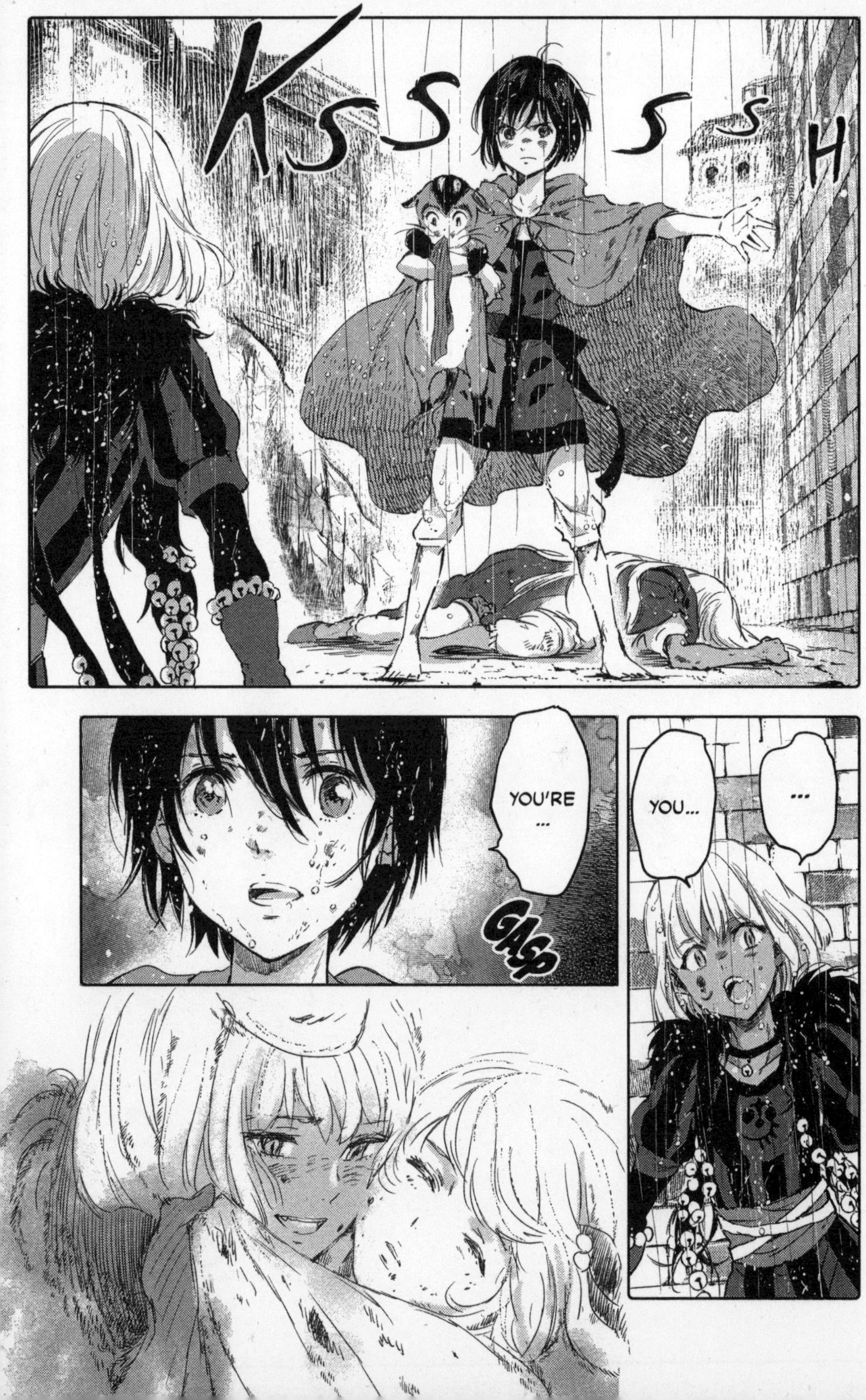
KSSSSH
...
YOU...
YOU'RE ...
GASP

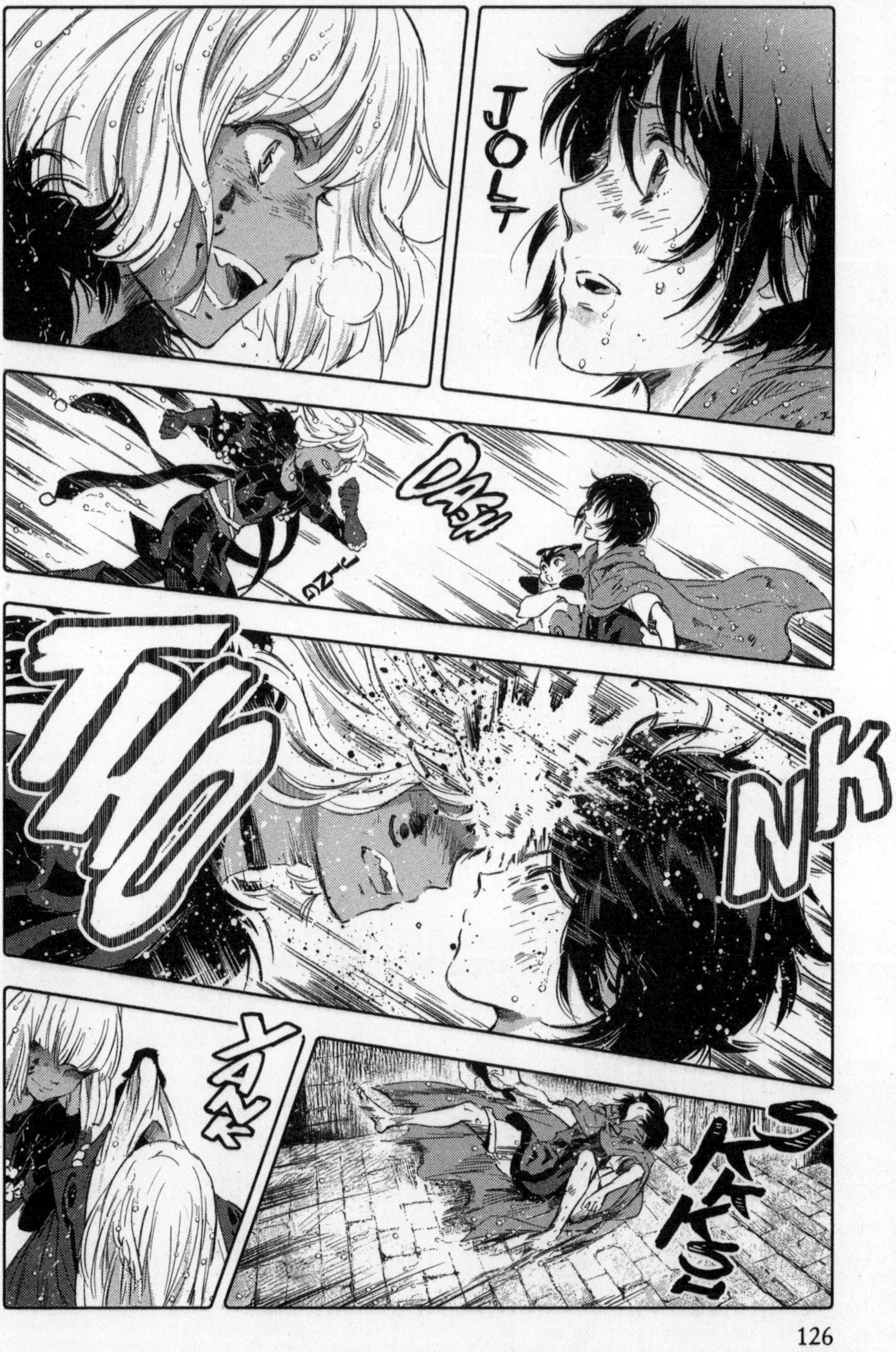
JOLT
DASH!
JING
THUNK
SKKSH
YANK

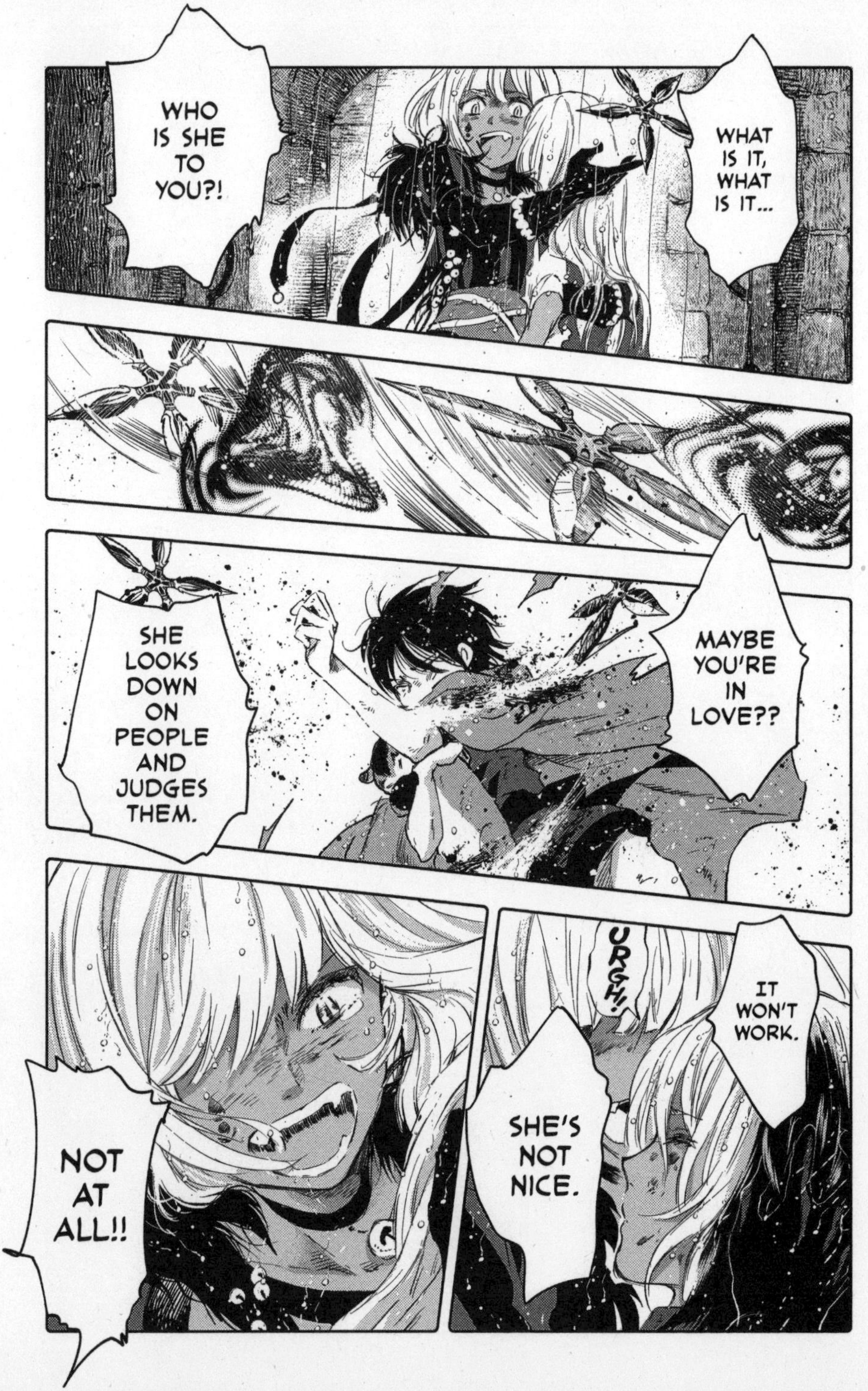
WHAT IS IT, WHAT IS IT...
WHO IS SHE TO YOU?!
MAYBE YOU'RE IN LOVE??
SHE LOOKS DOWN ON PEOPLE AND JUDGES THEM.
URGH!!
IT WON'T WORK.
SHE'S NOT NICE.
NOT AT ALL!!

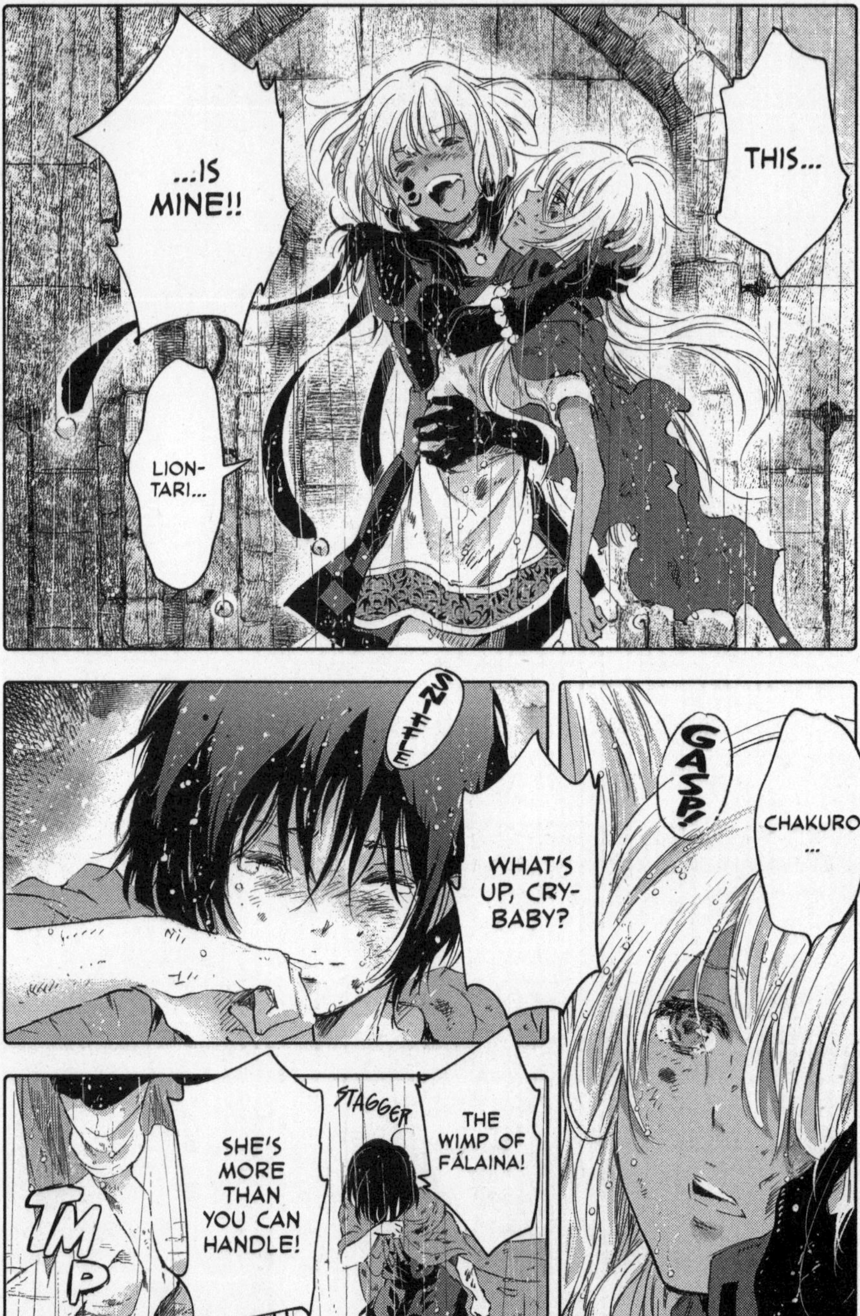
THIS...
...IS MINE!!
LION-TARI...
CHAKURO ...
GASP!
SNIFFLE
WHAT'S UP, CRY-BABY?
THE WIMP OF FÁLAINA!
STAGGER
SHE'S MORE THAN YOU CAN HANDLE!
TMP

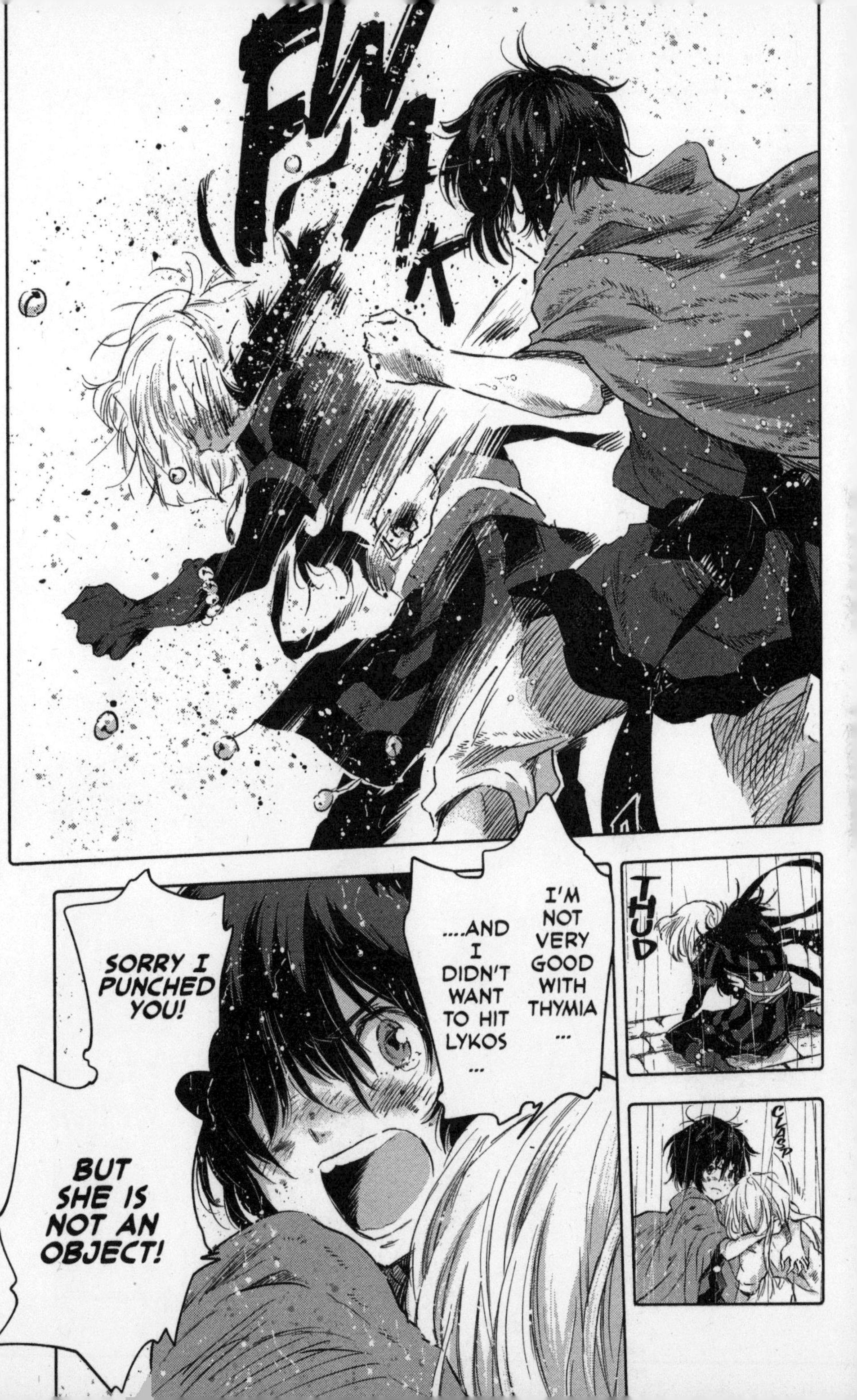
FWAK
THUD
CLASP
I'M NOT VERY GOOD WITH THYMIA ...
....AND I DIDN'T WANT TO HIT LYKOS ...
SORRY I PUNCHED YOU!
BUT SHE IS NOT AN OBJECT!

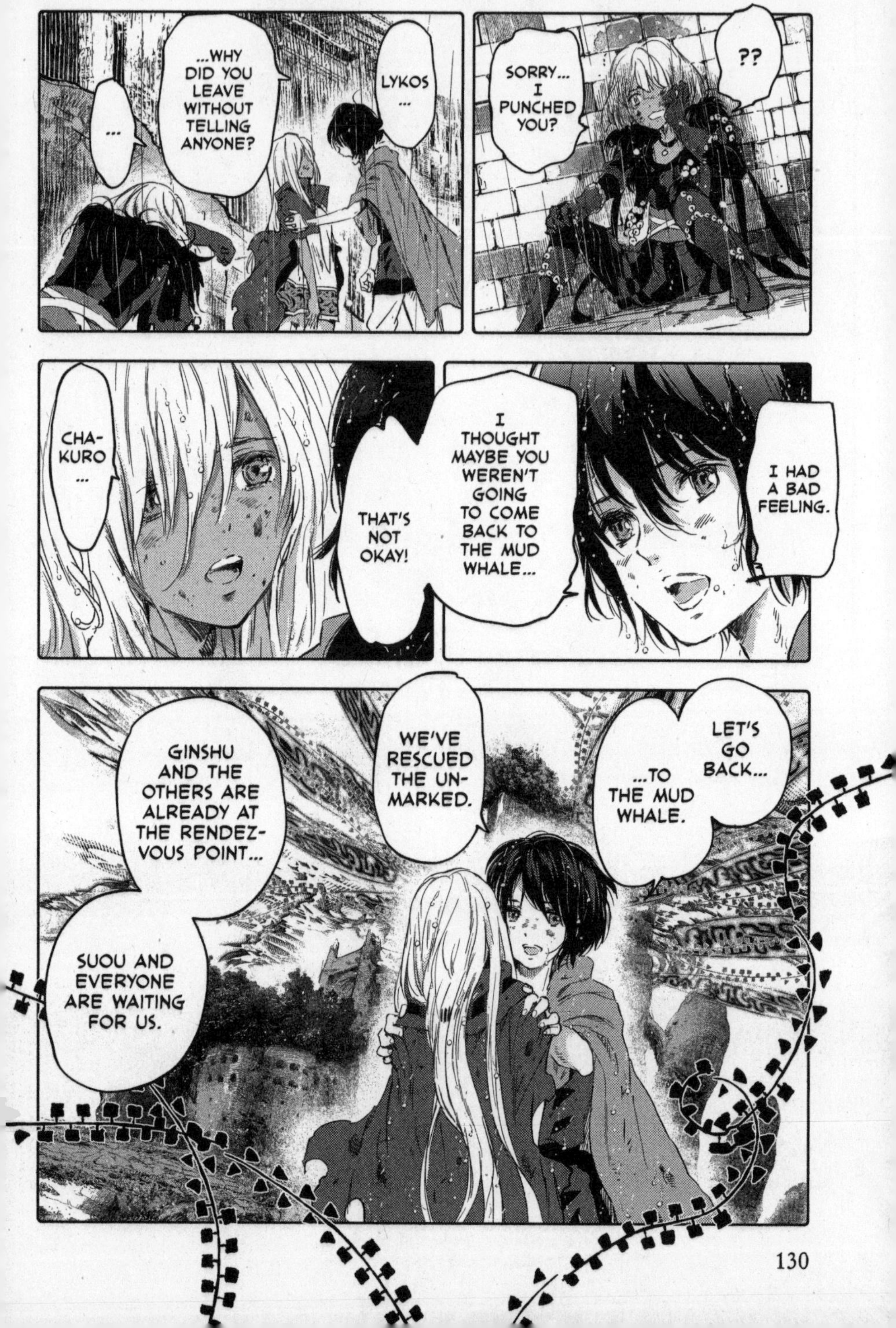
??
SORRY... I PUNCHED YOU?
LYKOS ...
...WHY DID YOU LEAVE WITHOUT TELLING ANYONE?
...
I HAD A BAD FEELING.
I THOUGHT MAYBE YOU WEREN'T GOING TO COME BACK TO THE MUD WHALE...
THAT'S NOT OKAY!
CHA-KURO ...
LET'S GO BACK...
...TO THE MUD WHALE.
WE'VE RESCUED THE UN-MARKED.
GINSHU AND THE OTHERS ARE ALREADY AT THE RENDEZ-VOUS POINT...
SUOU AND EVERYONE ARE WAITING FOR US.

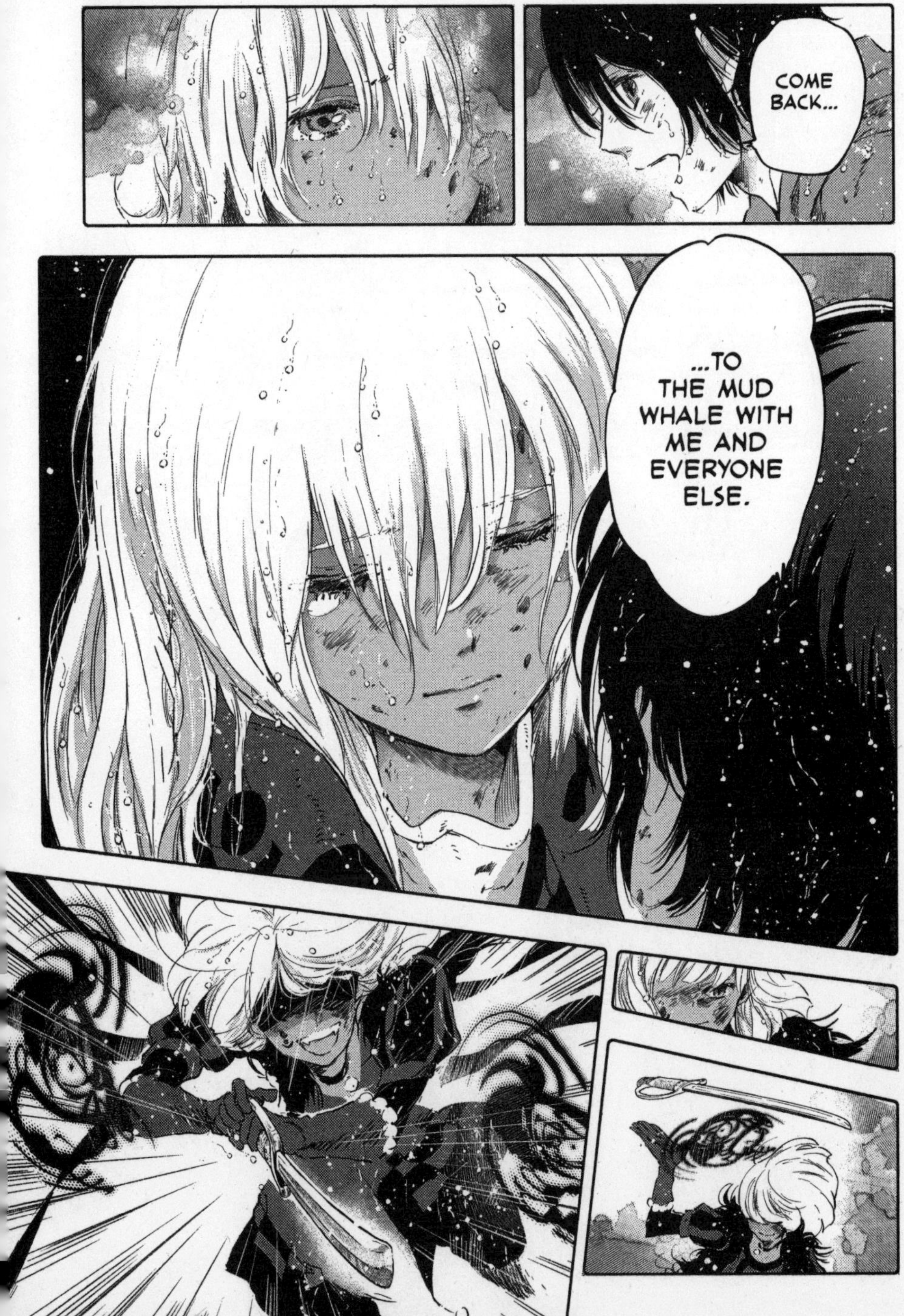
COME BACK...
...TO THE MUD WHALE WITH ME AND EVERYONE ELSE.

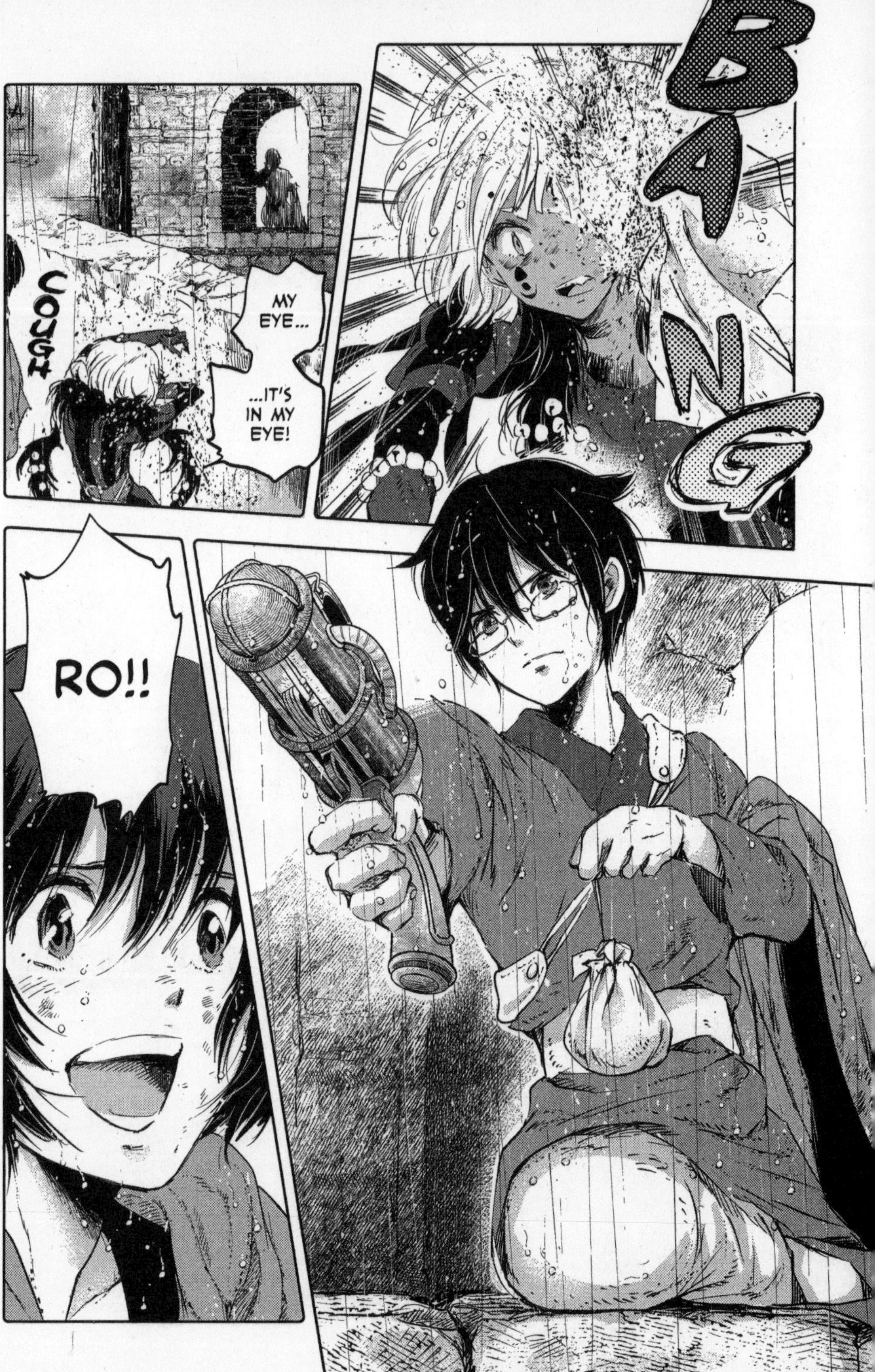
BANG
MY EYE...
...IT'S IN MY EYE!
COUGH
RO!!

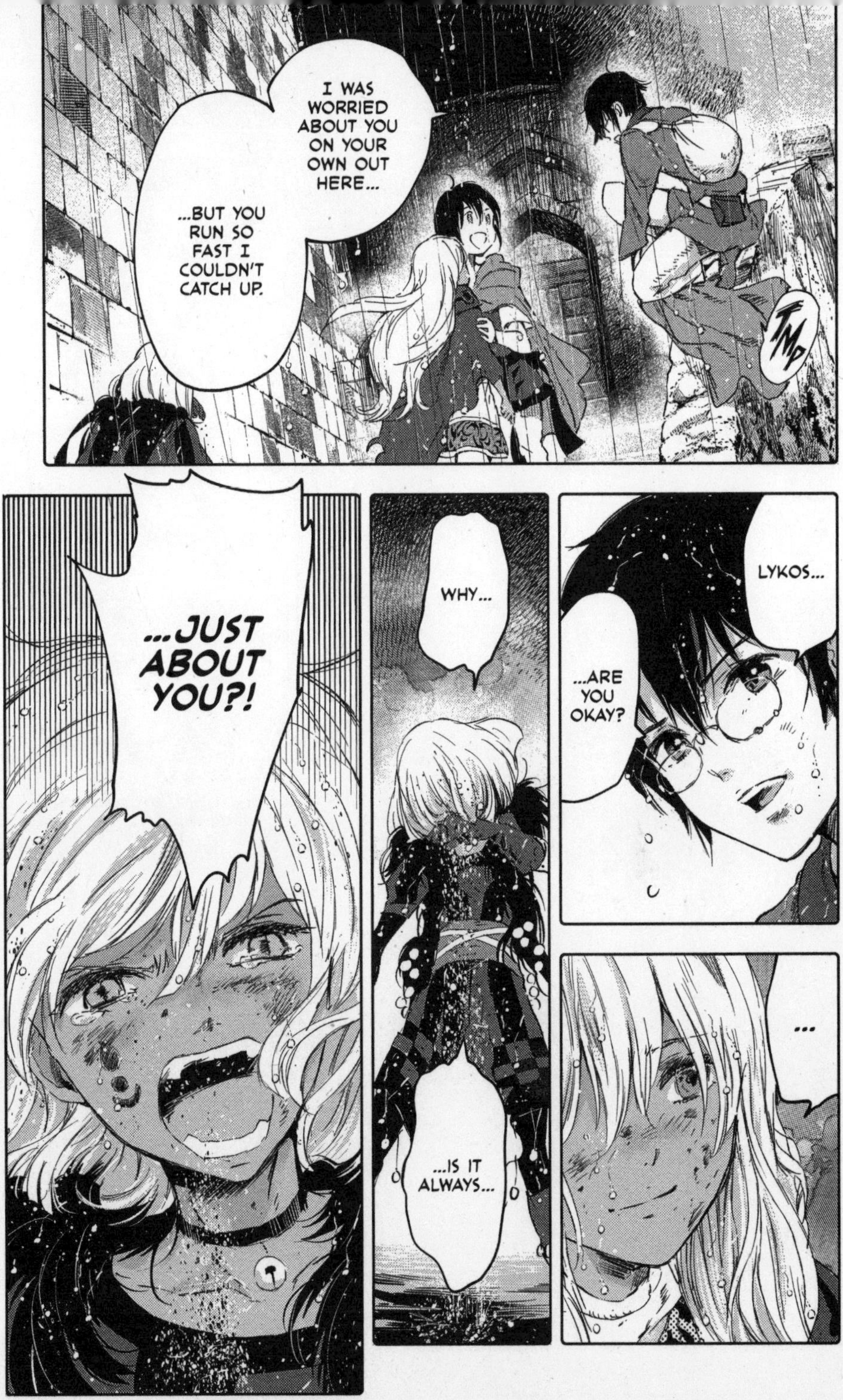
I WAS WORRIED ABOUT YOU ON YOUR OWN OUT HERE...
...BUT YOU RUN SO FAST I COULDN'T CATCH UP.
TMP
LYKOS...
...ARE YOU OKAY?
...
WHY...
...IS IT ALWAYS...
...JUST ABOUT YOU?!

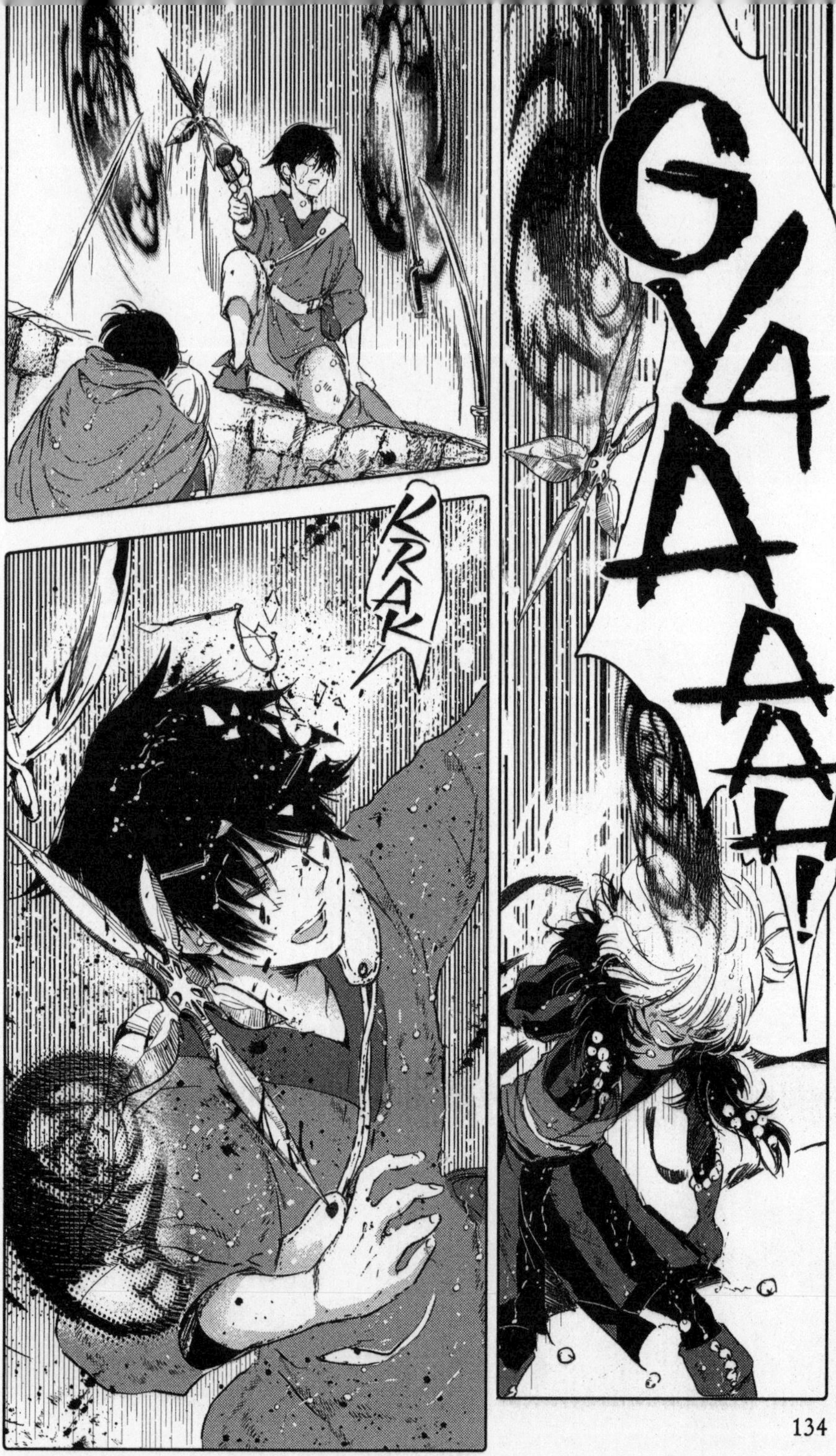
GYAAAAH!
KRAK

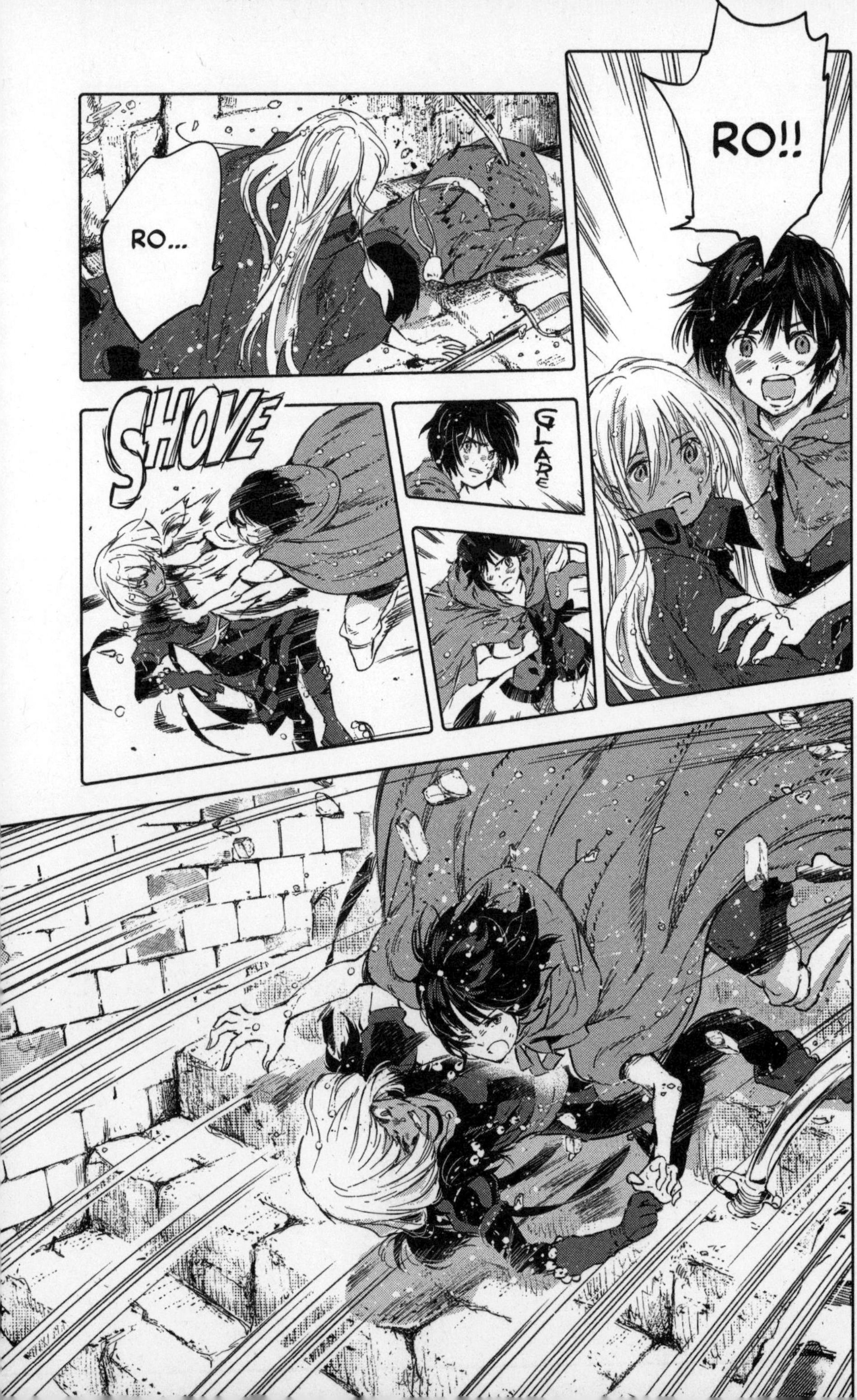
RO!!
RO...
GLARE
SHOVE

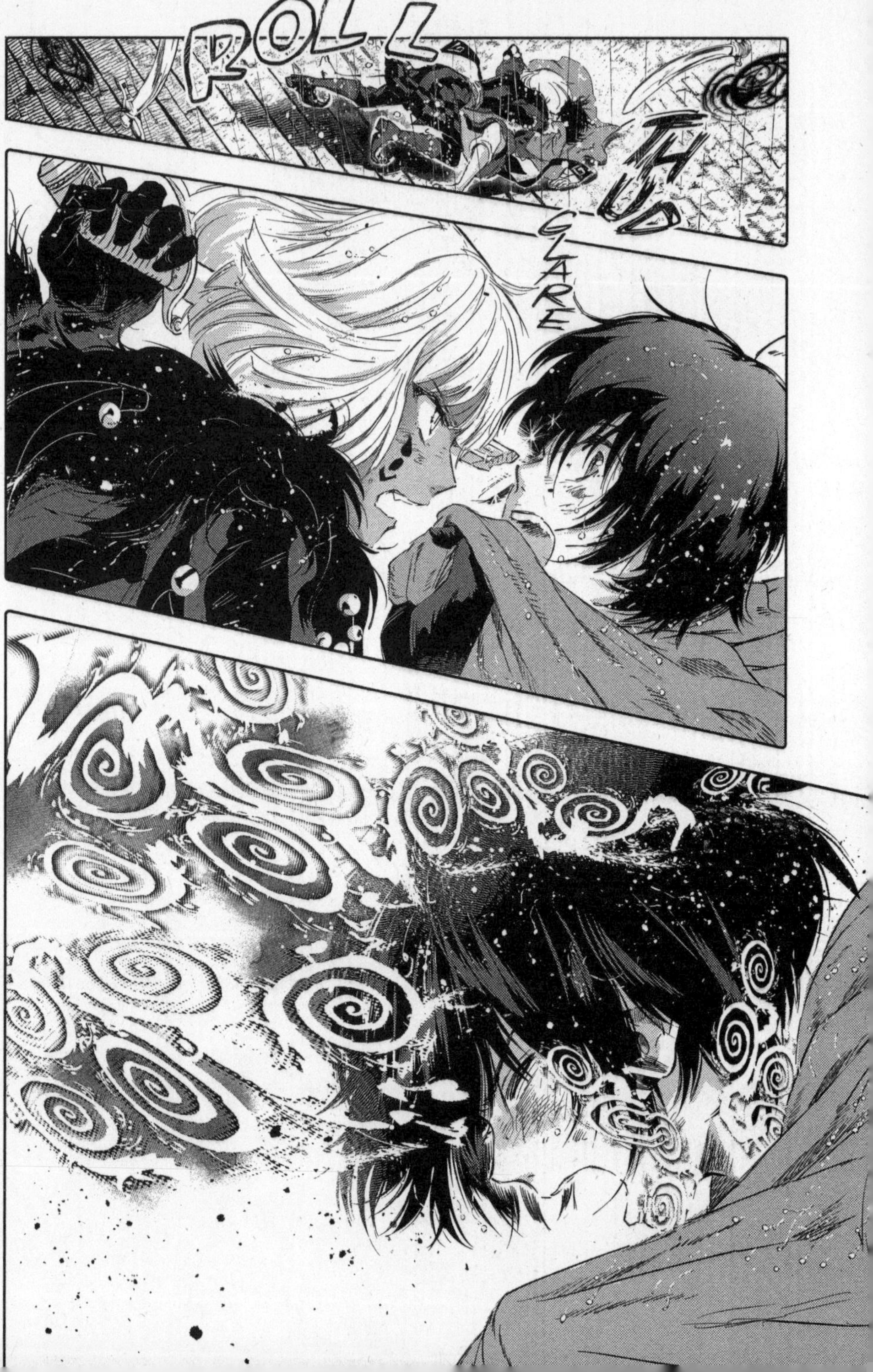
ROLL
THUD
GLARE

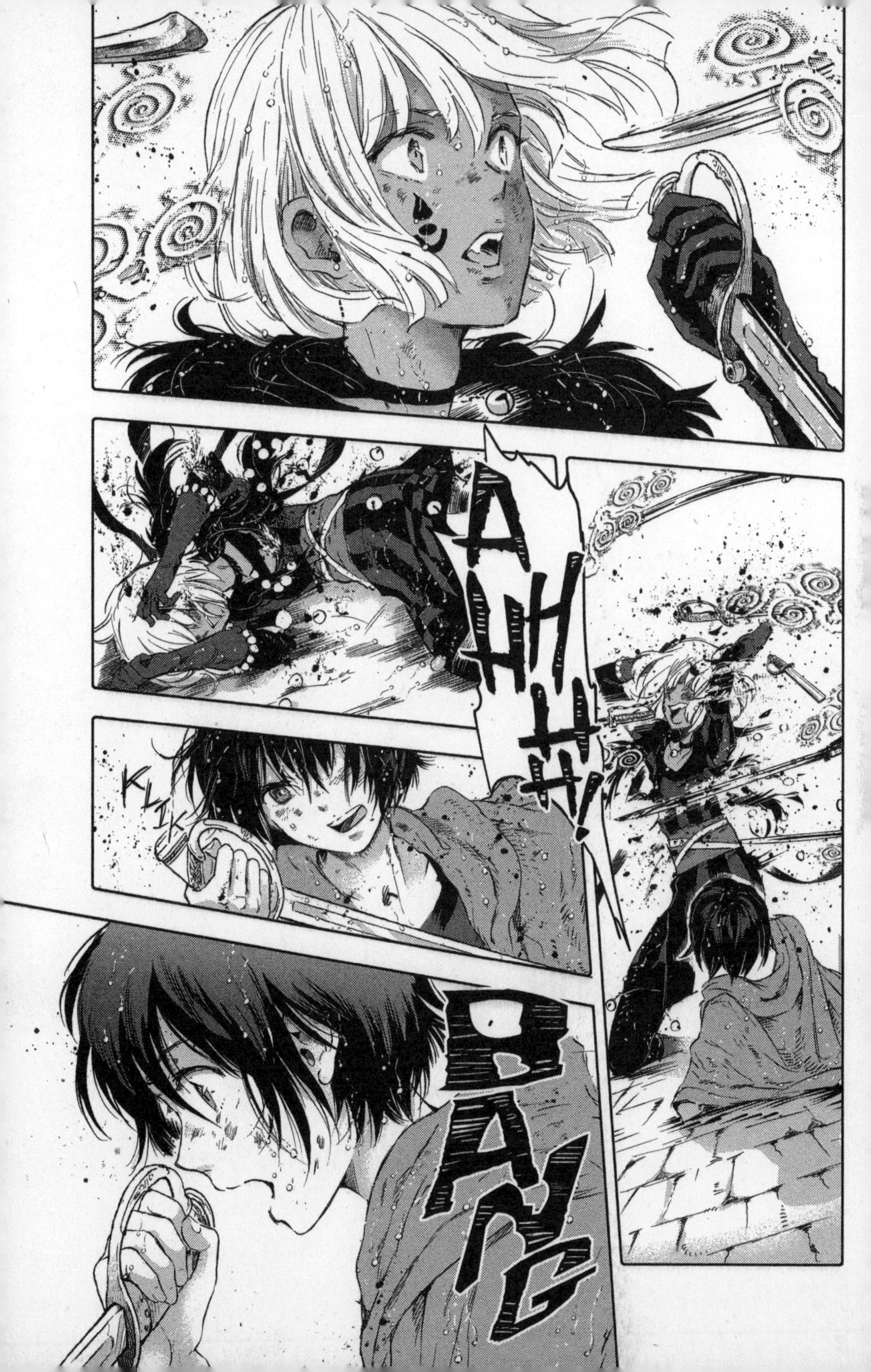
AHHHHH!
KLIK
BANG

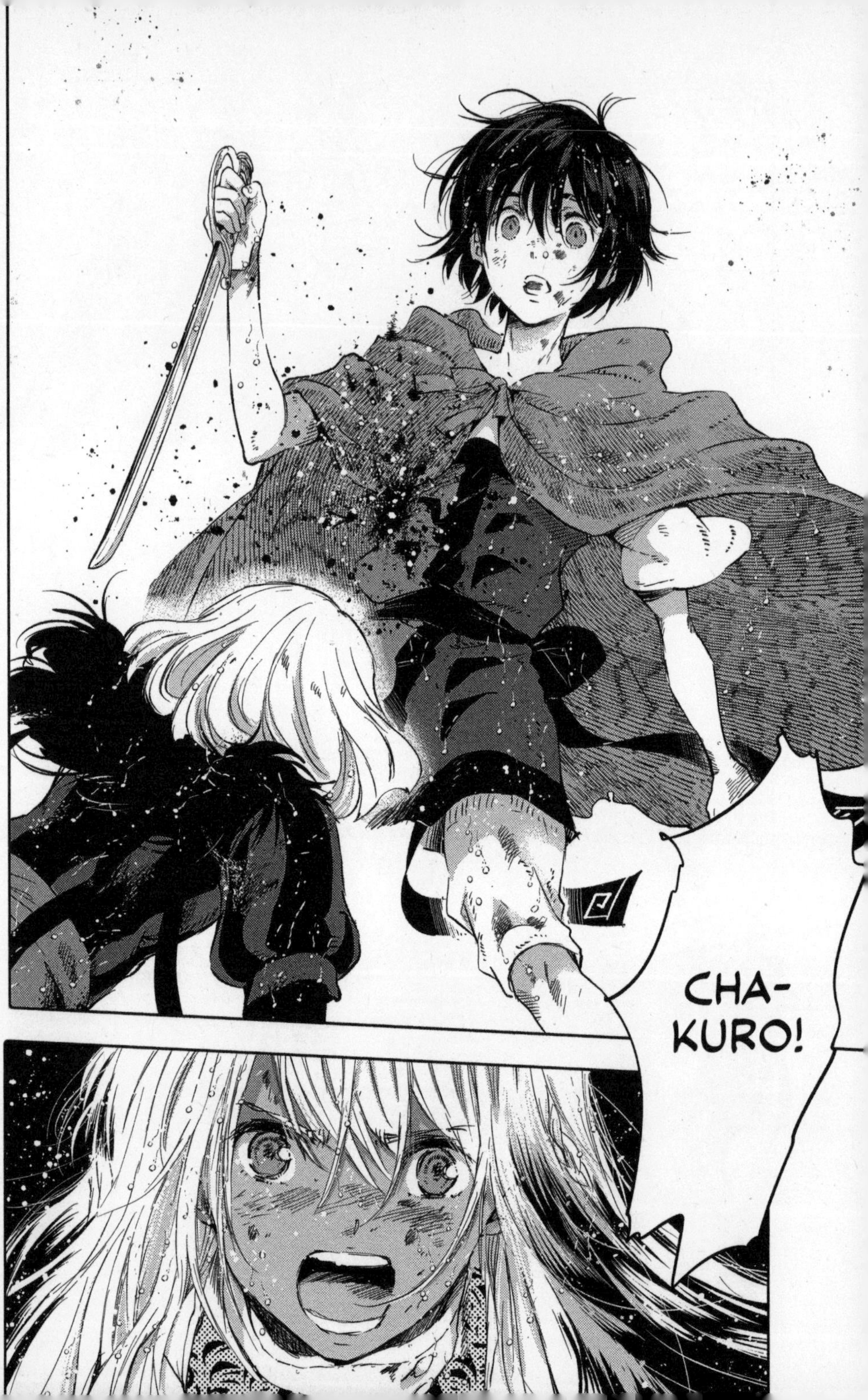
CHA-
KURO!

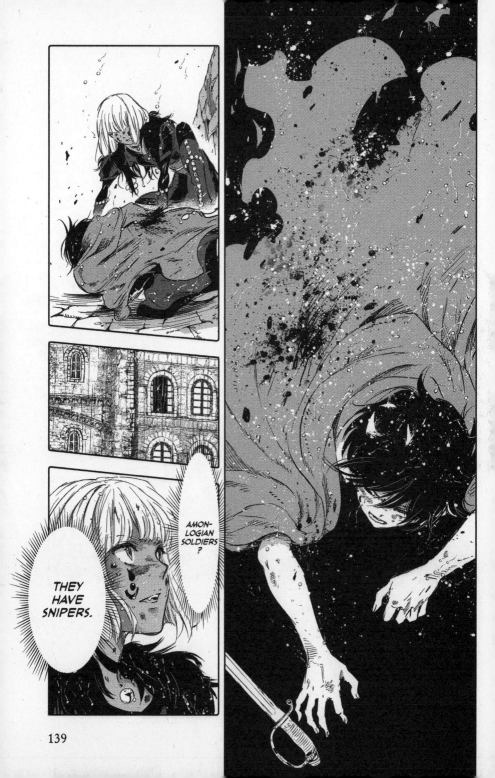

AMON-
LOGIAN
SOLDIERS
?

THEY
HAVE
SNIPERS.

139

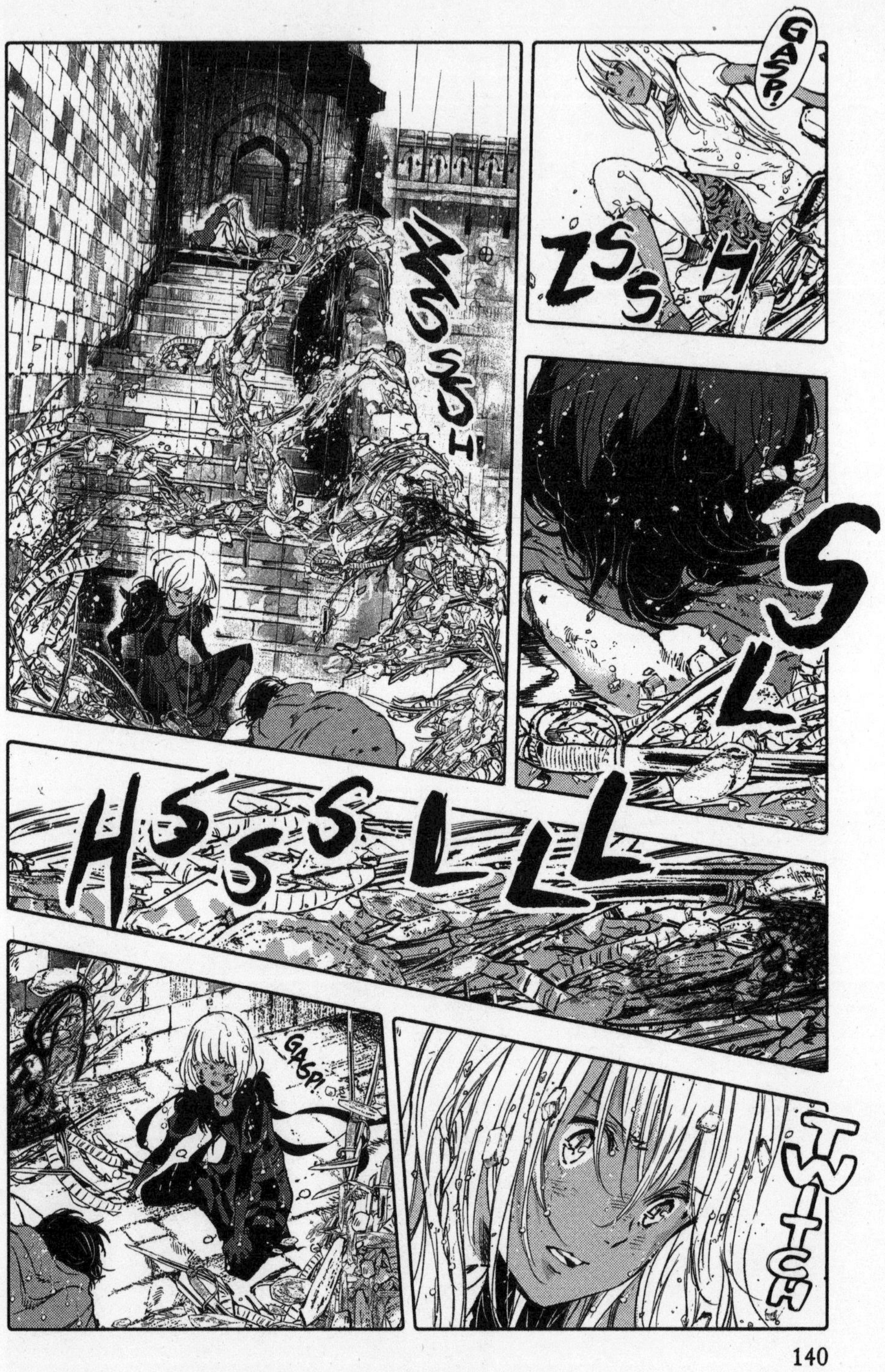
GASP!
ZSSH
SL
ZSSSH
HSSSLLL
TWITCH
GASP!

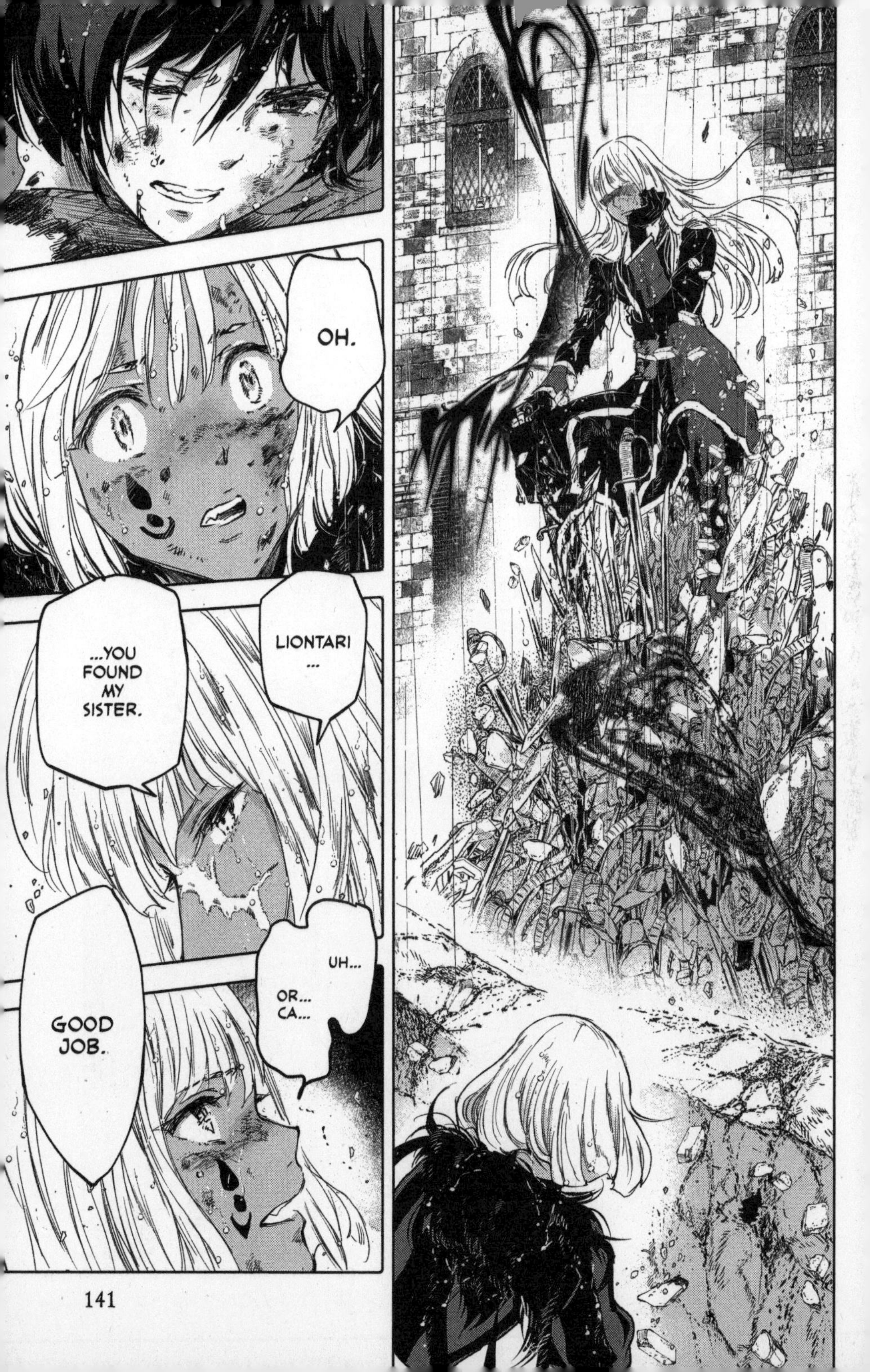
OH.
LIONTARI ...
...YOU FOUND MY SISTER.
UH... OR... CA...
GOOD JOB.

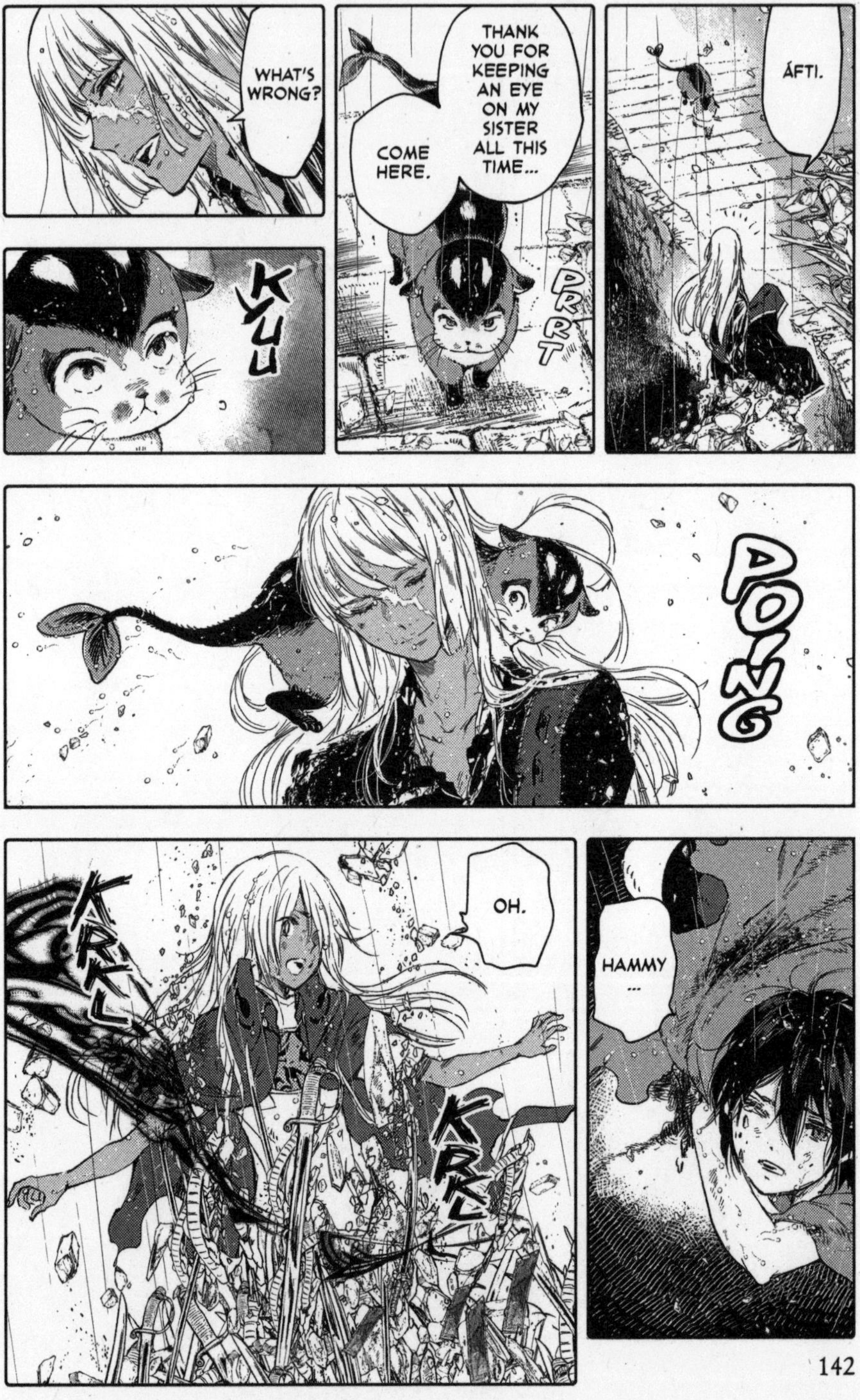
ÁFTI.
THANK YOU FOR KEEPING AN EYE ON MY SISTER ALL THIS TIME...
COME HERE.
PRRT
WHAT'S WRONG?
KYUU
POING
HAMMY...
OH.
KRKL
KRKL

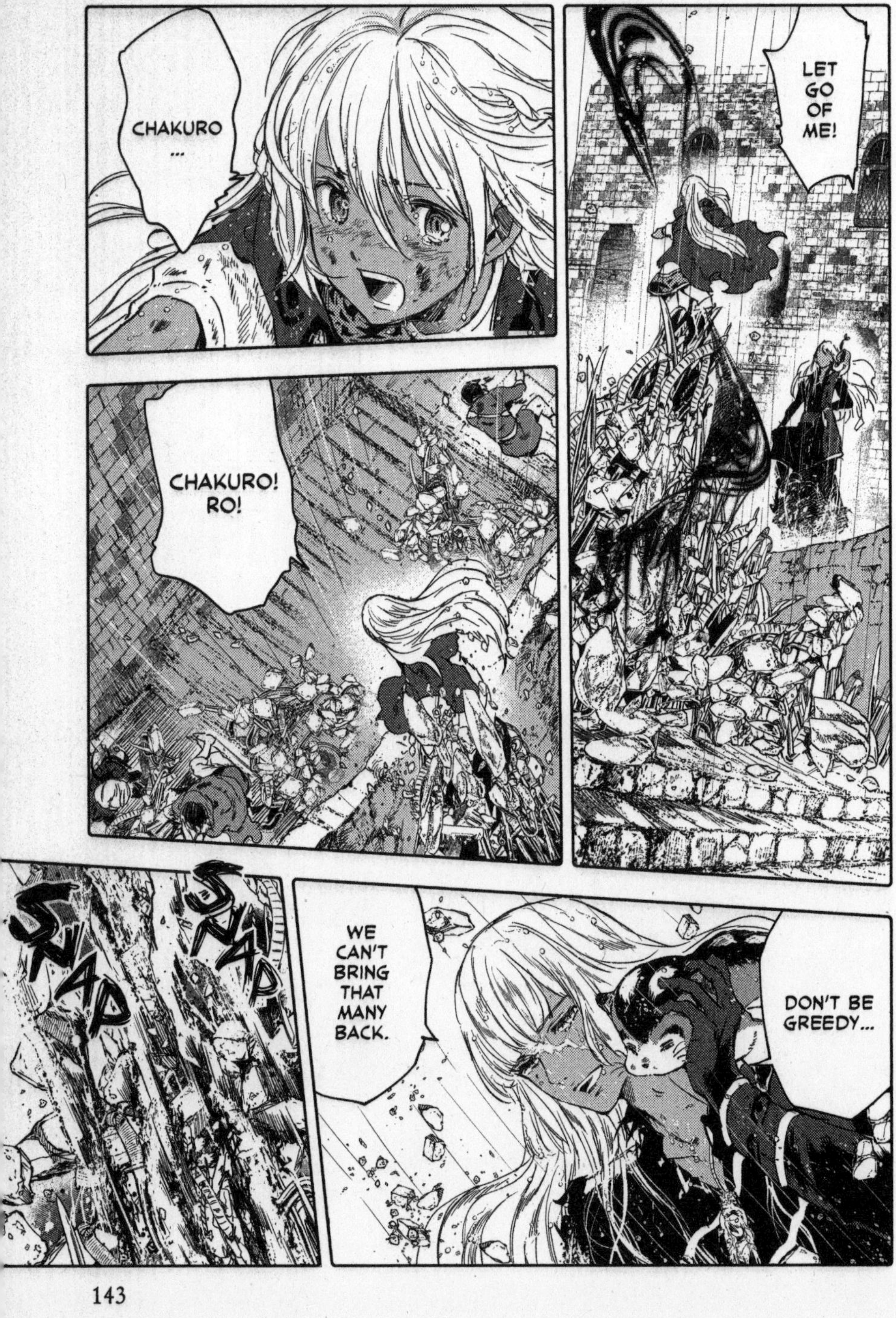
LET GO OF ME!
CHAKURO ...
CHAKURO! RO!
DON'T BE GREEDY...
WE CAN'T BRING THAT MANY BACK.
SNAP
SNAP

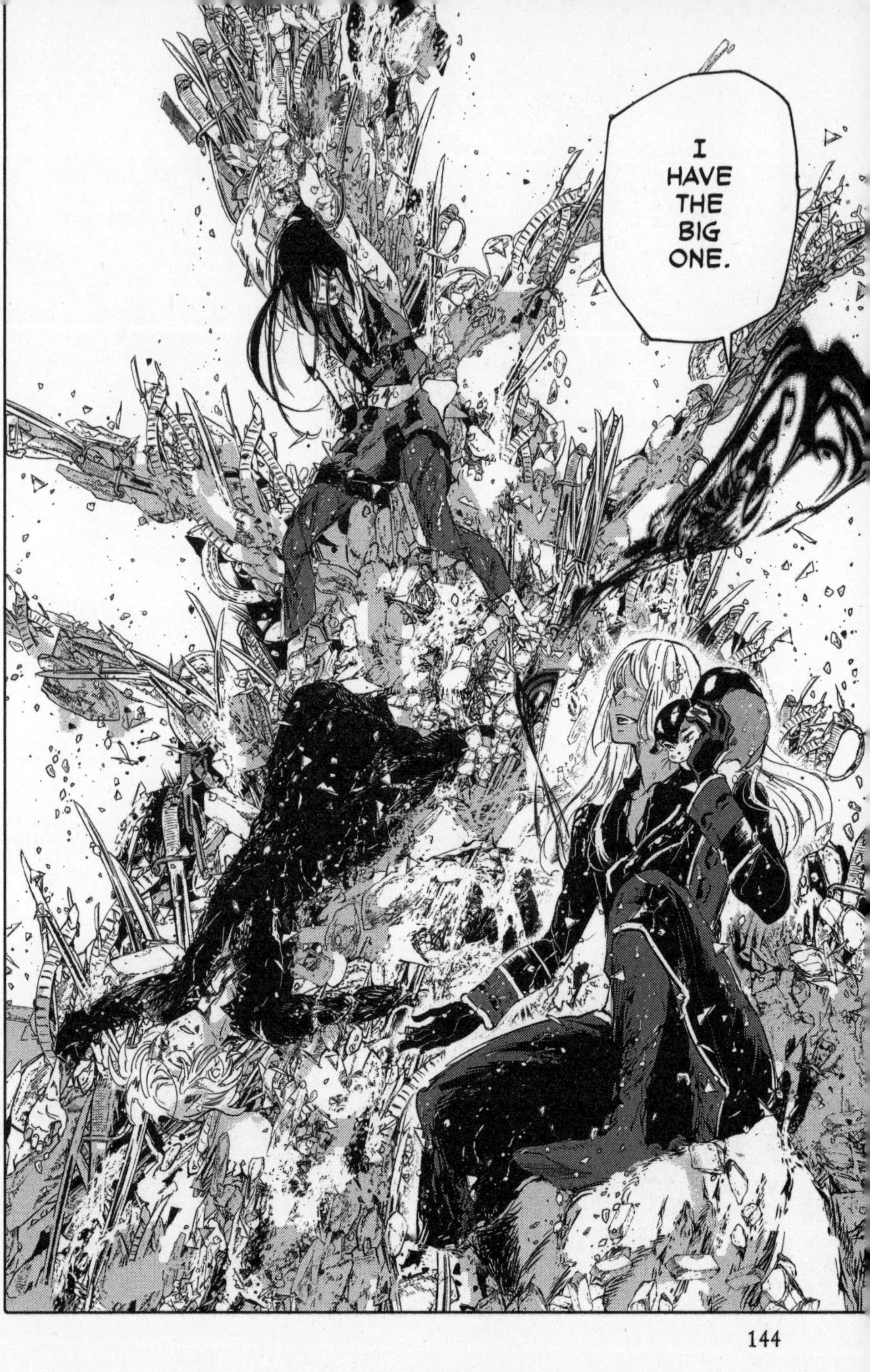
I HAVE THE BIG ONE.

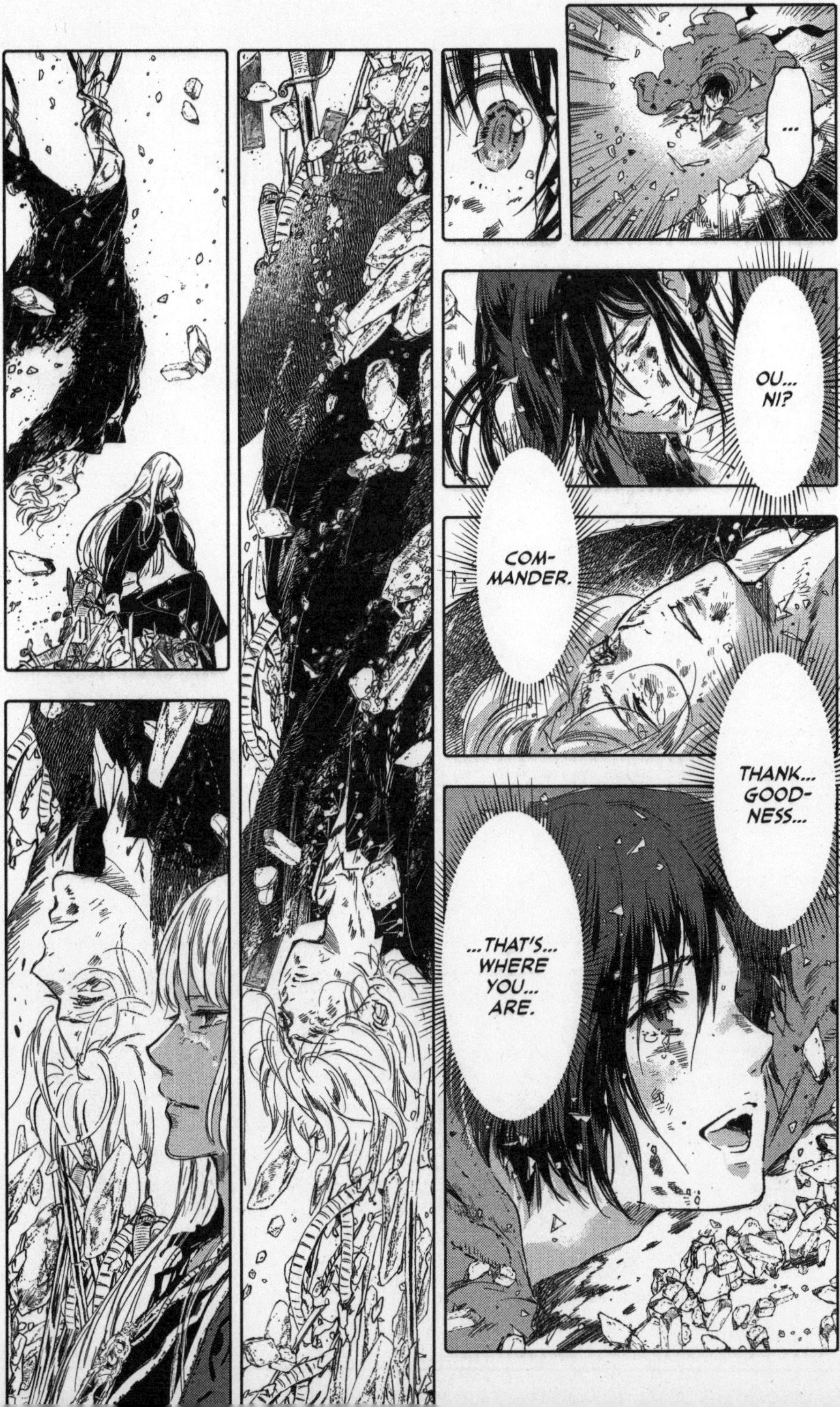
...
OU... NI?
COM-MANDER.
THANK... GOOD-NESS...
...THAT'S... WHERE YOU... ARE.

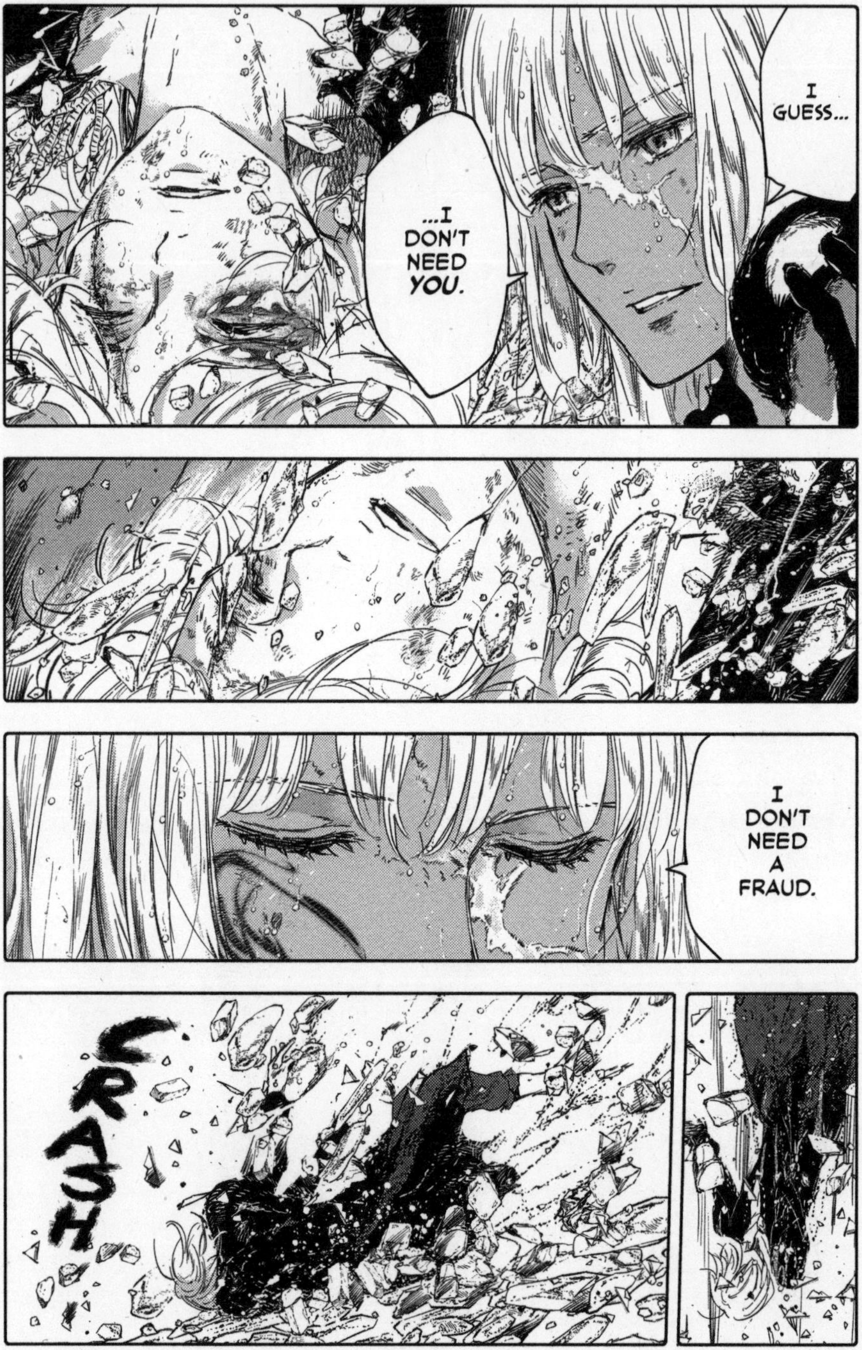
I GUESS...
...I DON'T NEED *YOU*.
I DON'T NEED A FRAUD.
CRASH

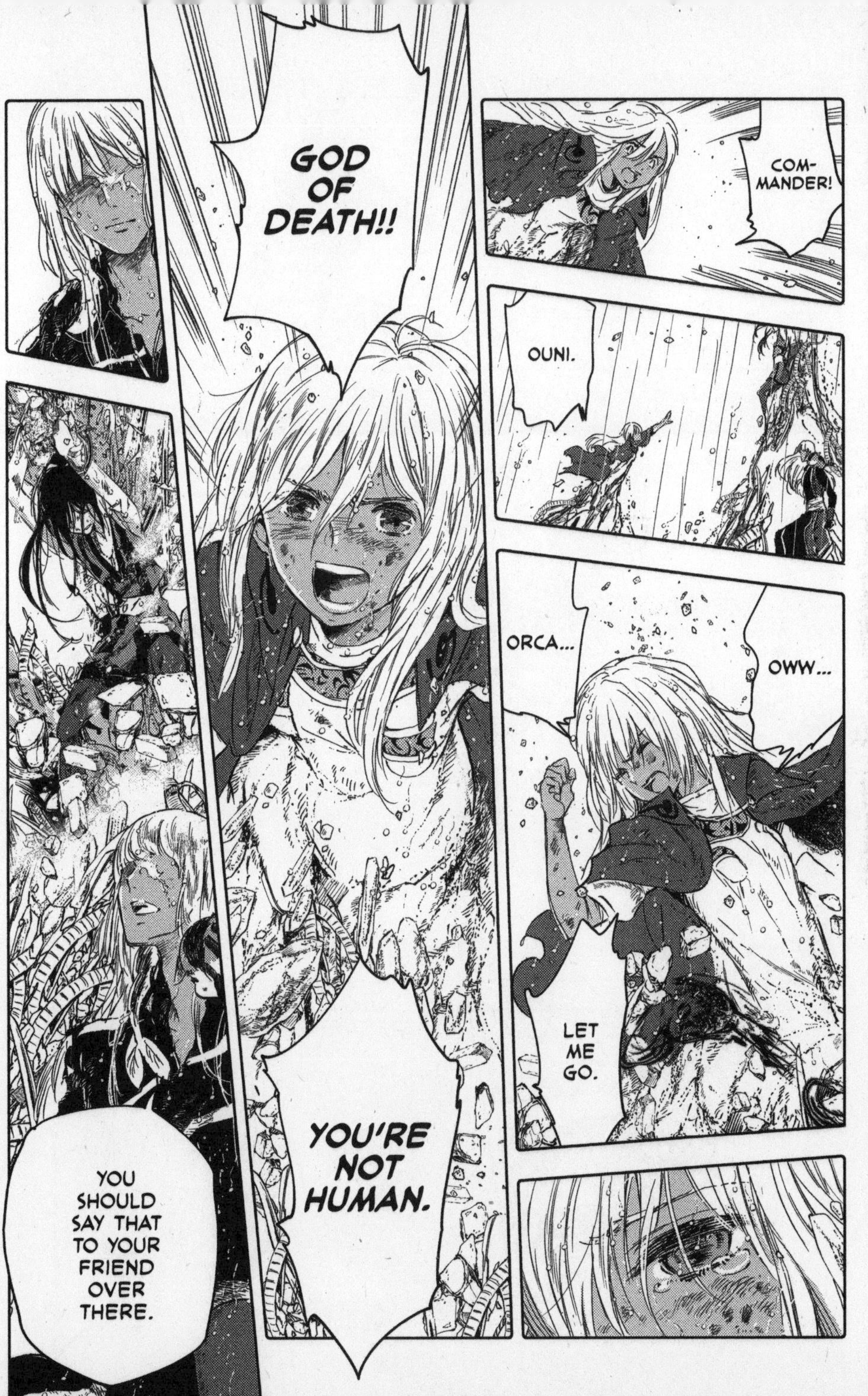
COM-
MANDER!
OUNI.
OWW...
ORCA...
LET ME GO.
GOD OF DEATH!!
YOU'RE NOT HUMAN.
YOU SHOULD SAY THAT TO YOUR FRIEND OVER THERE.

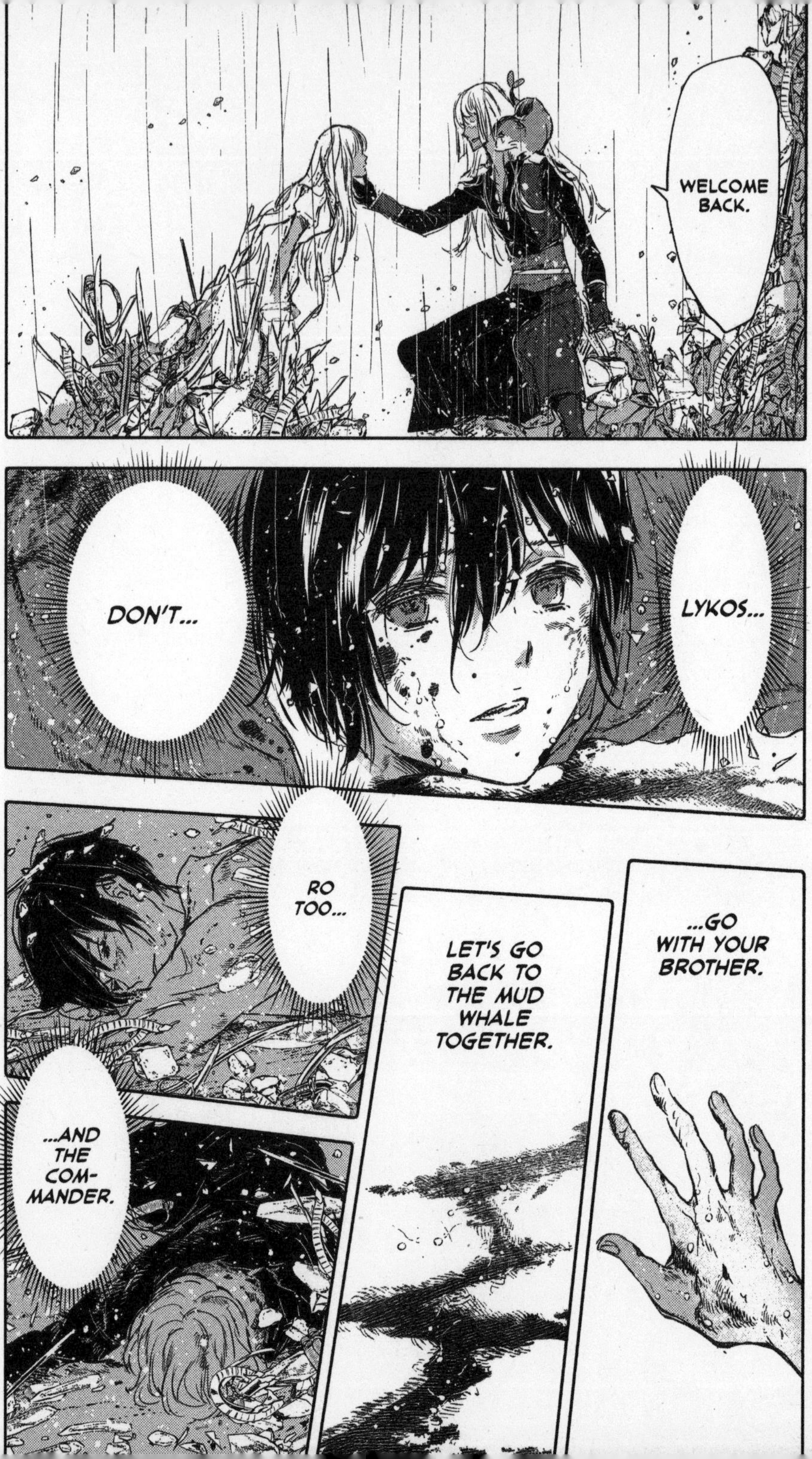
WELCOME BACK.
LYKOS...
DON'T...
...GO WITH YOUR BROTHER.
LET'S GO BACK TO THE MUD WHALE TOGETHER.
RO TOO...
...AND THE COM-MANDER.

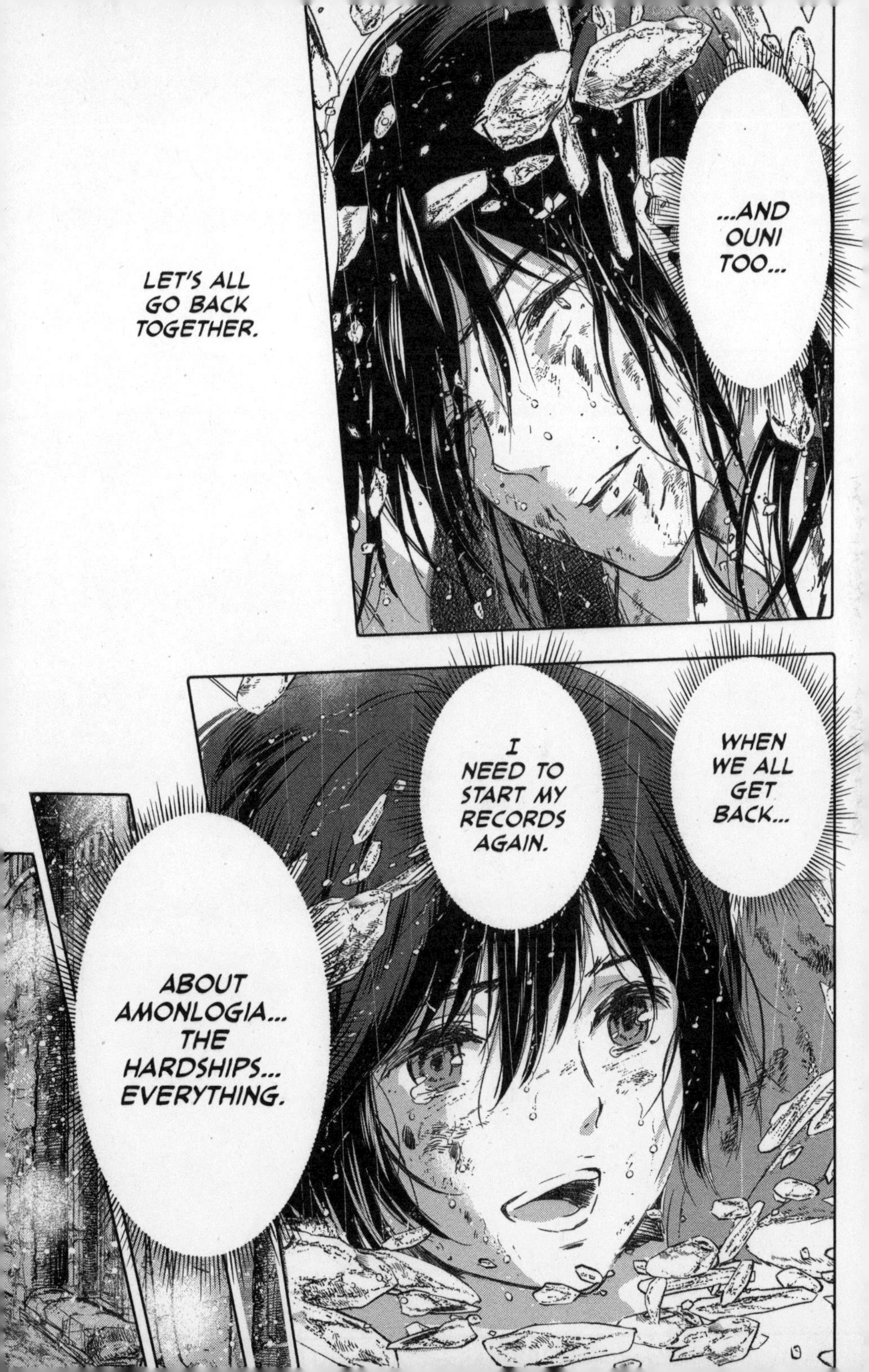
...AND OUNI TOO...
LET'S ALL GO BACK TOGETHER.
WHEN WE ALL GET BACK...
I NEED TO START MY RECORDS AGAIN.
ABOUT AMONLOGIA... THE HARDSHIPS... EVERYTHING.

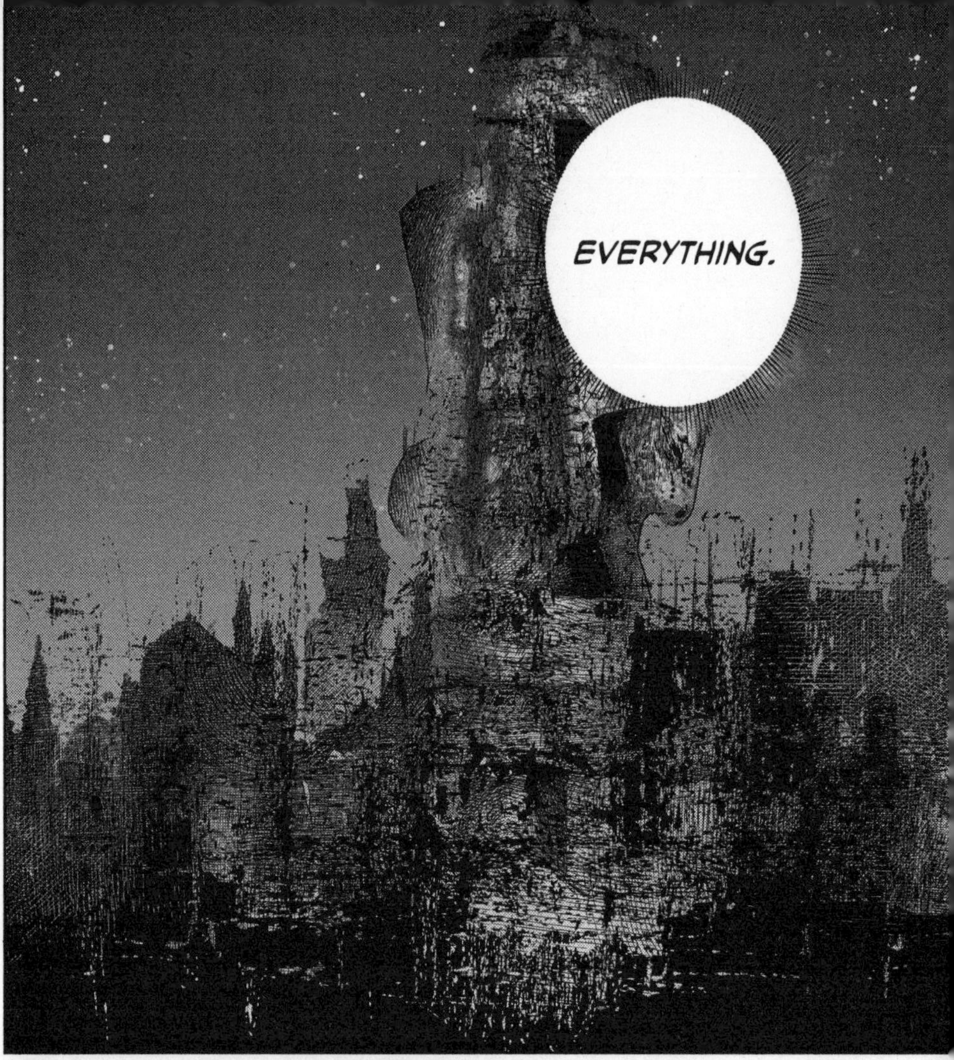
EVERYTHING.

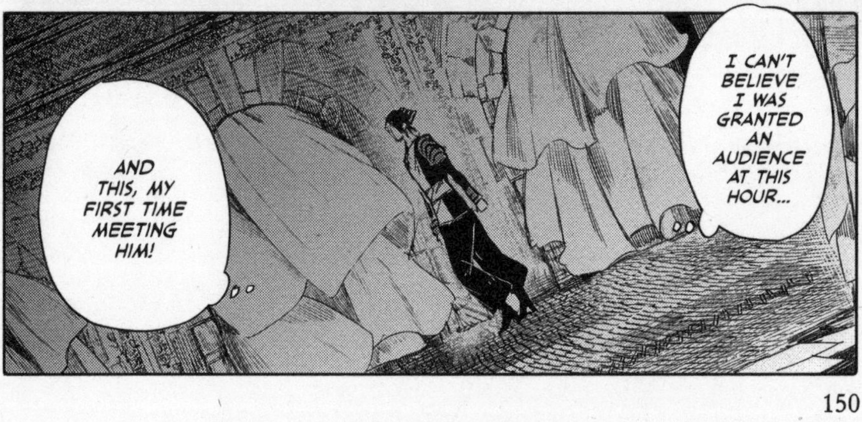
I CAN'T BELIEVE I WAS GRANTED AN AUDIENCE AT THIS HOUR...
AND THIS, MY FIRST TIME MEETING HIM!

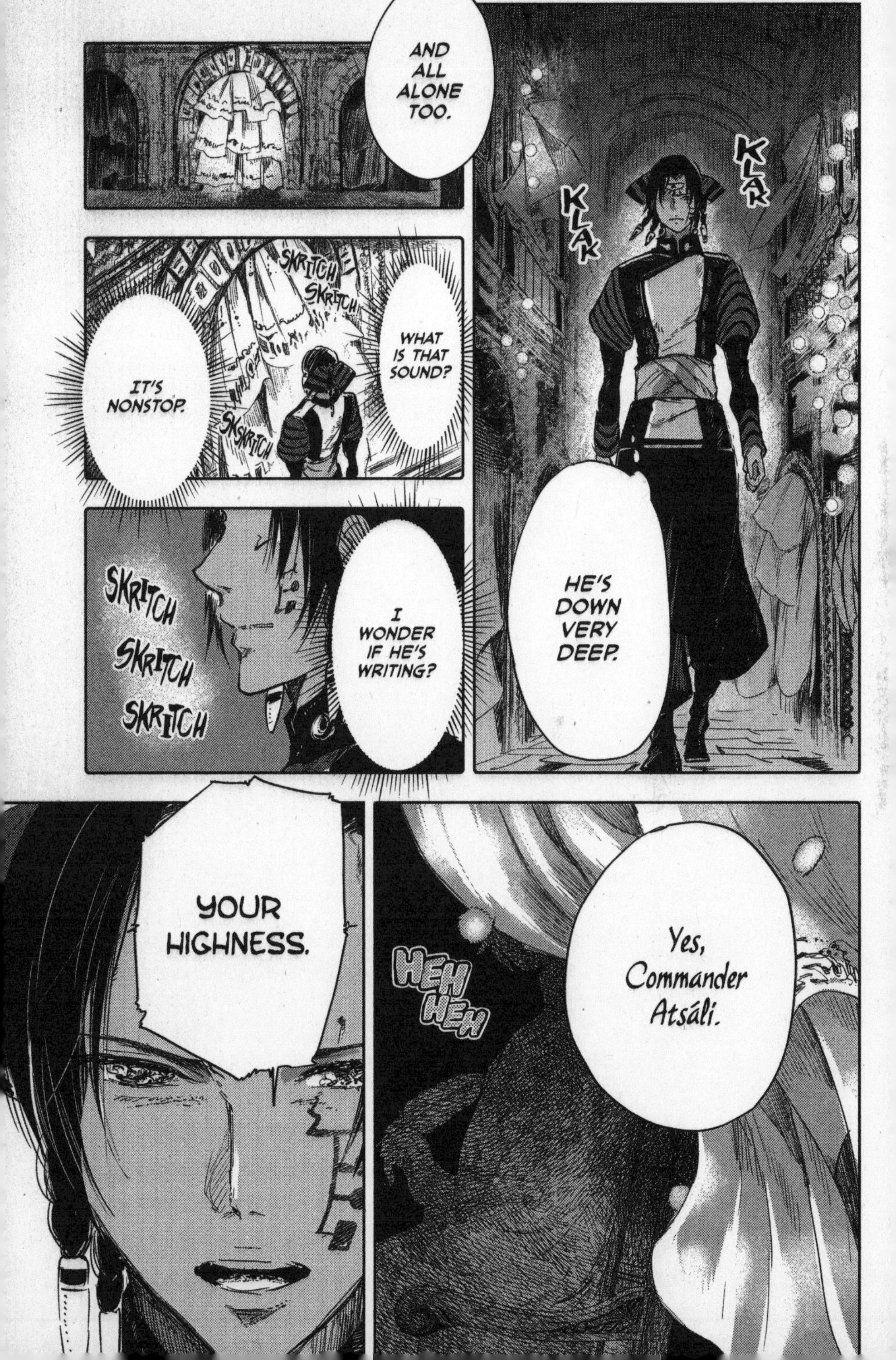
KLAK
KLAK
HE'S DOWN VERY DEEP.
AND ALL ALONE TOO.
SKRITCH SKRITCH
WHAT IS THAT SOUND?
IT'S NONSTOP.
SKSKRITCH
I WONDER IF HE'S WRITING?
SKRITCH
SKRITCH
SKRITCH
Yes, Commander Atsáli.
HEH HEH
YOUR HIGHNESS.

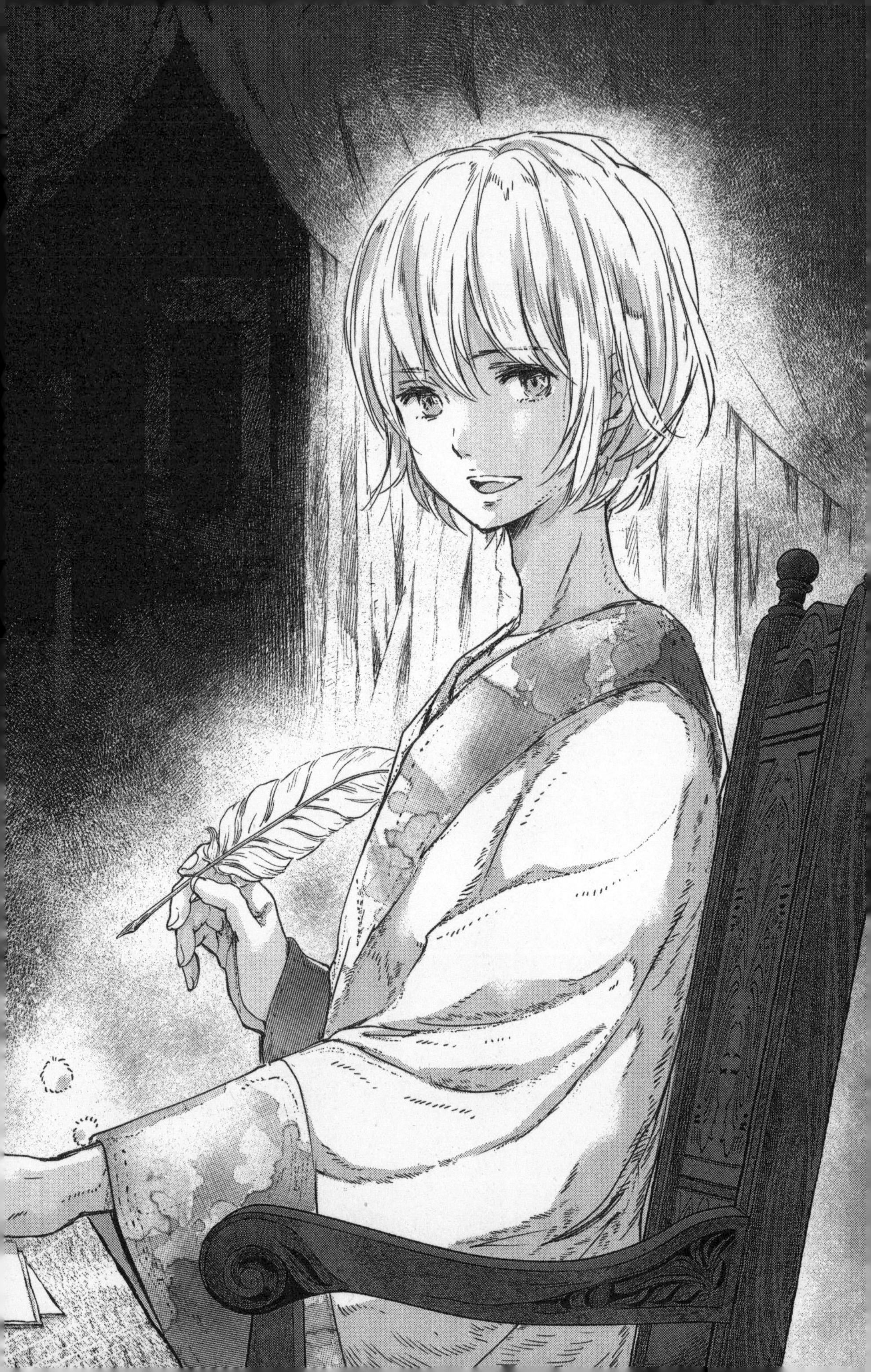

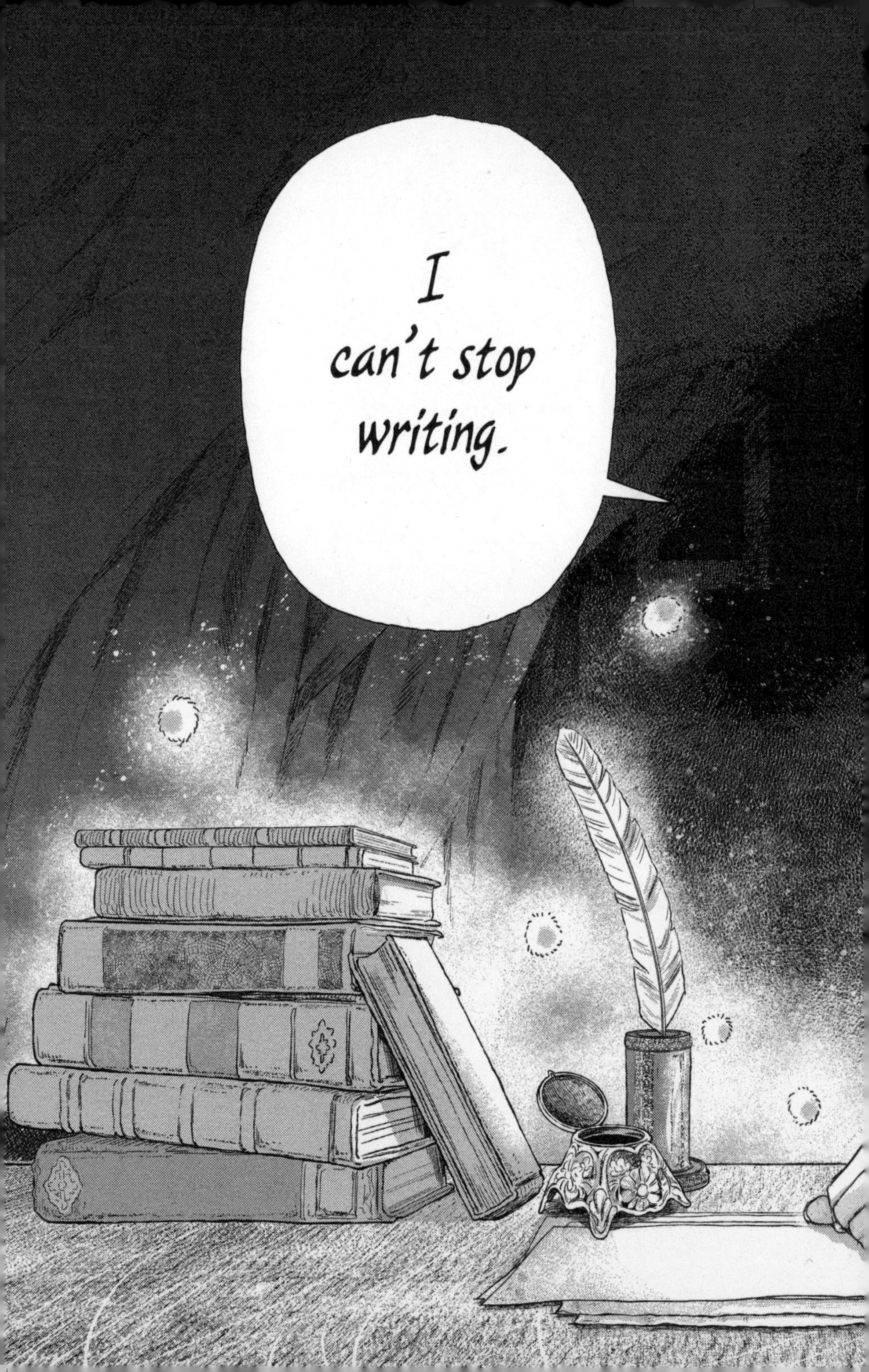
I can't stop writing.

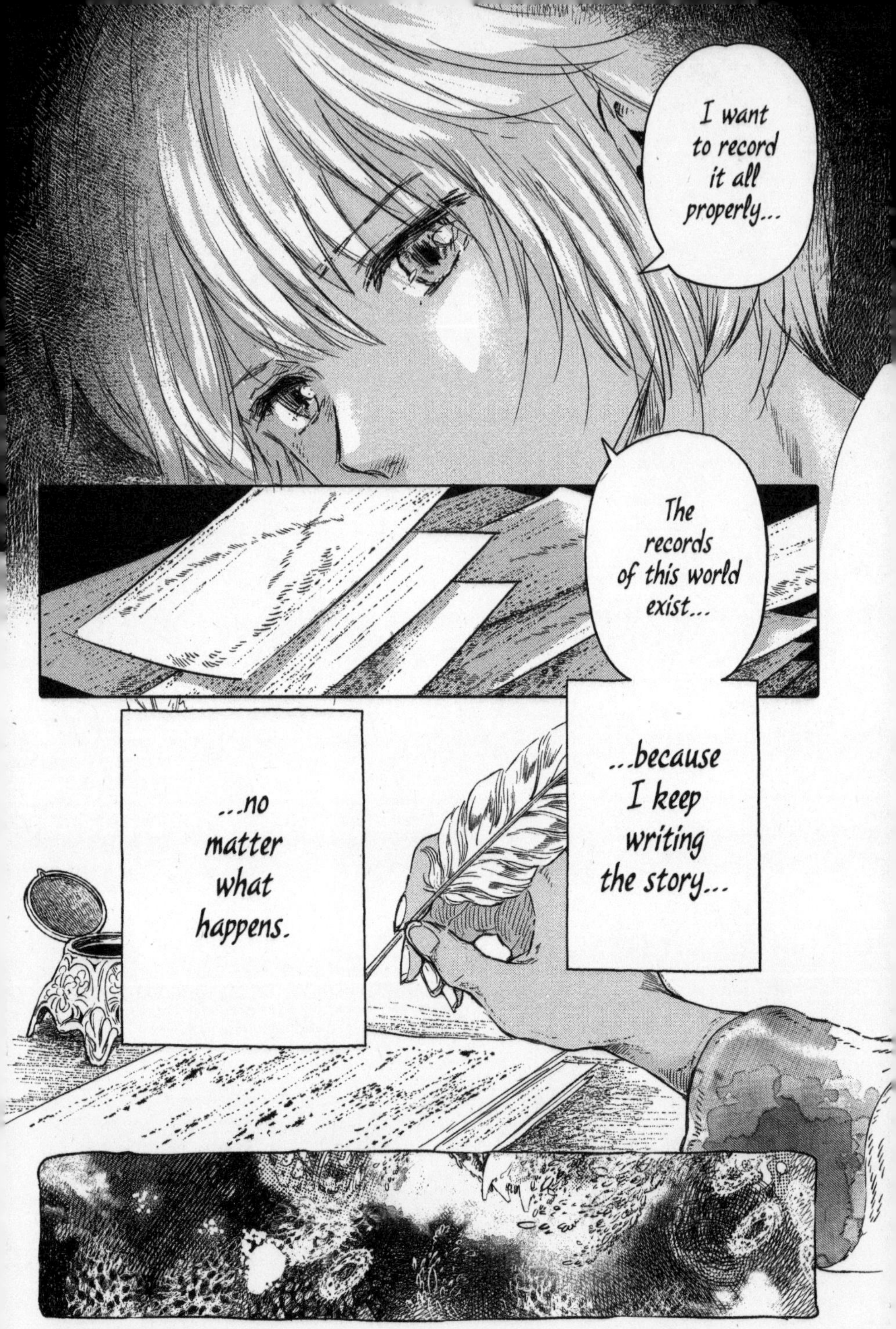
I want to record it all properly...
The records of this world exist...
...because I keep writing the story...
...no matter what happens.

One Who Records -The End-
Children of the Whales volume 12 -The End-

Current fashion on the Mud Whale

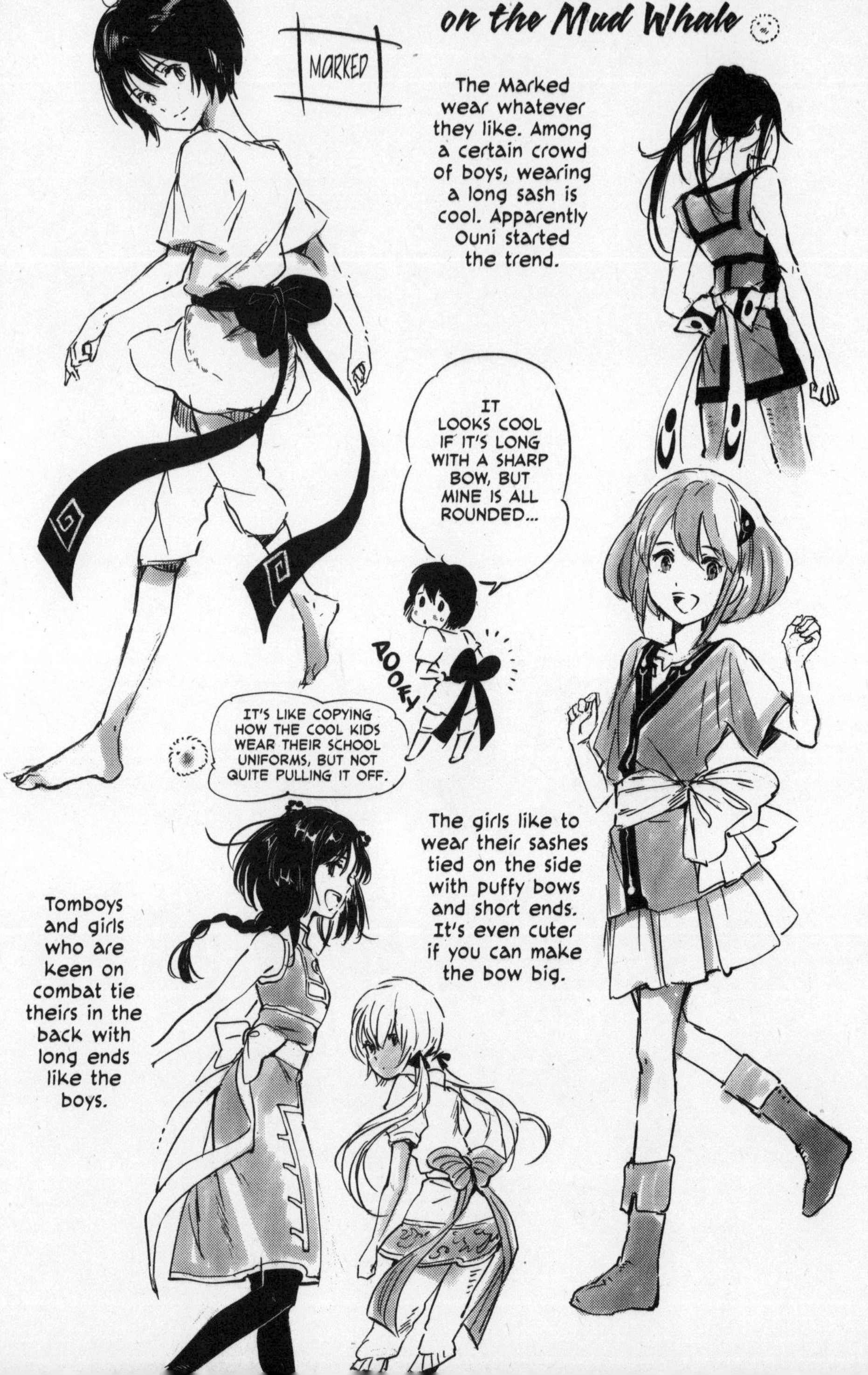
MARKED
The Marked wear whatever they like. Among a certain crowd of boys, wearing a long sash is cool. Apparently Ouni started the trend.
IT LOOKS COOL IF IT'S LONG WITH A SHARP BOW, BUT MINE IS ALL ROUNDED...
AOOFY
IT'S LIKE COPYING HOW THE COOL KIDS WEAR THEIR SCHOOL UNIFORMS, BUT NOT QUITE PULLING IT OFF.
The girls like to wear their sashes tied on the side with puffy bows and short ends. It's even cuter if you can make the bow big.
Tomboys and girls who are keen on combat tie theirs in the back with long ends like the boys.

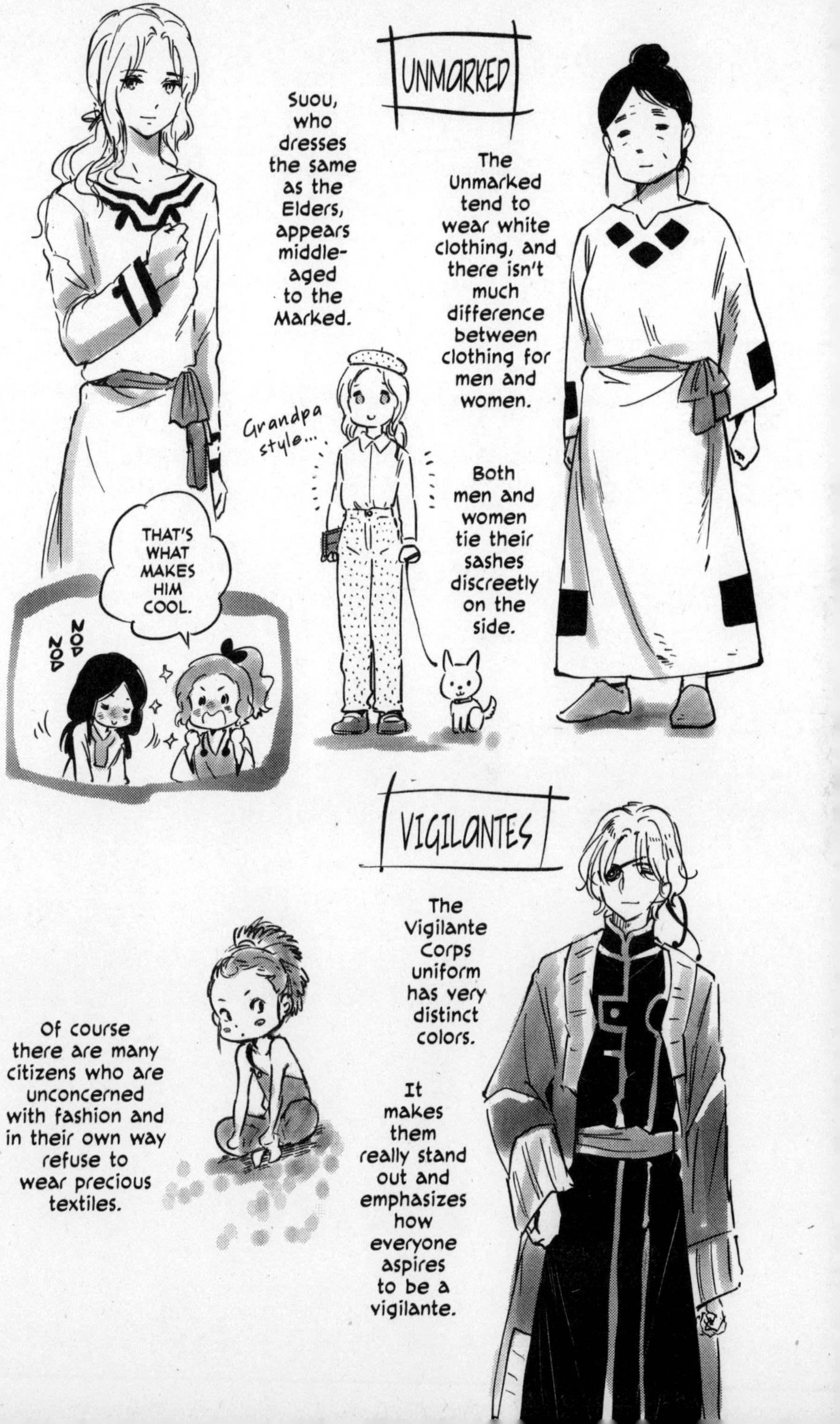
UNMARKED
The Unmarked tend to wear white clothing, and there isn't much difference between clothing for men and women.
Both men and women tie their sashes discreetly on the side.
Suou, who dresses the same as the Elders, appears middle-aged to the Marked.
Grandpa style...
THAT'S WHAT MAKES HIM COOL.
NOD NOD
VIGILANTES
The Vigilante Corps uniform has very distinct colors.
It makes them really stand out and emphasizes how everyone aspires to be a vigilante.
Of course there are many citizens who are unconcerned with fashion and in their own way refuse to wear precious textiles.

A NOTE ON NAMES

Those who live on the Mud Whale are named after colors in a language unknown. Abi Umeda uses Japanese translations of the names, which we have maintained. Here is a list of the English equivalents for the curious.

Aijiro	pale blue
Benihi	scarlet
Buki	kerria flower (*yamabuki*)
Byakuroku	malachite mineral pigments, pale green tinged with white
Chakuro	blackish brown (*cha* = brown, *kuro* = black)
Furano	from "flannel," a soft-woven fabric traditionally made of wool
Ginshu	vermillion
Hakuji	porcelain white
Jiki	golden
Kicha	yellowish brown
Kikujin	koji mold, yellowish green
Kogare	burnt muskwood, dark reddish brown
Kuchiba	decayed-leaf brown
Masoh	cinnabar
Miru	seaweed green
Nashiji	a traditional Japanese crepe weave fabric
Neri	silk white
Nezu	mouse gray
Nibi	dark gray
Ouni	safflower red
Rasha	darkest blue, nearly black
Ro	lacquer black
Sami	light green (*asa* = light, *midori* = green)

Shikoku	purple-tinged black
Shikon	purple-tinged navy
Shinono	the color of dawn (*shinonome*)
Shuan	dark bloodred
Sienna	reddish brown
Sumi	ink black
Suou	raspberry red
Taisha	red ocher
Tobi	reddish brown like a kite's feather
Tokusa	scouring rush green
Tonoko	the color of powdered grindstone, a pale brown
Urumi	muddy gray

I can describe the flavor of oomasagochiku, the main source of food on the Mud Whale, as if I've eaten it. But I haven't...

—Abi Umeda

ABI UMEDA debuted as a manga creator with the one-shot "Yukokugendan" in *Weekly Shonen Champion*. *Children of the Whales* is her eighth manga work.

CHILDREN OF THE WHALES

VOLUME 12
VIZ Signature Edition

Story and Art by Abi Umeda

Translation / JN Productions
Touch-Up Art & Lettering / Annaliese Christman
Design / Julian (JR) Robinson
Editor / Pancha Diaz

KUJIRANOKORAHA SAJOUNIUTAU Volume 12
© 2018 ABI UMEDA
First published in Japan in 2018 by AKITA PUBLISHING CO., LTD., Tokyo
English translation rights arranged with AKITA PUBLISHING CO., LTD. through
Tuttle-Mori Agency, Inc., Tokyo

Printed in the U.S.A.

Published by VIZ Media, LLC
P.O. Box 77010
San Francisco, CA 94107

10 9 8 7 6 5 4 3 2 1
First printing, September 2019

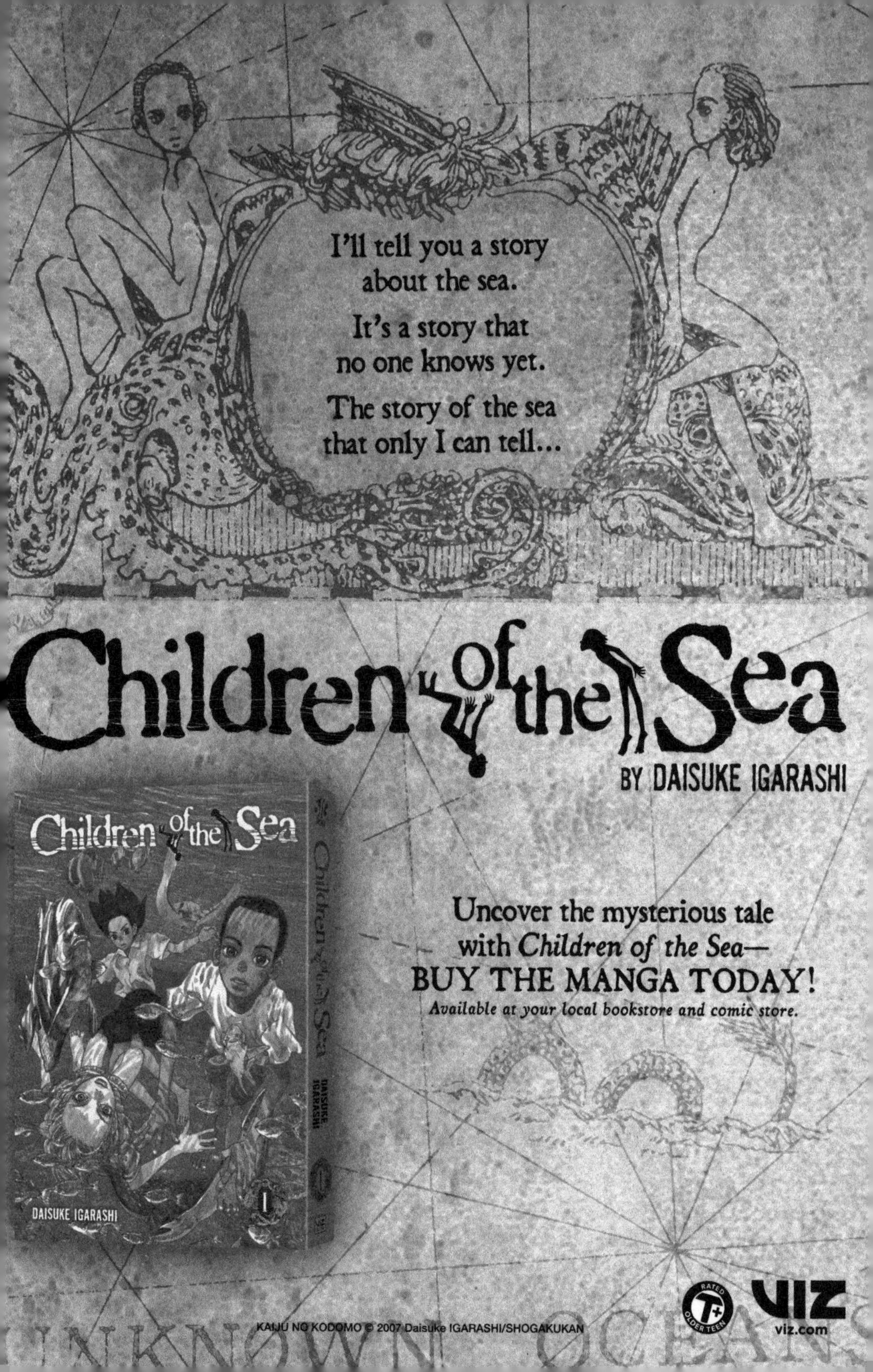

I'll tell you a story
about the sea.

It's a story that
no one knows yet.

The story of the sea
that only I can tell...

Children of the Sea

BY DAISUKE IGARASHI

Uncover the mysterious tale
with *Children of the Sea*—
BUY THE MANGA TODAY!
Available at your local bookstore and comic store.

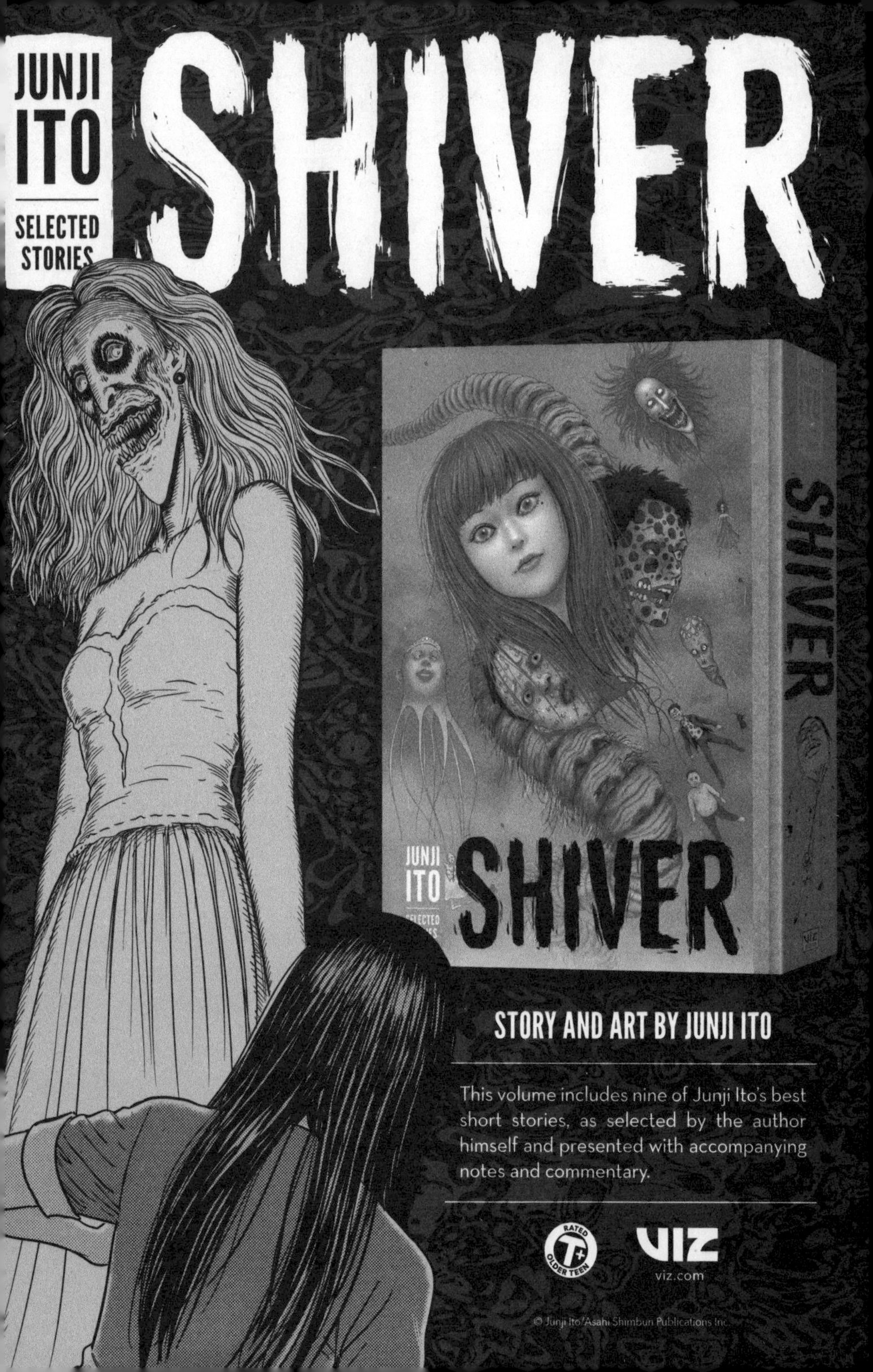
JUNJI ITO
SELECTED STORIES
SHIVER
JUNJI ITO
SELECTED STORIES
SHIVER
SHIVER
VIZ
STORY AND ART BY JUNJI ITO
This volume includes nine of Junji Ito's best short stories, as selected by the author himself and presented with accompanying notes and commentary.
RATED T+ OLDER TEEN
VIZ
viz.com
© Junji Ito/Asahi Shimbun Publications Inc.

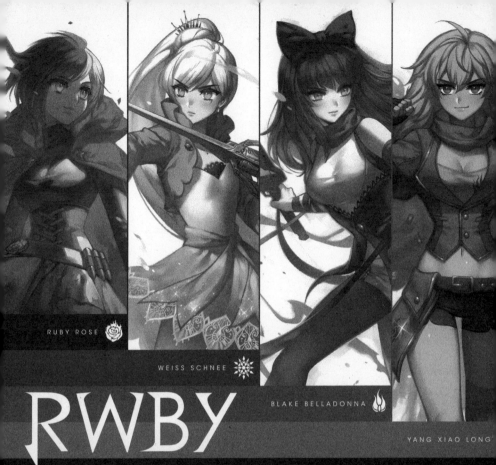

RUBY ROSE

WEISS SCHNEE ✳

BLAKE BELLADONNA 🔥

YANG XIAO LONG

RWBY

OFFICIAL MANGA ANTHOLOGIES

Original Concept by Monty Oum & Rooster Teeth Productions, Story and Art by Various Artists

All-new stories featuring Ruby, Weiss, Blake and Yang from Rooster Teeth's hit animation series

MOBILE SUIT GUNDAM THUNDERBOLT

In the Universal Century year 0079, the space colony known as Side 3 proclaims independence as the Principality of Zeon and declares war on the Earth Federation. One year later, they are locked in a fierce battle for the Thunderbolt Sector, an area of space scarred by the wreckage of destroyed colonies. Into this maelstrom of destruction go two veteran Mobile Suit pilots: the deadly Zeon sniper Daryl Lorenz, and Federation ace Io Fleming. It's the beginning of a rivalry that can end only when one of them is destroyed.

STORY AND ART
YASUO OHTAGAKI
ORIGINAL CONCEPT BY
HAJIME YATATE
AND **YOSHIYUKI TOMINO**

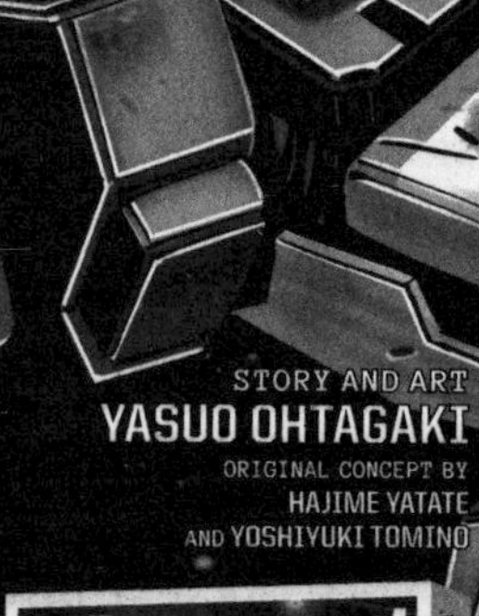

MOBILE SUIT GUNDAM
THUNDERBOLT

viz media
viz.com

ABARA
COMPLETE DELUXE EDITION
TSUTOMU NIHEI

A visually stunning work of sci-fi horror from the creator of **BIOMEGA** and **BLAME**!

ABARA

COMPLETE DELUXE EDITION

TSUTOMU NIHEI

A vast city lies under the shadow of colossal, ancient tombs, the identity of their builders lost to time. In the streets of the city something is preying on the inhabitants, something that moves faster than the human eye can see and leaves unimaginable horror in its wake.

Tsutomu Nihei's dazzling, harrowing dystopian thriller is presented here in a single-volume hardcover edition featuring full-color pages and foldout illustrations. This volume also includes the early short story "Digimortal."

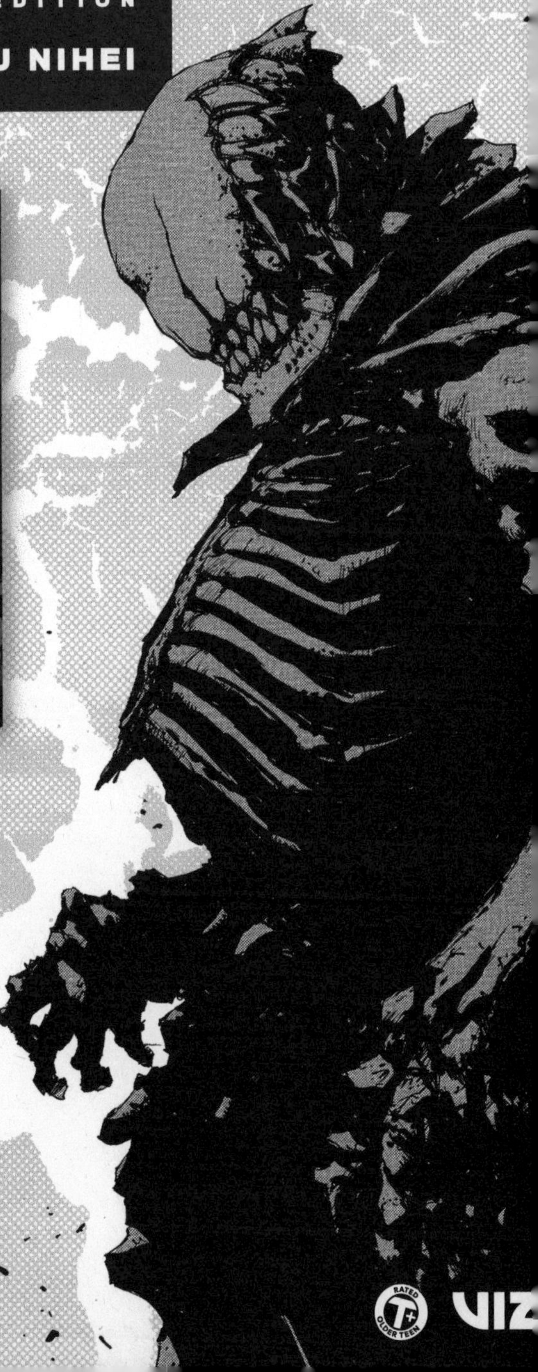

RATED T+ COLOR TEEN

VIZ

THIS IS THE LAST PAGE!

Children of the Whales has been printed in the original Japanese format to preserve the orientation of the original artwork.

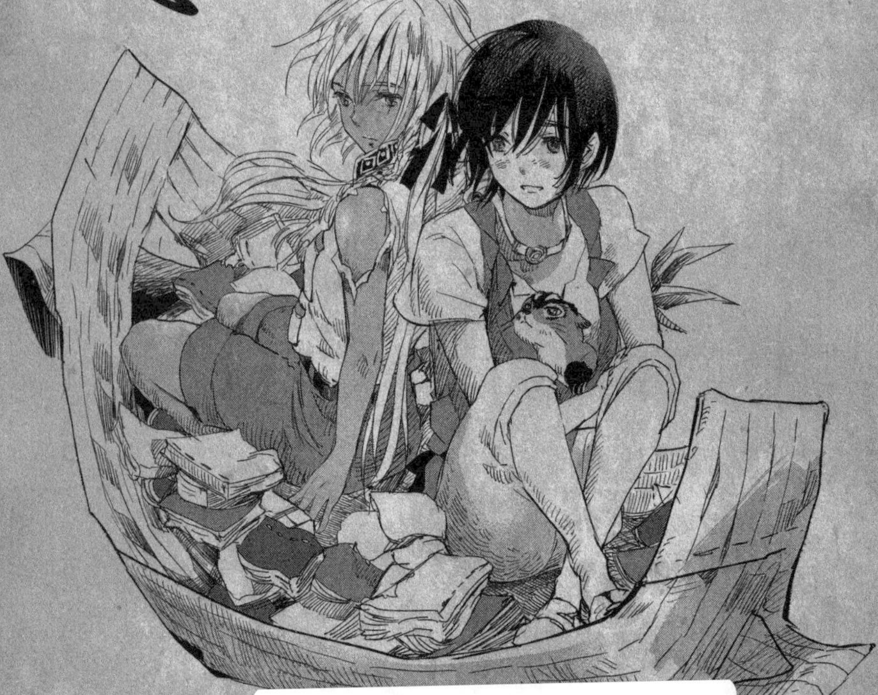